S0-BJO-185

THE
PERILS
OF
INVENTION

LYING, TECHNOLOGY, AND THE HUMAN CONDITION

ROGER BERKOWITZ, ED

BLACK ROSE BOOKS

Montréal•Chicago•London

Copyright © 2022

Thank you for purchasing this Black Rose Books publication. No part of this book may be reproduced or transmitted in any form, by any means electronic or mechanical including photocopying and recording, or by any information storage or retrieval system–without written permission from the publisher, or, in the case of photocopying or other reprographic copying, a license from the Canadian Copyright Licensing Agency, Access Copyright, with the exception of brief passages quoted by a reviewer in a newspaper or magazine. If you acquired an illicit electronic copy of this book, please consider making a donation to Black Rose Books.

Black Rose Books No. UU422

Library and Archives Canada Cataloguing in Publication

Title: The perils of invention : lying, technology, and the human condition / Roger Berkowitz, ed.
Names: Berkowitz, Roger, 1968- editor.
Description: Based on three Hannah Arendt Center Conferences: "Human Being in an Inhuman Age," "Lying and Politics," and "Truthtelling: Democracy in an Age without Facts" held at Bard College, Hannah Arendt Center.
Identifiers: Canadiana (print) 20210352183 | Canadiana (ebook) 20210352213 | ISBN 9781551647630 (hardcover) | ISBN 9781551647616 (softcover) | ISBN 9781551647654 (PDF)
Subjects: LCSH: Truthfulness and falsehood—Congresses. | LCSH: Technology—Social aspects—Congresses. | LCSH: Democracy—Congresses. | LCSH: Human beings—Congresses. | LCGFT: Conference papers and proceedings.
Classification: LCC BJ1421 .P47 2021 | DDC 177/.3—dc23

Cover design by Amanda Bartlett.

BLACK ROSE BOOKS

C.P.35788 Succ. Léo-Pariseau
Montréal, QC, H2X 0A4
Explore our books and subscribe to our newsletter:
blackrosebooks.com

Ordering Information

CANADA	USA/INTERNATIONAL	UK/IRELAND
University of Toronto Press	University of Chicago Press	Central Books
5201 Dufferin Street	Chicago Distribution Center	50 Freshwater Road
Toronto, ON	11030 South Langley Avenue	Chadwell Heath, London
M3H 5T8	Chicago, IL 60628	RM8 1RX
1-800-565-9523	(800) 621-2736 (USA)	+44 (0) 20 8525 8800
utpbooks@utpress.utoronto.ca	(773) 702-7000 (International)	contactus@centralbooks.com
	orders@press.uchicago.edu	

Table of Contents

For JLB who holds my reality together.

Acknowledgements

01110100 01101000 01100101 00100000 01110000 01100101 01110010 01101001 01101100 01110011 00100000 01101111 01100110 00100000 01101001 01101110 01110110 01100101 01101110 01110100 01101001 01101111 01101110

This book was born over a decade ago at two conferences I organized through the Hannah Arendt Center at Bard College. Mary Strieder, Bridget Hollenback, Debra Pemstein and many of colleagues at Bard College helped to make these conferences happen. Wyatt Mason in particular was a constant interlocutor, advisor, and friend, without whom these conferences and thus this book would not have been happened. Thomas Wild has been a grounding intellectual presence at the Arendt Center. I thank them along with my students and those who spoke at the conferences, many of whom have allowed me to print edited versions of their talks in this volume. Christine Stanton joined me at the Hannah Arendt Center after these conferences took place, but her dedication and incredible competency has enabled the Arendt Center to thrive in ways that have helped make this book a reality. I thank her along with David Bisson, Daniel Fiege, Craig Rothstein, Samantha Rose Hill, Jacob Rivers, Tara Needham, and Philip Lindsay for their incredible work with me at the Hannah Arendt Center. And of course, my wonderful wife and partner, Jenny Lyn Bader, has inspired and edited most everything I write. Finally, this book would never have come to be without the enthusiasm and interest of Jason Toney, a former student, former Hannah Arendt Center Fellow, and now my editor at Black Rose Books. Jason, along with Clara Swan Kennedy, have shepherded this book through to completion amidst a global pandemic. I am extremely grateful for their dedication and excellent work.

— Roger Berkowitz

Introduction:
The Perils of Invention

Roger Berkowitz

01110100 01101000 01100101 00100000 01110000 01100101 01110010 01101001 01101100 01110011 00100000 01101111 01100110 00100000 01101001 01101110 01110110 01100101 01101110 01110100 01101001 01101111 01101110

Reality is in retreat. Amidst an incredible explosion of technological inventiveness, predictive algorithms sell us products we didn't know we wanted; algorithms also provide data to institute regulations of social control based on insights no human being could know. As we allow algorithms to think and plan for us, we imagine a future with the incredible potential to improve our lives and we fear a dystopian future in which we submit our human freedom to the control of quasi-intelligent machine algorithms. In both cases the world we inhabit is an invention, a world where reality is unknowable by human intelligence.

Our reality is equally threatened by our human capacity to invent alternative meanings and alternative worlds. An entire legal and political apparatus tells us that President Joe Biden won the 2020 election, but millions of Americans, mobilized by former President Donald Trump, are convinced the election was stolen and are intent on stealing it back. Our world is warming and that is caused by human activity; yet many deny this fact even as others embrace as 'science' unproven and unsettled claims that a climate change will bring about the end of civilization if not the end of the world. Nearly ten percent of Americans now believe, without a shred of evidence, that leading politicians are members of a secret pedophilia ring that has taken over the United States government. All the data confirm that anti-bias trainings don't work and may even be counterproductive, and yet organizations worried about perception over reality insist on them. Divided by social media bubbles and structured by virtual architectures, we live in social and political worlds that are increasingly tailored to our wants and needs.

Amidst the loss of a common tradition and the virulent polarization of politics, there is a yearning for experts to take control. Experts can be valuable for tasks such as helping us understand historical complexities or envision future possibilities. But on matters of policy, experts will frequently disagree amongst one another. As the COVID-19 pandemic has shown, some will sometimes be demonstrably wrong; some will make misleading comments to advance larger public health or political purposes; and sometimes, experts will simply disagree. Indeed, it may be the case that experts are particularly ill-suited to making policy or predicting the future.

The crisis of expertise that destabilizes institutions emerges from this basic fact that experts can and do disagree. Just as science has failed to provide a solution to the death of God, so too does the turn to experts fail to resolve our political polarization. To the contrary, as experts contribute to the invention of purportedly scientific or technocratic narratives and counternarratives struggling over the interpretation of reality, they add to the confusion over the complicated and deeply human meaning of reality itself.

Beyond experts, the human capacity to imagine and realize theoretical worlds is greater than ever. DeepFake technology can produce videos of someone saying words they never said, creating the possibility that video evidence will be employed to discredit and even re-make reality. Nanotechnology offers the potential to digitize water, blood platelets, and matter so that rivers, blood, and rocks can be programmed—and re-programmed—to conform to our wishes. The real world when it is uncomfortable or painful is increasingly open to being edited, produced, and re-produced according to our wants and in response to our fears. We are living through a revolt against reality.

Doubt regarding reality is, since René Descartes, baked into the modern age. With the rise of modern science, we humans understood that our senses had long been deceiving us. Our eyes show us the sun rises and travels across the sky, but science corrects that error. Our ears pick up only a fraction of the sounds around us that resound on wavelengths imperceptible to human hearing. Our faculties of taste, smell, and touch are all easily tricked. Even our sense of free will is questioned by scientific assertions of neurological and environmental determination. Common sense—that famous sixth sense that for Hannah Arendt fits the five senses into a common world we share with others—comes to be less and less reliable as we realize that we have been deceived by our trust in our sensual reality.

Against the simple idea that science is based on observation stands the truth that science is predicated on the suspicion of senses and the submission of the sensible world to scientifically discoverable laws of nature and laws of society. Free from the world of our senses, scientific humanity can imagine new worlds and create them, whether they be utopias here on earth, virtual worlds in a networked online life, or new colonial civilizations in space. The world, our world of scientific innovation, is increasingly one liberated from physical and sensual reality.

The loss of the real world is bound up with the fraying of political truth. In her essay "Truth and Politics," Arendt argues that the loss of truth is more catastrophic for the human activity of politics than is the loss of justice. We can live in a world without justice; but a world without truth, Arendt writes, would cease to be a human world: "What is at stake is survival, the perseverance in existence (*in suo esse perseverare*), and no human world destined to outlast the short life span of mortals within it will ever be able to survive without men willing . . . to say what is."[1] To "say what is," what Herodotus called the activity of the historian, is also the activity of politics, because in saying what is the politician and political actors affirm their shared world amongst their many differences. Since politics is that activity that unites a multitude of plural individuals around a common center, there is no politics once what is common is lost. In fact, politics is most essentially the public search for and collective discovery and maintenance of "what is" or "what we cannot change." Included in what we cannot change is the necessity of change, the newness and natality that Arendt celebrates in human freedom. But the opening of the new can only happen on the foundation of something that endures, which is why politics is, above all, the building and nurturing of a common world. Speaking metaphorically, politics is the ever-necessary acknowldgement and nurturing in speech and action of "the ground on which we stand and the sky that stretches above us."[2]

* * *

The Perils of Invention addresses two threats to the human encounter with reality. The first is the rise of modern propaganda, fake news, and conspiracy theories that weaponize facts and invent a coherent fictional reality in the pursuit of political power. Propaganda and mass lying respond to the human need to simplify the world and make certain the uncertainty of our political and social worlds. In simplifying the world, propaganda embraces ideologies that interpret the complexity of the world by a single, simple idea. Ideologies are, as Arendt argues, "a very recent phenomenon" and "known for their scientific character."[3] As the very word ideology suggests, it is the "logic of an idea."[4] In demanding that reality conform to logical laws, ideological thinking replaces ungovernable reality with logical deductions; the dominant ideologies of the modern era—racism and communism—promise to solve the complicated problems of our world by promising a simple solution by eliminating a certain race or class.

The rise of competing ideologies today means that a contradictory and uncomfortable reality is denied and denigrated, replaced by empowering ideological fictions. Against a worldly reality of incredible economic inequality and also an extraordinary elitism on the part of those who are convinced that their educational status empowers them to govern, we are witnessing a revolt that challenges any one version of reality. The flight from reality encompasses not only those who join movements (reactionary, progressive, and social justice movements), but also those who aim to understand the world through social theories (for example global warming, neo-liberalism, and decolonization) that abstract from facts and construct theoretical castles impervious to the constraints of the real. The essays in Part One of this volume ask: how can we maintain a commitment to truth and a common factual world when lies and ideologies offer simpler, more comforting, and preferable answers to the human craving for a meaningful life?

The second threat to our encounter with reality is the rise of artificial intelligence and predictive algorithms. Even as we flee reality through lies, we also seek to overcome the real and worldly limits of our humanity through the invention of new technologies. The human faculty of invention to improve the world is old; but the human power to fundamentally alter and create alternate realities is new. We now carry around the libraries of the world in our pockets, searchable in mere seconds, giving us infinite recall. We implant neural enhancers in our brains that smooth out our movements and augment our intelligence. We can extend life quite possibly as long as we want, challenging our human mortality. We can create simulated realities that become more real than the once-real world. We live in a world we create rather than one given to us by a god or by fortune. As our world becomes populated by rationally-minded machines, as more of our ethical and political thinking is tested through computers employing rational choice models, as our cars our driven by computers, as surgeries and diagnostics are handled by robotic doctors, and as these machines are designed, built, and serviced by other machines, the question arises: what is the role of a pre-given and natural human reality in an increasingly inhuman and humanly created world?

Our addiction to technology—to remaking reality—and our fanaticism for lying—to denying and re-imagining reality—reveal that we have a true contempt for our real limitations in the face of a world that is given to us and is beyond our control. Religious thinkers escape this world through the inventions of a heaven. Philosophical theories impose a logical meaning to the human mystery. And political visionaries imagine that pain and suffering can be vanquished through rational rules and regulations. Against the messiness of reality, the human capacity for invention answers to a profound human need to make the world fit our desires—to remake the world as a humanly made world.

Modern lying and modern technology share a disdain for the complexity and messiness of the human world. They have in common a desire to "fix" our real human limitations and failings. Seduced by our capacity to invent, we too easily disdain what we have and even who we are. Craving the fantasy of coherent ideology, we willingly deny the dissonance of the real. The perils of invention name the nihilistic willingness to destroy what is in the name of some fabulous hope that the real might conform to our ideal.

* * *

In 1949, when Hannah Arendt went to Germany as part of the Jewish Cultural Reconstruction Commission, she was struck by the way the Germans showed an "at times vicious refusal to face and come to terms with what really happened."[5] This "escape from reality," as Arendt named it, meant that the reality of the Holocaust and the death factories was spoken of as a hypothetical, a mere potential. And when the truth of the Holocaust was admitted, it was diminished: "The Germans did only what others are capable of doing."[6] The Germans, at times, simply denied the facts of what had happened. One woman told Arendt that the "Russians had begun the war with an attack on Danzig."[7] What she encountered was a "kind of gentleman's agreement by which everyone has a right to his ignorance under the pretext that everyone has a right to his opinion." The underlying assumption for such a right is the "tacit assumption that opinions really do not matter." Opinions are just that, mere opinions. And facts, once they are reduced to opinions, also don't matter. This confusion of fact and opinion alongside the diminution of opinions as mere opinions together lead to a situation in which there is a "flight from reality."[8]

The focus of Arendt's lifelong engagement with the human flight from reality is her encounter with ideologies, specifically Nazism and Bolshevism. In *The Origins of Totalitarianism* and other texts (especially her essay "On the Nature of Totalitarianism"), Arendt defines an ideology as a system of explanation that seeks to explain "all the mysteries of life and the world" according to one idea.[9] Nazism is an ideology that blames economic disaster, political loss, and the evils of modernity on the Jews. The Jews are not simply enemies, but are vermin, inhuman flotsam who must be exterminated to allow a master race to flourish. Bolshevism, in turn, "pretends that all history is a struggle of classes, that the proletariat is bound by eternal laws to win this struggle, that a classless society will then come about, and that the state, finally, will wither away."[10] The bourgeoisie are not simply class traitors, they are a dying class and killing them only supports a law of history. As ideologies, both Nazism and Bolshevism insist on explaining the events of the world according to theories "without further concurrence with actual experience."[11] The result, Arendt argues, is that ideologies bring about an "arrogant emancipation from reality and experience."[12]

Because an ideology "looks upon all factuality as fabricated," it "no longer knows any reliable criterion for distinguishing truth from falsehood."[13] As reality recedes, ideologies organize society to transform its ideas into a living reality. If antisemitism as an ideology says that all Jews are beggars without passports, the fact of wealthy and established Jews must simply be eliminated. If Bolshevism says that the bourgeoisie are corrupt, they must admit their corruption or be killed. The realization of such ideological realities can be accomplished, of course, through terror, by which Jews are dispossessed and expelled and the bourgeoisie are destroyed.

But even before a totalitarian movement takes power and mobilizes the secret police in the machinery of terror, ideological movements can employ propaganda to deny and nullify facts, to change facts. The Nazis, she writes, "did not so much believe in the truth of racism as desire to change the world into a race reality."[14] Similarly, the Bolshevist ideology that classes were dying was not something real, but something that had to be made real. The purges and terror that Stalin unleashed were to "establish a classless society" by exterminating all social groups that might develop into classes.[15] In both instances, the point of the ideology was to transform a mere opinion—race consciousness or class consciousness—into "the lived content of reality."[16]

The point, as Arendt concludes, is that "ideological consistency reducing everything to one all-dominating factor is always in conflict with the inconsistency of the world, on the one hand, and the unpredictability of human actions, on the other."[17] What ideology demands is that man—an unpredictable and spontaneous being—cease to exist, that all humans be subjected to laws of development that follow ideological truth. That is why the turn from an unreliable reality to coherent fantasy requires an absolute elimination of human spontaneity and freedom.

What distinguishes the modern lie from the long history of human mendacity is its capacity to deny and replace reality. The modern lie is ideological in that it rejects all contrary evidence and all inconvenient facts. It involves, as Arendt writes, the "mass manipulation of fact and opinion" towards the totalizing end of "rewriting history" and the present to fit one idea. Traditional lies sought to hide the truth; the modern lie "deals efficiently with things that are not secrets at all but are known to practically everybody."[18] It seeks to deny facts that are obvious and present and replace them with an alternate image that, even though it is obviously unreal, is accepted as real because it is seen and felt to be more true and more palatable.

The modern lie can succeed because when faced with the anarchy, loneliness, and senselessness of modern life, "the masses probably will always choose" the consistent and logical certainty of an ideology. The choice of a coherent fiction over the messiness of reality is "not because they are stupid or wicked, but because in the general disaster this escape grants them a minimum of self-respect."[19] The fictional realities ideologies offer—be they the reality of a racial superiority or a class-based right to rule—promises to their adherents a "lying world of consistency which is more adequate to the needs of the human mind than reality itself."[20]

The burgeoning field of research into "motivated reasoning" confirms that the desire to find meaning in membership in a group will lead adherents to hold onto the tenets of that collective ideology even in the face of clear factual evidence to the contrary.[21] Human thinking, as Arendt argues, is concerned not with truth, but with meaning. It is meaning, not truth, that Arendt holds to be the basic human need. That is why for Arendt, the most fundamental of human rights is the right to have rights, the right to speak and act in a political world so that one is meaningful. But this means that being part of a group, a people, a nation, or even a political party is often more humanly significant than the truth. We are all motivated to believe facts selectively in line with our political and social needs.

Arendt's writing is marked by what Jerome Kohn, in his essay in this volume, calls a "passion for political reality—*the reality of the realm of politics.*" Kohn cites Montaigne's essay "Of Liars," where Montaigne writes that "If falsehood, like truth, had only one face, we would know better where we are . . . But the reverse of truth has a thousand shapes and a limitless field . . . . A thousand paths miss the target, only one path leads to it." Montaigne sees that the inventiveness of lies allows the liar to tailor their account to the needs of the human psyche in a way that reality cannot. Because lies and ideologies can appeal to our deepest desires, they have a competitive advantage over and against the truth of the real world.

Beyond Nazism and Bolshevism, the examples of the modern lies that Arendt offers include lies of highly respected statesmen such as Charles de Gaulle and Konrad Adenauer; they were, she writes, "able to build their basic policies on such evident non-facts as that France belongs among the victors of the last war and hence is one of the great powers, and 'that the barbarism of National Socialism had affected only a relatively small percentage of the country.'"[22] Similarly, Stalin had not only to defeat his opponents, but deny that they ever existed; when Leon Trotsky was excised from the Russian Revolution, the widely known fact of his leading role in the Revolution was simply denied. This could only be accomplished—to the extent possible at all—if and when Trotsky would disappear, either into a hole of oblivion or an anonymous death. In either case, the distinction of the modern lie does not simply hide or conceal an unwelcome truth. It seeks to destroy it and replace it with a more palatable and thus more believable lie.

Writing this introduction in January 2021, I am witness to one of the greatest examples of modern lying, President Donald Trump's semi-successful effort to convince his followers that he won the 2020 Presidential election. The facts that the 2020 election was fair, clean, and honest are widely available. State after state has certified the results and court after court has thrown out challenges. The U.S. Justice Department and numerous state justice departments have investigated asserted irregularities and none of them have been found credible.

And yet President Trump continues to say that he won the election. He spreads false and refuted reports of election tampering. He claims that the election was stolen. He is peddling a simple narrative that excites and coddles his supporters. And exit polling in Georgia and other national polls have found that 40% of the U.S. population believes that President Trump won the election. His lie has been so impactful that thousands of Americans—convinced that their country has been stolen—stormed the U.S. Capitol building seeking to disrupt the certification of Joe Biden's election.

Conspiracy theories, as Jonathan Kay writes in this volume, "act as a bridge between political ideology and reality." It might be better to say that they act as a way to cancel an unwelcome reality. Kay offers the example of those Obama Birthers who had spent their entire lives "believing that America is a right-wing country, and that it would never elect a left-wing Harvard type like Barack Obama—a community organizer from Chicago." When the election defies their convictions it "shatters [their] worldview." It is comforting, Kay writes, "to think that somehow that historical episode never happened, that it is illegitimate, that it is a hoax, that somehow if you do enough investigation, and if you count enough pixels on a PDF of Barack Obama's electronic birth certificate, you can somehow discover 'the truth.'"

Similarly, for someone who believes that Democrats and some mainstream Republicans are socialists and pedophiles, the idea that President Biden could defeat President Trump is a challenge to their fundamental view of the United States. Confronted with a reality so threatening to their self-image, these Americans would rather believe an obvious lie than face up to reality.

Indeed, conspiracy theories feed upon their patent rejection of socially accepted facts. We see this in the contemporary denial of President Biden's electoral victory. Every presentation of facts—whether by state election officials or by the media or government—is met with fantasies. Voting machines were hacked. Felt tip pens were incorrectly used. Dead people voted. As each conspiratorial claim is refuted, those holding the conspiracy are brought closer together to form a band of the elect, those who can see the hidden truth behind the real world.

The embrace of conspiracy theories is often seen as an affront to democracy. And yet democracy is always tempted by untruth, by lies that tempt the masses and the elites alike. In democracies, George Kateb argues in this volume, "the influence of truth is small in proportion to the need for it. People need it but often don't want it." We have to confront the fact that democratic politics has a tenuous and frequently hostile relation to truth. This is also why, as Peg Birmingham argues, facts are so easily denied in a political world founded upon a moral vision. The American ideology of a "city on the hill" allows for lies that are understood to support a political ideal rather than tell the truth.

To confront the truth of the reality of politics is, as Jerome Kohn argues in his essay below, to recognize that the passion for reality is rare and that it is more often than not subordinated to the comfort of lies. The act of lying treats the world as if it were not real and deprives the political realm of its stability and reality. It is for this reason that political lying, while it can be powerful and active, is more often a semblance of action that can in fact ruin action.

What is more, the effort to correct ideological errors can backfire. As Linda Zerilli writes in her contribution below, fact-checking usually does not lead to an embrace of facts, but often works to destroy the idea of a factual world. Zerilli argues that fact-checking "undermines the truth of opinion that Arendt argues to be crucial to caring about factual truths at all." All that fact-checking accomplishes is to undermine "our allegiance to a fact-based reality." The difficulty with truthtelling today is not that we disagree about facts, it is the deeper problem that we no longer inhabit and share a common world.

Similarly, Marianne Constable argues in her contribution to this volume that fact-checking loses its power to correct misstatements when those who lie simply dismiss the meaning of their words. The former President, Constable argues, uses words not to engage in meaningful public exchange, but simply to undermine the very idea that words and how we use them matter.

In their essays below, Uday Singh Mehta and Wolfgang Heuer ask what it would mean to tell the truth amidst the deep human need for comforting lies. Mehta turns to Gandhi whose idea of *satya* (truth) is rooted in devotion to God. Truthtelling is not easy, Mehta argues, but it demands courage, a willingness even to sacrifice one's life for one's truth. Similarly, Heuer argues that Arendt also connects courage and telling the truth. If for Gandhi courage is found in religious devotion, for Arendt it emerges from the transcendence of the self into a public world one shares with others.

The root of the modern susceptibility to the modern lie is the rise of what Arendt calls mass loneliness. While loneliness is not a new phenomenon, it has transformed itself in the modern age. Throughout human history, Arendt observes, loneliness was a "borderline experience usually suffered in certain marginal social conditions like old age." In our time, however, loneliness "has become an everyday experience of the evergrowing masses of our century."[23] Yes, there were lonely people, but most people were not lonely most of the time. Beginning in the modern age, however, loneliness becomes a mass phenomenon with a metaphysical dimension. Increasingly people feel adrift amidst the purposeless of human life, amidst the death of God, and amidst the break in tradition. Arendt describes the feeling of loneliness as *Verlassenheit*, or abandonment. "The Foundational experience on which terror rests as the essence of totalitarian domination and ideological-logical thinking as the principal of its action is abandonment."[24]

Modern loneliness begins in the shattering of collective dreams and common hope. Hope gives life purpose and shape. In this sense, hope is a story that one sees oneself within. It can be the story of religious salvation or the story of a family tradition. It can be a national story or the story of a clan or tribe. Or it can be a cosmopolitan story in which one imagines oneself a part of a world community. It is this hopeful story that is the breath of life. The loss of hope is like the loss of dreams. And such loss is the beginning of loneliness. "The foundations for loneliness begin in the dreamscapes you create. Their resemblance to reality reflects disappointment first."[25] To be abandoned is to be lost in the world and it is this being-lost that is the foundation for the rise of the modern lie that rejects reality and invents a new and more palatable world.

***

If the human capacity for inventing fictional worlds turns man against reality, so too does the drive to invent ever newer and more powerful technologies that alter our world and even ourselves. The rise of automation, the yearning for intelligent machines, the ability to create life in a test tube, the potential to create artificial planets so that human life could be separated from its earthly home, and the desire to augment human potential through artificial intelligence all promise to free humanity from the real limitations that have till now been part of the human condition. We humans are mortal; we are fallible; and we are prone to exhaustion and irrational outbursts. Technology offers a path beyond our weaknesses and the potential of an alternate reality, one in which we merge with machines and artificial enhancements to cure us of human deficiencies.

The promise of modern science answers an ever-present-but-only-now-realizable drive to make life and man artificial, to cut "the last tie through which even man belongs among the children of nature."[26] With the possibility of making life one of the many artifices that humans create, we humans of the scientific age are breaching the last barricade that characterized a distinctively human way of life, one given to us by birth and by fate. Even man, as with all of nature, will be a product of human hands. We will soon "produce superior human beings." We will be able "to alter [their] size, shape and function."[27] Thus, humanity loosens its tether to a shared and given reality.

The desire and the imminent possibility of making life itself artificial is indicative of a profound "wish to escape the human condition." one expressed in the "hope to extend man's life-span far beyond the hundred-year limit."[28] What Mankind wants, Arendt sees, is to free himself from nature and biology. This is what she means with her citation of the Russian Cosmonaut that "mankind will not remain bound to the earth forever."[29] There is a desire, and increasingly the ability, to improve upon if not reject our human imperfections.

In pointing to modern technology, the launch of Sputnik, and the possibility to "produce superior human beings," and to extend the human "life-span far beyond the hundred-year limit," Arendt shows us what the loss of our earthly nature is. It is, she argues, the loss of our humanity insofar as we humans are, as humans, subject to chance, fate, and fortune. She writes:

> *"This Future man, whom the scientists tell us they will produce in no more than a hundred years, seems to be possessed by a rebellion against human existence as it has been given, a free gift from nowhere (secularly speaking), which he wishes to exchange, as it were, for something he has made himself."*[30]

Human existence, at least as it was for thousands of years, is not something humans make or control. Unlike the artificial world we create, we ourselves are a free gift. In a religious register, that gift can come from God. In a secular world, the free gift of human existence is a matter of fate, chance or *fortuna*. In religious or secular terms, however, the human condition is one of finitude and mortality. It is this aspect of our humanity that science threatens, insofar as science internalizes a way of thinking that yearns to fully master all elements of the earth, including humans themselves.

The earth, then, is Arendt's name for that one aspect of man's reality—his mortal finitude—that must remain if man is to remain subject to the human condition as it has been known for thousands of years. While humans may cultivate crops and domesticate animals, while we may build dams and form polities, we cannot, as humans, shed our mortal coil. To be alive, man, just as animals and plants, must be born and he must die and this life process is an organic and natural event that must remain free from the artifice and fabrication that humans bring to all other aspects of earthly existence. The mortal course of human life, Arendt writes, "is outside this artificial world." The rise of modern science is built upon a denial of our human subjection to an infinitely unknowable and uncontrollable reality.

Our flight from reality is met by our desire to master it so that we simply reject the power of reality. The tree in the forest, and with it the real world, dissolves "into subjective mental processes."[31] As the world comes to be processed through our calculating and rational minds, common sense retreats, and the commonality of the real world—what we all share by being part of a real world because it was common to all—comes to be replaced by the simple commonality of our "faculty of reasoning."[32] It is this faculty of reasoning beyond the real world of common sense that Arendt calls "the playing of the mind with itself, which comes to pass when the mind is shut off from all reality and 'senses' only itself."[33] Humans finally become, in the age of science, rational animals, understood now with a "terrible precision." They are deprived of a grounding in the real and common world, "no more than animals who are able to reason, 'to reckon with consequences.'"[34]

As we rational animals submit the world to our reasoning, we are "freed . . . from given reality altogether—that is, from the human condition of being an inhabitant of the earth."[35] The rise of science—and with it the upending of commonsense assumptions about the world—means that we humans stand before a political choice: are we so alienated from the world in which we have lived that we are willing to remake the world—ourselves included—to conform to our own perfectionist desires?

As Babette Babich writes in her essay in this volume, the eros of the transhumanism movement is not that robots are perfected as robots, but that they improve upon human life. Buried in the transhumanist desire to supplement and surpass humanity with machines and implants is, in Babich's account, a profound shame regarding our human limitations. What transhumanism disdains are the limits of our given abilities.

Nicholson Baker finds a different eros in his love for machines of all kinds, from escalators to street sweepers. Machines, he writes, destabilize us; while we create them, they throw us off course. For that very reason machines make us think about them and ourselves so that machines are actually a reminder of our human capacity to think.

The drive of artificial intelligence is, as Davide Panagia writes below, to "stay the ocean of uncertainty." The effort is to replace the uncertainty of the real world with an artificial world of human control. Exploring the rise of cyberculture, Panagia argues that we are witnessing the rise of a new "way of life that ushers a fundamental ontological shift that transforms the relationship between technology and governance, and thus the relationship between humans and political action." In this new world, humans may well create a world impervious to human action.

Looking at the language of the environmental movement, Marianne Constable argues in her contribution "The Rhetoric of Sustainability" that in the effort to preserve the natural world we humans justify further intrusions into that world. In the name of sustaining nature, we expand our human power "over both nature and artifice, earth and world." In the very effort to save and preserve the natural world we further impose upon that world so that, increasingly, the line between the real and the artificial—the natural world and the human world—blurs into oblivion.

Against the transhumanist vision of humanity Rob Riemen raises a cry of rebellion. In his contribution, Riemen reminds us that human beings are moral beings, and that the idea of an intelligent or a human machine can only be seductive once we have forgotten that human beings are spiritual beings. Riemen dares to ask the question of what happens to the human soul in an age of transhumanism.

***

There may be nothing more terrifying to the human mind than reality, what Nietzsche called the stone of the past. The past is the one thing that human invention can't change, it is a reality that the will cannot master. When the past is horrific or simply oppressive, it stands against us and over us. We can tell stories that re-frame the past. But like a heavy stone along the path, it remains an immovable part of our collective world.

In the face of the past, Nietzsche counsels reconciliation with what is. What is best, Zarathustra says, is that one love even what he most despises. To unlearn the spirit of revenge—the gnashing of teeth at the "it was" of the past—is to learn "reconciliation with time and something higher than reconciliation."[36] To reconcile oneself with time and with the stone of the past is to learn to affirm what is. That is man's redemption, to "recreate all 'it was' into a 'thus I willed it'." The highest will of the overman, the eternal return of the same, is what Nietzsche names reconciliation with time. For Nietzsche, the love of what is requires us to "see as beautiful what is necessary in things," and thus to elevate the natural to the beautiful.[37]

Where loving affirmation of what is real remains impossible—when one is not yet strong enough to be merciful to oneself or to others—then one should pass by. The path to the overman entails the overcoming of revenge and its replacement with love, the gift-giving virtue. For those who cannot yet give affirmation to others, we can, at least, be thankful for what he have, and pass by.

Following Nietzsche, Arendt understands reconciliation and "passing by" to be closely connected. As she writes: "In reconciliation or passing by, what another has *done* is made into what is fated to me, that which I can either accept or that I can, as with everything that is sent to me, move out of its way."[38] Faced with a wrong or an unwelcome reality, Arendt suggests that we have the choice of either reconciliation—affirming one's acceptance of the existence of a world that includes such a wrong—or at least passing by—silently allowing the wrong to exist. In either case, the judgment is made that reconciles oneself to the existence of the wrong and the persistence of the wrongdoer.

A third choice is available as well: namely, in the face of that irreconcilable reality, to deny reconciliation. "Reconciliation has a merciless boundary, which forgiveness and revenge don't recognize—namely, at that about which one must say: This *ought* not to have happened."[39] Arendt explains what she means by reference to Kant's discussion of the rules of war, where Kant says that actions in war that might make a subsequent peace impossible are not permitted. Such acts, whether in war or peace, are examples of "radical evil;" they are "what ought not to have come to pass." Such acts are also those that cannot be reconciled, "what cannot be accepted under any circumstances as our fate."[40] Nor can one simply silently pass by in the face of radical evil. Thus, Arendt's judgment to accept a fateful wrong will differ meaningfully from Nietzsche's fatalism. For both, reconciliation with what is—wrong or right—is to be affirmed or accepted. For Arendt, however, there is a limit to reconciliation that Nietzsche does not seem to recognize.

For Arendt, reconciliation is a political act of solidarity with the existence of others.[41] When I decide to reconcile with the world as it is, I affirm my love for the world and thus my solidarity with the world and those who live in it. In this sense, reconciliation is the precondition for the being of a *polis*: It is the judgment that in spite of our plurality and differences, we share a common world. To reconcile with a wrong is to affirm one's solidarity with the world as it is and is, therefore, to help bring into being a common world. Arendt thus turns to reconciliation as "a new concept of solidarity."[42]

Arendt's most famous example of a judgment of reconciliation is her judgment not to reconcile with Adolf Eichmann. Faced with an epic wrong and a wrongdoer who refuses to repent, reconciliation would affirm a world in which something like the Holocaust could happen. Reconciliation, therefore, would be powerless to remake the human community shattered by the Holocaust. For Arendt, reconciliation with Eichmann is impossible.

When Arendt turns to reconciliation her touchstone is Hegel: "The task of the mind is to understand what happened, and this understanding, according to Hegel, is man's way of reconciling himself with reality; its actual end is to be at peace with the world."[43] In *Truth and Politics*, Arendt raises the problem of a thoughtful reconciliation to reality alongside a reference to Hegel: "Who says what is always tells a story. To the extent that the teller of factual truth is also a storyteller, he brings about that 'reconciliation with reality' which Hegel, the philosopher of history *par excellence*, understood as the ultimate goal of all philosophical thought."[44] Reconciliation, she writes in *The Life of the Mind*, affirms that "the course of history would no longer be haphazard and the realm of human affairs no longer devoid of meaning."[45] There is a basic truth to Hegel's idealism: that the real world only is for humans insofar as we humans understand that world and reconcile ourselves to it.

Hegel's view of reconciliation is, however, in need of revision. He argues that reconciliation allows us to make peace with the world as it is. But peace may not be the adequate response to the world. While reconciliation is necessary to be at peace with the world, we today may no longer be in position to seek peace in the world: *"The trouble is that if the mind is unable to bring peace and to induce reconciliation, it finds itself immediately engaged in its own kind of warfare."*[46] Arendt questions whether reconciliation and the peace it would bring are possible. Against Hegel, she asks: What happens when reconciliation fails?

In asking after reconciliation Arendt is raising the problem of how to approach reality when amidst the "break in tradition" and the "death of God." The Marxian response—to force reality into a new progressive reason guided by science—goes down the path of totalitarianism. Instead, Arendt counsels a new idea of reconciliation: reconciliation to a world without political truths, one in which politics is closer to a kind of unwinnable warfare—one specifically suited to the human mind.

Against "Hegel's gigantic enterprise to reconcile spirit with reality,"[47] Arendt reimagines reconciliation as a facing up to the basic fact of the modern world. We must reconcile ourselves to the fact that there is no truth in politics, and all politics is a struggle among opposing opinions. This does not mean there are no political facts or that truth is politically irrelevant, but there are fewer political facts than most people think. Further, such facts as there may be are themselves cemented only by persuasion and opinion. They are settled political facts that come, by weight of overwhelming persuasiveness, to be part of the shared common world. We must reconcile ourselves, she argues, to a world of plurality absent authority and absent all but the most foundational truths.

Arendt's rethinking of reconciliation follows her conviction that sometime in the early part of the twentieth century, philosophy and thinking ceased to be able "to perform the task assigned to it by Hegel and the philosophy of history, that is, to understand and grasp conceptually historical reality and the events that made the modern world what it is."[48] A gap emerges between reality and thinking. This gap between thinking and reality is not new, and it is even "coeval with the existence of man on earth." But for centuries and millennia, the gap was bridged over by tradition.[49] Reconciliation demands that we forgo the will to absolute knowledge or scientific mastery of the world. We must instead reconcile ourselves to the reality of the gap between thinking and acting. We must, in other words, reconcile ourselves to our irreconcilability to the world.

Thinking today requires accepting the irreconcilability of the world. It demands that we continually recommit ourselves to the loss of a knowable and hospitable world and instead commit ourselves to the struggle of thinking and acting in a world without banisters. Reconciliation is a political judgment to love the world in spite of its evil and inclusive of its irreconcilability. Reconciliation is a necessary political response to the alienation and resentment that mark our times. The grave danger of the modern world is that we humans will resent our reality—our moral, political, and personal limitations and weaknesses—and strive to cure ourselves of human weakness with the aid of science and technology. The dream to perfect the earth and ourselves is, as Arendt writes in *The Human Condition*, "the wish to escape the human condition."

***

The essays in this volume respond to our failure to reconcile ourselves to the irreconcilability of our world. They address the all-too-human wish to escape our human condition through technological and ideological invention. Most of the essays have their origins either in two conferences sponsored by the Hannah Arendt Center at Bard College between 2010 and 2011 or as a response to those conferences. The conference "Human Being in an Inhuman Age" (2010) took seriously the transhumanist claim not simply that intelligent machines would change humanity, but that it would make humans better. Responding to a keynote address by the futurist Ray Kurzweil, participants asked what it means for humanity that we increasingly live in an age where humans can remake the natural and given world, including our own humanity. "Truthtelling: Democracy in an Age Without Facts" (2011) explored the loss of factual truth in the political realm and the invention of the modern lie, whereby reality is replaced by coherent fictional narratives. Together, these conferences and the essays that emerged from them reflect on the perils of invention.

Endnotes

1 Hannah Arendt, "Truth and Politics," in *Between Past and Future* (Penguin Books: New York, 2006) 225.

2 Id. 259.

3 Hannah Arendt, *The Origins of Totalitarianism* (A Harvest Book: New York, 1976) *468*.

4 Id. 469.

5 Hannah Arendt, "The Aftermath of Nazi Rule: Report From Germany," in *Essays in Understanding*, ed. Jerome Kohn (New York: Harcourt Brace & Company, 1994) 249.

6 Id. 250

7 Id. 251.

8 Id.

9 Hannah Arendt, "On the Nature of Totalitarianism," in *Essays in Understanding*, ed. Jerome Kohn (New York: Harcourt Brace & Company, 1994) 349.

10 Id. 349.

11 Id. 350.

12 Id.

13 Id.

14 Id. 351.

15 Id.

16 Id.

17 Id. 350.

18 Hannah Arendt, "Truth and Politics," in *Between Past and Future* (New York: Penguin, 1968) 247.

19 *Origins of Totalitarianism*, 352.

20 Id. 353.

21 Julie Beck, "This Article Won't Change Your Mind," *The Atlantic*, March 13, 2017. https://www.theatlantic.com/science/archive/2017/03/this-article-wont-change-your-mind/519093/

22 "Truth and Politics," 248.

23 *Origins*, 478.

24 Hannah Arendt, "Ideologie und Terror," in *The Modern Challenge to Tradition*, edited by Barbara Hahn and James McFarland, with the support of Ingo Kieslich and Ingeborg Nordmann. (Göttingen: Wallstein Verlag, 2018) 18.

25 Claudia Rankine, *Don't Let Me Be Lonely: An American Lyric* (Minneapolis: Graywolf Press, 2004) 121.

26 Hannah Arendt, *The Human Condition* (Chicago, IL: University of Chicago Press, 1998), 2.

27 Id. 2

28 Id.

29 Id. 1-2.

30 Id.

31 Id. 282.

32 Id. 283.

33 Id. 284.

34 Id.

35 Id. 285.

36 Friedrich Nietzsche, *Also Sprach Zarathustra, Kritische Studienausgabe* v. 4 (Giorgio Colli & Mazzino Montinari eds., 1988) 181

37 Friedrich Nietzsche, *Die Fröhliche Wissenschaften, in Kritische Studienausgabe*, v. 3 (Giorgio Colli & Mazzino Montinari eds., 1988) §276, 523

38 Hannah Arendt, *Denktagebuch*, ed. Ursula Ludz and Igeborg Nordmann (München: Piper Verlag, 2003) I. 6.

39 Id. 7. The text here says *"umbarmherzige"* which I read as a typographical error for *"unbarmherzige."*

40 Id. 7.

41 Hannah Arendt to Karl Jaspers, August 6, 1955, in *Hannah Arendt Karl Jaspers Correspondence 1929-1969*, ed. Lotte Kohler and Hans Saner, trans. Robert and Rita Kimber (New York: Harcourt Brace Jovanovich, 1992), 264.

42 Ibid.

43 *Between Past and Future*, 7.

44 Id.

45 Hannah Arendt, *Life of the Mind* (New York: Harcourt Brace Jovanovich, 1978) 2:46.

46 *Between Past and Future*, 7 italics added.

47 *The Human Condition*, 300–301.

48 *Between Past and Future*, 8.

49 Id. 13.

01110100 01101000 01100101 00100000 01110000 01100101 01110010 01101001 01101100 01110011 00100000 01101111 01100110 00100000 01101001 01110110 01100101 01101110 01110110 01100101 01110100 01110100 01101001 01101111 01101110

Truthtelling

01110100 01101000 01100101 00100000 01110000 01100101 01110010 01101001 01101100 01110011 00100000 01101111 01100110 00100000 01101001 01101110 01110110 01100101 01101110 01110100 01101001 01101111 01101110

Reality Wobbles:
When A Lying Way of Life
Comes Home To Roost

Roger Berkowitz

01110100 01101000 01100101 00100000 01110000 01100101 01110010 01101001 01101100 01110011 00100000 01101111 01100110 00100000 01101001 01110110 01110110 01100101 01110110 01110110 01100101 01110110 01110100 01101001 01101111 01101110

O n May 28, 1975, then Senator Joe Biden wrote a letter to Hannah Arendt:

> *Dear Miss Arendt,*
>
> *I read in a recent article by Tom Wicker of a paper that you read at the Boston Bicentennial Forum.*
>
> *As a member of the Foreign Relations Committee of the Senate, I am most interested in receiving a copy of your paper.*
>
> *Thank you.*
>
> *Sincerely,*
>
> *Joseph R. Biden Jr.*
>
> *United State Senator*

The paper to which Senator Biden referred is "Home to Roost," a lecture Arendt read on May 20, 1975 at Faneuil Hall, which also was broadcast five days later by National Public Radio.[1] The lecture was then published in the *New York Review of Books*. Arendt died suddenly a few months later in December of 1975, making the speech her last public appearance and "Home to Roost" her last finished essay. "Home to Roost" is republished in a remarkable collection of essays *Responsibility and Judgment*.[2]

"Home to Roost" gathers together Arendt's lifelong concerns with totalitarian lying and theoretical obfuscation, alongside her deep fear about the corruption and failure of the American republican tradition of free self-government. Invited to speak at the Bicentennial ceremony billed as a birthday party for America, Arendt focused on recent "years of aberration" in which the country had seen its prestige and power wane. Her hope, expressed in the final sentences of her talk, is that when the facts of the country's corruption come 'home to roost' in the crises facing the republic, we would "try at least to make" the facts welcome. "Let us not try to escape into some utopias—images, theories, or sheer follies." For the sake of freedom, Arendt asks, let us seek to confront the facts of who we are and where we have fallen short of our ideals.

The facts of the crises facing the United States are myriad in Arendt's telling. Just nine months earlier President Nixon had resigned in the wake of Watergate and was pardoned by President Ford. Add the defeat in Vietnam, the crisis of McCarthyism, the bankruptcy of New York City, and the "destruction of a reliable and devoted civil service." All of which were followed by the appearance of the "ugly American" in imperialist foreign affairs. Which is why Arendt mused that for the two hundredth birthday of the Republic of the United States, "I fear we could not have chosen a less appropriate moment."[3]

Forty-five years after Senator Biden wrote to Hannah Arendt, now President Biden oversees another moment of crisis for the democratic and constitutional Republic of the United States. The facts of our current crises include the impeachment of the former-President for abuse of power by the House of Representatives, a cultural and political war pitting educated elites against lower status Americans, rebellions against expert rule and a professional civil service, a continued reckoning with over 200 years of chattel slavery, 100 years of Jim Crow, and the racism that justified both, a pandemic that has turned into a partisan battle with deadly consequences, and the most unequal recession in US history, barely impacting those who work from their screens while causing depression-era misery for millions at the bottom of the economic pyramid.

What unites these two moments of crisis separated by half a century is the flight from reality that Arendt understood to be at the center of our modern predicament. She connects this aversion to reality first to the instinct of pundits and intellectuals to search for "deeper causes" of what went wrong. The speculations by intellectuals are "often far-fetched and almost always based on assumptions which are prior to an impartial examination of the factual record." It is in the nature of such speculative theories to "to hide and to make us forget the stark, naked brutality of facts, of things as they are."[4]

Arendt also traces the modern flight from reality to the doctrine of progress, the "premise underlying this whole age" that we have to keep growing and getting bigger and more efficient.

For both socialism and capitalism, there is a belief that we must get ever richer and bigger. Not because there is anything good or beautiful in bigness, but because we are terrified of what we will find if we stop moving forward.

"[T]o stop going, stop wasting, to stop consuming more and more, quicker and quicker, to say at any given moment enough is enough would spell imminent doom."[5]

Most importantly, Arendt argues that the refusal of reality is tied to the "mass manipulation of fact and opinion,"[6] which she attributes to the "decisive" consequences of the rise of public relations that has "invaded our political life."[7] Arendt's prime example of the dominance of image-making in politics is the Vietnam War. To look at the Vietnam War is to be confronted with a reality that is "unbelievable": the horror of the war, the failures of U.S. policy; the lies and corruption; and the atrocities committed. This "not very honorable and not very rational enterprise was," she writes, "exclusively guided by the needs of a superpower to create for itself an *image* which would *convince* the world that it was indeed 'the mightiest power on earth.'"[8] The war in Vietnam was fought for neither "power nor profit." It did not aim at imperialist domination. Not even influence in Asia was the goal. "The terrible truth" revealed by the Pentagon Papers was that the "only permanent goal had become the *image* itself." The war was fought for "audiences" according to imagined "scenarios" and how they would be perceived. And at the end, the entirety of the effort was not to avoid losing, but "to avoid *admitting* defeat and to keep the *image* of the 'mightiest power on earth' intact."[9]

Today, our infatuation with *images* and our flight from the real world is all around us. The former President lied about the size of the crowds at his inauguration. He lied to the American people about the coronavirus. He is now lying about the threat of voter fraud. He appeared at campaign rallies after having tested positive for Covid-19. The audacity of Trump's lies is at times difficult to fathom. What needs to be understood, however, is that the President's lies are not attempts to convince or persuade; his lies are designed to buttress his image. His lies about the inauguration are to protect his image as a powerful leader. But above all, his lies that attack experts, civil servants, the intelligence agencies, and our political institutions are aimed to burnish his image as a truthteller.

It is a twist of irony that the greatest liar ever to hold the office of the Presidency won in large part because people saw him as telling the one big truth—that the system is broken and corrupt. Donald Trump can appear as a truthteller because he rejects the expert-and-pundit-driven theories and speculations that have come to justify globalization, imperialism, systemic racism, rape culture, and media objectivity. Globalization and free trade have been sold as an unqualified good by the cosmopolitan classes who jet around the world attending conferences and opening factories, while millions of people in the lower and middle classes see their incomes diminished with little benefit. United States intervention in foreign nations is defended by the foreign policy elite as necessary to uphold the liberal world order, but the people who fight those wars are almost exclusively those on the bottom of the economic and social ladder.

Systemic racism and white privilege embrace a theory of collective guilt, ignoring differences of class, origin, and hardship, and forgetting that where all are guilty, none are guilty—all of which leads to a public relations strategy of admitting an abstract guilt divorced from consequences. The claim from the #MeToo movement to "believe women"—rooted, of course, in the longstanding silencing of women—makes the ideological demand that all women be believed, until, of course, someone like Tara Reade accuses Joe Biden of rape or popular feminist professors are accused of harassment, at which point the at-least-sometimes hypocrisy of the #MeToo movement is exposed. And the embrace of "resistance journalism" by much of the media elite has, finally, made clear the real bias of mainstream journalism that largely ignores and diminishes the worldview of those outside the centers of urban and elite culture. There is no greater example of this than the continued belief by many in the press that the former President colluded with Russia and that his election in 2016 was illegitimate, even after the Mueller Report found no evidence of such collusion.

The problem today is not simply that former President Trump lies incessantly. It is not only that those on the left insist on theories and speculations that defy common sense. It is easy to focus on the specific lies the ex-President tells because they are so brazen. Conspiracies are thriving and not only on the fringes of our society: There is the Qanon claim about a pedophile ring throughout the reaches of the U.S. government; the fantasy of #Obamagate that President Obama and Vice-President Biden conspired to prevent President Trump from winning the election; there is the fictional claim that President Obama and now Representative Ilhan Omar are not U.S. citizens; Holocaust deniers are in ascendence and #Russiagate purveyors insist that President Trump is controlled by Moscow. To point out that conspiracies impact both the left and the right is not to state an equivalency; it is, however, to recognize that there is a flight from reality across our social and political worlds: lying today has become a way of life.

"Lying as a way of life,"[10] Arendt observes, was "quite successful in countries under totalitarian rule." In totalitarian regimes, lying was guided by ideologies and enforced by terror. Only a totalitarian regime can make bold and obvious lies believable. They do so, first, by choosing plausible but simple ideological fictions—that a conspiracy of Jews controls world politics—and organizing a logical coherent narrative around that fiction. These "facts" are not objective, but they are believed as part of ideological fantasy, they become as "real and untouchable an element in their lives as the rules of arithmetic."[11] And since the "fact" of a Jewish conspiracy is not a fact but the linchpin of a logically coherent world, it is foolproof against reality-based arguments.

In totalitarian states, lying was guided by an ideology and thus had a logical consistency that fully divorced the lies from reality, which is always complicated and never logical. Totalitarianism promises to lonely masses what they want: a logically coherent fantasy that replaces a messy and uncomfortable reality. But the totalitarian states could only cement their lies through terror—by normalizing a "sheer criminality" by which lies would be certified by mass murder. For one sure way to "prove" the fact of Jewish world conspiracy is to exterminate the Jews and make them into the enemy you claim that they are. By bringing criminality into the political process on a gigantic scale, Nazi Germany secured belief in the fictional ideological reality.

Arendt did not believe that totalitarianism as it existed in Nazi Germany or Bolshevist Russia was a threat in the United States. Aware of the dangers of totalitarianism, public opinion in the United States, she saw, was not prepared to condone mass murder, camps, and terror. And yet, writing in the wake of the blatant lying in Vietnam, the burglaries and cover-ups of Watergate, rampant inflation and urban decay amidst the refusal to own up to the economic crises in the country, she does believe that public opinion appeared ready to condone "all political transgressions short of murder."[12] In other words, if "lying as a way of life" might not support the kinds of criminality evidence in totalitarian states, it might serve to obfuscate and justify a lower level of criminality in a declining American Republic.

American politicians consistently get away with lying and even blatant criminality. Arendt's primary example is Richard Nixon and Watergate. While Nixon's crimes "were a far cry from the sort of criminality with which we once were inclined to compare it," the facts are clear that Nixon's administration included many persons who—if not criminals—were so attracted to the "aura of power, its glamorous trappings," that they came to see themselves as above the law.[13] Nixon, and those around him, assumed that they could and would get away with their crimes because they believed that "all people are actually like them."[14] They thought that all people are, in the end, corruptible. Thus, they believed that judges, the press, and politicians could be bought or cowed. They sought to deny the reality of their crimes by spreading the *image* of human corruptibility—all men would have done the same.

Against the logical ideological coherence backed by terror that supports the big lie in totalitarian states, Arendt sees that the lying in the American Republic of the 1970s was based upon the hidden persuasive power of an image: namely, the image that those who became "accomplices in criminal activities" in the pursuit of power were normal, just like everyone else, and "would be above the law."[15] What Nixon sought was to replace the totalitarian support of lying on principle by the rule by terror with a culture of lying as a way of life that could persist because nobody would care. He and his cronies imagined that lying as an everyday activity in the pursuit of power would be as acceptable to their fellow citizens as it was to them. And to Nixon's shock, the public was not amenable to such pressure and manipulation by the Executive. The press and the American republican institutions did fight back. "Nixon's greatest mistake—aside from not burning the tapes in time—was to have misjudged the incorruptibility of the courts and the press."[16]

The kind of lying Arendt saw emerging in the United States—lying as a way of life—was not a traditional political lie that was intended to keep secrets of state. It did not concern "data that had never been made public."[17] Rather, the modern lie that emerged in the 20th century "deals efficiently with things that are not secrets at all but are known to practically everybody."[18] Everyone might know that Nixon was a criminal: the question is—Would they care?

Similarly, everyone today knows not only that ex-President Trump lies, but also that he is a con man at best and a criminal at worst: The former President avoids taxes; he pays hush money to prostitutes; he harasses women; he bullies and intimidates contractors and employees to accept less money than they are owed; someone else took his SAT; he encourages foreign leaders and American corporations to do business at his hotels, thus profiting off the presidency; and he abuses his power to seek political advantage. He is a con man and we are all in on the con. His lies simply give plausible deniability to his truth, that he is a con man who is powerful enough to get away with taking control of the most powerful country on earth. His lies are not designed to be believable. They are designed to foment chaos and instability, all in the name an image of power.

Consider one of former President Trump's many bald-faced lies. Amidst protests over the murder of George Floyd by a white Minneapolis police officer on May 25th, 2020, a protester named Martin Gugino approached a line of police in Buffalo, New York. The police line, with officers wearing tactical riot gear, was moving forward, to clear protesters from Buffalo's Niagara Square at 8:10 pm, ten minutes after the 8 pm curfew. Gugino, a 75 year-old man and a "longtime peace activist and gentle person," approached the line of police.[19] Two officers brandishing batons pushed Gugino back and he toppled and fell backwards, hitting his head. Blood began trickling from his ear. The police formed a cordon around Gugino. Eventually he was brought to a hospital, where he recovered.

Five days later, President Donald Trump tweeted that Gugino "could be an ANTIFA provocateur" and that he appeared to "scan police communications in order to black out the equipment." The President also wrote:

"Buffalo protester shoved by Police could be an ANTIFA provocateur. 75 year old Martin Gugino was pushed away after appearing to scan police communications in order to black out the equipment. @OANNI watched, he fell harder than was pushed. Was aiming scanner. Could be a set up?"[20]

The President's tweet was quickly refuted by mainstream news outlets[21] and even by a smattering of Republican Senators.[22] No one in the mainstream press or political life of the country believed the President. So why does the President tell such lies?

There are at least three answers to the question of why the President can lie so obviously. The first is that lying is simply a part of politics. "Truthfulness," as Arendt famously remarked, "has never been counted among the political virtues."[23]

Political action seeks change; it must begin something new. But change is not possible if we cannot "remove ourselves from where we physically are located and *imagine* that things might as well be different from what they actually are."[24] Thus all political activism and change demand the imagination, the capacity to deliberately deny "factual truth—the ability to lie."[25]

Not only can we say that the sun shines when it is raining, we can say that "all men are created equal" when we know for sure that they are all incredibly different and unique. Without this "mental freedom to deny or affirm existence," Arendt writes, no action and no politics is possible.[26] Lies are at the center of the political enterprise.

The second reason the President can lie without consequence is that political facts are contingent; they depend upon agreement and persuasion. Even the President's seemingly clear lie in his tweet about Mr. Gugino can be spun as a true statement. His tweet is expressed in the subjunctive: Gugino "*could* be an ANTIFA provocateur." Gugino "*appeared*" to scan police communications. The President asks a question: "*Could* it be a set up?" To call the President a liar or to fact-check his statements may well lead to a parsing of the facts in such a way that reduces all facts to statements of opinion. This transformation of fact into opinion can destroy the common world. It reminds us "facts" are contingent and only are "true" when they are believed by enough people in a political community.

Finally, the President's lying displays the cancerous growth of the public relations machine to encompass all areas of political and economic life such that lying and the evasion of reality are made into matters of principle. When lying becomes a way of life, the very idea of truth is transformed into a battle of competing images. The question of whether there is voter fraud ceases to have a true answer; it is transformed into contest between dueling images. Is wearing a mask medically sound? It is, rather, a partisan statement, an image representing one's political commitments. "The result of a consistent and total substitution of lies for factual truth," Arendt writes, "is not that the lies will now be accepted as truth, and the truth be defamed as lies, but that the sense by which we take our bearings in the real world—and the category of truth vs. falsehood is among the mental means to this end—is being destroyed."[27]

The end goal of lying as a way of life is not that the lies are believed, but the cementing of cynicism. When cynicism reigns, not only is everything permitted; but also everything is possible. Cynicism is the fertile ground in which power grows unstoppable absent the constraints of reality.

And for such cynicism, Arendt worries, "there is no remedy."[28] What consistent lying achieves is the "experience of a trembling wobbling motion of everything we rely on for our sense of direction and reality is among the most common and vivid experiences of men under totalitarian rule."[29] But if in totalitarian government reality wobbles as a result of terror enforcing lies, in the corruption of our present politics, reality wobbles because the image having overtaken truth has become persuasive.

Arendt offers a metaphor of sitting around a table to understand what it means when the real world is lost. So long as the table is there, we are all part of a conversation, connected by the table that creates as it were the world that unites us. Remove the table and we are isolated individuals sitting in space. Similarly, stories we tell and songs we sing bring us together and guide us in living together as a collectivity. Institutions we respect and symbols we revere inspire in us a shared sense of purpose. And celebrations and memorials offer us a common liturgy that builds a foundation upon which we stand, a shared ground in spite of our many differences. The building and nurturing of this shared common world is the activity of politics; politics is the telling of stories and building of institutions that unite a multitude of individuals into a common and meaningful project.

The political world needs a shared reality that in turn is based upon a factual world; and yet political facts are contingent, they depend upon agreement and persuasion. The fact that the earth is warming because of human activity, the fact that abortion is a constitutional right, the fact that we live in a constitutional democracy, and the fact that systemic racism disadvantages black Americans are facts that could be otherwise and can be contested. But factual truths are "always related to other people" and such truths only exist when they are spoken about.[30] They are only "facts" when they are believed by enough people in a political community so that they come to be part of the public world.

It is in speaking with one another that we come to share common reference points and in our talking amongst ourselves conjure the factual world into being. At that point the facts become part of our shared truths, "the ground on which we stand and the sky that stretches above us."[31]

The tendency to "transform fact into opinion, to blur the dividing line between them," can lead to a situation where "simple factual statements are not accepted," and even the most basic facts dissolve into the diversity of viewpoints.[32] When this happens, there is no permanence and no durability to the world. A world without durability and permanence is an inhuman world and ceases to be a home and a haven for mortal beings.

While Arendt wonders if there may be no remedy for cynicism, she also offers a faith that amidst the ruin of our human world, a new world can be reborn. She holds a fundamental belief in the power of talking. She writes: "We become more just and more pious by thinking and talking about justice and piety."[33] But why is this so?

First, in talking about the world with others, with those who disagree, we make the world visible in its complexity. Second, in talking about the world, we also make judgments and decisions about the world. Those decisions, Arendt admits, "may one day prove wholly inadequate." But even absent agreements on the nature of a crisis and how to solve it, the act of speaking with one another about the crises of our times will, she argues, "eventually lay the groundwork for new agreements between ourselves as well as between the nations of the earth, which then might become customs, rules, [and] standards that again will be frozen into what is called morality."[34] In talking with one another we create the kinds of shared experiences and common points of connections that might, over time, become the building blocks of a new shared world that can give birth to new traditions and thus a new moral order.

This potential rebirth of a new common ethical world is not only possible, but likely. It depends, however, on the courage to speak honestly and openly with one another absent ideological rigidity. If and when we do, we will come to understand what we share and where we disagree. If and when we do open such a common world, we will begin the process of bringing that world into existence. That is the source of Arendt's optimism: "I personally do not doubt that from the turmoil of being confronted with reality without the help of precedent, that is, of tradition and authority, there will finally arise some new code of conduct."[35] The only way to engage the crisis of our wobbling world is to confront the reality and talk honestly about it with others.

Endnotes

1 The article then Senator Biden had read was "The Lie and the Image," by Tom Wicker, which appeared in *The New York Times* on May 25, 1975.

2 Citations to "Home to Roost" are from *Responsibility and Judgment*, ed. by Jerome Kohn (Schocken Books: New York, 2003).

3 Home To Roost, 257.

4 Id. 261.

5 Id. 262.

6 Hannah Arendt, Truth and Politics (Penguin Books: New York, 1977), 247.

7 Home to Roost, 263.

8 Id.

9 Id.

10 Id. 264.

11 Hannah Arendt, *The Origins of Totalitarianism* (Harcourt: New York, 1976), 363.

12 Home to Roost, 266.

13 Id. 268.

14 Id.

15 Id.

16 Id.

17 Arendt, Truth and Politics, 247.

18 Id.

19 Joshua Rhett Miller and Lia Eustachewich. "Martin Gugino, Buffalo Man Pushed by Police, Is Long-time Peace Activist," *New York Post*, June 5, 2020. https://nypost.com/2020/06/05/martin-gugino-buffalo-man-pushed-by-police-is-long-time-activist/.

20 Alan Feuer, "Trump Falsely Targets Buffalo Protester, 75, as 'Antifa Provocateur'," The New York Times, June 9, 2020. https://www.nytimes.com/2020/06/09/nyregion/who-is-martin-gugino-buffalo-police.html)

21 Id.

22 Marianne Levine and Burgess Everett, "'Ugh': Republicans Cringe after Trump's Attack on 75-year-old Protester," Politico, June 9, 2020. https://www.politico.com/news/2020/06/09/republicans-deflect-questions-after-trump-tweet-75-year-old-protester-309075)

23 Truth and Politics, 233. Also in "Lying and Politics" in *Crisis of the Republic* (Harcourt: New York, 1972), 4.

24 Lying and Politics, 5.

25 Id.

26 Id. 5-6.

27 Truth and Politics, 252-53.

28 Truth and Politics, 253

29 Truth and Politics, 253.

30 Truth and Politics, 234.

31 Truth and Politics, 258.

32 Truth and Politics, 232, 233.

33 Hannah Arendt, "The Crisis Character of Modern Society," in *Thinking Without a Bannister*, ed. Jerome Kohn (Schocken Books: New York, 2018), 331.

34 Id. 331.

35 Id. 330.

Democracy and Untruth

George Kateb

A common belief is that one main reason for the superiority of representative democracy to all other political systems is that it works by procedures that compel officials to be held accountable. They must take responsibility for their conduct in office and submit to the judgment of the electorate on the basis of their record. Ideally, they would fail at re-election not only because they pursued bad policies but also because they did not pursue the policies that they had pledged to pursue if elected. Accountability is thus made up of two questions that are rightly asked of elected officials. Always the first question is: What have you done? It can be asked every day as well as on Election Day, the day of judgment. But there is also a second question, for both Election Day and every day, barely less important than the first one: Have you done what you said you would do or try to do? Both of these questions deal with the past and present. There is a third question for Election Day, which pertains to the future conduct of those who want to hold onto their offices or who want to win an office for the first time: What do you plan to do or try to do?

Obviously, this picture is simple to the point of being almost useless. The actuality doesn't sustain the aspiration: the ideal of democratic accountability appears to endure such a hard fate that it is to an appreciable extent fictitious. Democracy, with the greatest freedom to speak and the greatest amount of public speech, seems to operate by means of untruth much more than any other contemporary political system. By *untruth* I mean not just outright lying by false description or denial, but also such devices and practices as secrets or the withholding of knowledge, propaganda, exaggeration and other kinds of distortion, simplification, and construction of plausible stories and solemn narratives.

If accountability is to exist, citizens must want it, and people holding office or seeking election to office must provide it. If people want it intensely enough, democratic citizens would press the political stratum to provide it in order to avoid being punished by electoral defeat. The essential form of accountability is transparency. That is, citizens must want, and officials and would-be officials must provide, intelligible descriptive statements that are also honest or sincere. Sincere, intelligible statements must describe what officials in power have done and why, or must explain what they intend to do and why; and similarly, those who seek office must intelligibly and sincerely say what they would do, if elected. Naturally, changing circumstances can throw any intended policy off course. Public policies are at the mercy of unexpected events at home and abroad; statements of intention and purpose cannot be ironclad contracts or promises. But when events deflect officials from their stated purposes, these officials must be transparent in explaining why they did not or cannot do what they said they intended to do. On the other hand, citizens must care about being dealt with honestly, and allowing for the play of circumstances, hold officials to their word. When accountability is haphazard or arbitrary, it would then seem that representative democracy could well be replaced by any political system that got desirable results. The initial judgment is thus that citizens must want and expect transparency, and find its lack unacceptable, if the political stratum is to feel urgency in providing it to the fullest extent possible.

Of course, many of us are not conscientious and attentive as citizens. We make an undesirable situation much worse in many areas of policy in which technical knowledge is not demanded of the citizen and where greater transparency than actually exists is possible. My main interest is in the area of foreign policy, where the failure to insist on transparency intensifies the inveterate disposition of those who make foreign policy not to provide it. And because the results of foreign policy, though always of significance to American citizens, are only episodically or selectively or intermittently visible and palpable, the people remain fairly inattentive.

We will return to foreign policy as the most important field for discussion regarding the lack of transparency in democracy. But I would like to turn first in a general way to the deficiencies of democratic citizens.

Untruth plays a large role in American politics, so large a role that we could be led to contemplate the possibility that our democracy is intrinsically tenuous. But the plain fact is that untruth plays a large role in American democratic culture, in American life altogether. We the people bear a good deal of the responsibility for that condition. Some main institutions in American life proceed on the assumption that the mental level of the American people is low and that their moral level is perhaps not higher. I have in mind especially politics and advertising. Much of the time, power holders in these institutions can and do assume that people don't want very much transparency, as long as things go tolerably well. In democratic politics and culture, much of the blame for the ubiquity of untruth must fall on the people. How else could advertising, with its deception, inaccuracy, and exaggeration, prosper? How else could the political stratum get away with its lies, distortions, withholdings, secrets, ingrained partisan bias, and ideological misrepresentations, and even flourish because of them? Partisanship is a particularly virulent source of disregard for truth. To be sure, partisanship supplies ideological emphasis, and emphasis is often needed to get important events and conditions noticed with an appropriate seriousness. But when emphasis turns into inflamed exaggeration and then into outright mendacity that is repeated tenaciously as if it were a helpless obsession, partisanship soils public discourse indelibly. An adversarial partisanship might right the balance politically, but two gross falsehoods do not add up to a truth, and a midway compromise between them may be no better than a half-truth.

Must we say, then, that there is a greater prevalence of untruth in modern mass democracy than in all other political systems, except for 20th-century totalitarian rule? Where the people are the ultimate judges because of mass enfranchisement, and where numerous mass media cater to the people by pitching their wares at the most profitable level—that is, a low average level— politics and the whole ambient culture will be bathed in untruth. After a certain point, the larger the audience, the coarser or simpler the discourse must be. If politics is confined to the elite or at most a few segments of the population where discussion is therefore pitched at a much higher level and to a much smaller audience, and where the ambient culture is dominated by the standards of the comparative few, then perhaps untruth in all its forms would be much less necessary, and consequently, more candor would be in circulation in political life and elsewhere. Fewer outside the elite would be able to notice the candor; and if they somehow managed to have access to it, it would not register, or if it registered, it would not be likely to spread; it would look too unfamiliar. The truth would be unblushing in an oligarchic political system with restricted media of communication, but there would be much to hide, whenever there was a need to hide it. Exclusion of most of the population from political life reduces the need until some patent crisis occurs, and then the unscrupulousness of the elite is strained to the limit to improvise explanations that do not make things worse. Once a larger public engages in even minimal discussion, untruth must change its forms: secrecy no longer suffices; unembarrassed lies and distortions must be risked.

The irony is great and was theoretically noticed before by the early Frankfurt school. The means of enlightenment in an open society, which is also a mass democratic society, are abundantly available. Someone or other will speak or write practically every truth that is relevant to discussion of public policy, the stuff of political life. Of course, not every secret will be disclosed, but nearly all the truth can be found in some medium or other; you have to look tirelessly, however, and even so, those who are committed to the truth may on occasion innocently offer untruth. At the same time, the means of false enlightenment or semi-enlightenment are far more abundant because the popular demand for them is far in excess of the demand for enlightenment. Truth is often not nearly as attractive as untruth, which has unlimited seductive power. To be sure, freedom of speech and press is a standing encouragement to expression on all matters of life, including public affairs. The sheer abundance of expression is staggering. How could one wish it otherwise? Nonetheless, the fact remains that the volume of untruth crowds out truth and makes the truth about the facts—I don't refer to diverse opinions about the facts—just one more strand in public discourse. The influence of truth is small in proportion to the need for it. People need it but often don't want it.

The people appear to get the elites they deserve or need or want. The harms and injuries inflicted by the elites on the people are the responsibility, to a considerable extent, of the people themselves. Untruth serves various interests and passions of the elites, whether in office or in society—the powerful and advantaged classes, in short. Where power is untransparent, accountability is a sham. The real motives of policy makers are obscured, and often what the policy makers have actually done or failed to do or intend to do is unclear or secret. When policies are difficult to identify or discuss, attribution of responsibility is hard, if not impossible, to determine; it becomes diffuse or murky. An incurious or non-vigilant people are not served; they are even sacrificed. The situation would be better if people wanted the truth more than they seem to, and tried harder to understand it when it was actually provided. In a democracy, popular deficiencies of attention and understanding set systematic untruth in motion.

Since democratic control is often crude or belated or nonexistent, it does not serve to transform psychologically the power holders and power seekers and thus create a stratum *radically* different from power holders and power seekers in oligarchic and other nondemocratic forms of government. Let us posit the fairly constant disposition in all those who are attracted to political power, that whatever the form of government, they desire as much discretionary power as possible. I do not say that they are normally driven by the will to tyrannize, or that they have no regard for ends other than acquiring and maintaining their power and feeling the pleasure that comes from making things happen and giving orders to people who are subordinate to them, or that they must love to the point of compulsion such accompaniments of power as prestige or glory. The point is that those in any political stratum are not usually dominated by the intellectual appetite to understand their own motives or to understand what it means for others to suffer the consequences of their deeds. They are not committed to truth and find the appetite for untruth in citizens gratifying. They love having secrets. Is that their greatest delight, more than lying or distorting?

The long and short of it is that the solution to the problem of transparency and, hence, accountability is not found in either more democracy or less, more popular power or less. If you want more democracy or less or none, you have to use some standard other than the principle of accountability. If we were better citizens, our political stratum would be better, more true to the spirit of constitutional democracy. But bad citizens with democratic rights are better than subjects. Left to themselves to rule completely as they please, autocratic rulers or mostly closed elites would be likely to do worse things than democratic officials who are slackly controlled or controlled for irrational or unjust purposes—certainly in many important areas of public policy. I characterize the situation we have as a grim and fundamentally un-improvable mixture: a combination of democracy and oligarchy and of democracy and nondemocratic features inherent in any system of government and therefore shared by all of them. But even this general description is not adequately pessimistic when we consider the making of foreign policy.

***

I now turn to a particular area of public policy, foreign policy, because I believe that the lack of transparency and accountability in that area is most acute, and the effects most serious. This is not to say that transparency by itself would be a panacea; much would depend on what citizens made of transparency or even whether they paid receptive attention to an appreciably greater amount of it.

From the early 20th century on, foreign policy has been the most important area of public policy in the United States (to leave aside other Western democracies). This is because the United States has become, with ever-growing determination, an imperial power; if you prefer a euphemism, a country with global ambitions and global reach. The greatest American land grabs came earlier, in the 19th century, and were at the expense of Mexico, a neighbor, and of indigenous peoples already here. They prefigured global exertion. In an empire, of whatever sort, foreign policy can never be absent from the minds of those in high office, those around them, those who report on them, and those who aspire to high office.

Foreign policy, no matter how unadventurous, wreaks havoc on modern constitutional democracy. An active foreign policy increases the damage; then, when a constitutional democracy has an imperial foreign policy of global reach, every problem of transparency discussed so far is intensively and systematically aggravated. Such a foreign policy establishes a second polity attached to the first supposedly democratic one, and thereby creates a kind of strange hybrid with no name. This second polity is not merely a large oligarchic element in an otherwise democratic polity but rather tends to be a despotic element (but not in Tocqueville's sense of democratic despotism). It is not exactly a state within the state, the core or cabal (like the old Prussian military), or a parallel political apparatus imposed on the formal state (like the Bolshevik party). It includes but is more than a collection of secret agencies or a delegated privatized part of the state.

The people as a body of citizens are for the most part out of the story of foreign policy, except as resources—bodies and taxes—and as sources of psychological support, sending back to the foreign policy elite the elite's dispositions, but now magnified, simplified, and made more urgent or gross by mass sentiment. To be sure, various sectors of the population have a particular interest in the conduct of foreign policy toward one or another state for ethnic or religious reasons, and supply a fairly steady pressure that cannot be ignored by officials or those who observe or report the action. It is quite common for a particular interest to see foreign menace to the favored ethnicity or religion all over the globe; thus, one source of the momentum for imperialism can be pressure applied upward from particular groups of citizens.

How shall we judge such ethnic and religious loyalty? Is it rational, or not? Is group identity rational, or not? How could it be rational? It is certainly true that such loyalty consists in part in adherence to an imaginary whole or entity, an entity imagined as a person that is surpassingly greater than any individual person; each member is incorporated as an indissociable part of the "superperson" (in Isaiah Berlin's term), absorbed into it to such an extent that the person has identity only through the group. But the superperson disregards national boundaries just as it transcends individual selves. The hold of group identity is one of the greatest sources of the will to live in untruth. It rests on an inexhaustibly potent metaphor that is never seen through.

Group identity, however, is not confined to those who feel it toward their fellow ethnics or co-religionists and across boundaries. Group identity lies at the heart of a more general sentiment, nationally confined patriotism, which may subsist alongside a particular ethnic or religious loyalty. Once in a contest, patriots want their country to win, or not to lose. The uncanny fact is that all countries are patriotic. Passions (commitments, attachments) define a country; different passions make different countries. But when it comes to conflict between countries, the same kind of passion dominates all countries. Populations are *inwardly* interchangeable when national group identity takes over, and yet each population is devoted to a country that is prized for its cultural particularity or distinctiveness. Recall Lincoln's bemused mention in his second Inaugural Address of this tragic absurdity: "Both [sides in the civil war] read the same Bible, and pray to the same God; and each invokes His aid against the other . . . The prayers of both could not be answered."

To be sure, patriotism is at heart a sort of agonism; it delights in a pure contest that is valuable apart from any tangible gains, in which the point is to prevail after struggle. Foreign policy thus rests on a merger in the people of the tribally primitive and the abstract. Abstraction is the foundation of the primitive. Sometimes, the will is to prevail at any cost to one's side and to the other's; but sometimes the aim could be to prevail by displays of virtues and skills that are also valued, apart from tangible gains. A democracy cannot be imperialist without a strong agonistic spirit in the people. Of course, the elite also shares that spirit; to them, foreign policy can feel like a game, but one that is more rarified and far more brutal than team sports. The relevant point is that agonism is not the monopoly of the elite. In foreign policy, untruth can be a potent auxiliary to agonism by hiding or disguising it; more than that, agonism feeds the appetite for sustained and flattering untruth. The constant price of the foreign policy of any country is untruth, gladly paid.

Foreign policy makes vividly clear that in modern democracy, the people are masters who are also slaves. Their energies are needed but are turned against their interests because of their passions. Slaves to their passions, the people are made slaves to the interests of elites. They are seduced or manipulated by the several forms of untruth, but often feel as if their energies are being spent in the direction they desire. The people corrupt and are corrupted by the elite along lines that serve the elite more than the people.

***

The discretionary power of officials is a good deal greater in foreign policy than it is in domestic policy. Truth scarcely seems to exist in the domain of foreign policy except when there is no possibility that untruth could succeed. The facts come home, even if many facts may beg for explanation or interpretation. But all the action that precedes and flows from brute, undeniable facts is interwoven with official accounts that manifest one or another form of untruth. In assertions that officials make concerning their motives and their purposes or strategies that impel or guide their policies, and in the descriptions they give of events that took place, are taking place, and are planned for the future, observers can count on the proliferation of untruth, and they do so without cynicism. Yes, U.S. President George W. Bush lied the country into a war of aggression against Iraq, but he was reelected anyway. To whom in the United States did the system of lies matter as lies, let alone matter in the vast destruction, dislocation, and dispossession inflicted on the Iraqi people?

Untruth answers to the desire of the people. Whenever I think about American imperialism, I am drawn to the idea of overdetermination, Freud's theory of the manifest content of dreams, especially as Althusser explicated it. Let us say that the rhetoric of imperialism, which is manifold in its un-truthful representations, is overdetermined: the representations, the accounts given by those who make policy systematically misrepresent their motives and purposes. The spokespersons of imperialism tell a typical story. The aim is to give a reassuring account of the pattern of policy or action. In this ac-count, every motive of the elite is honorable (un-self-interested, high-minded, and well-intentioned) while the motives of the other side are evil, inhuman, or not humanly recognizable. The shortcomings of one's side are owed to a general human weakness or fallibility, not to the will to power or the will to prevail or to crude or narrow interests, while the other side is cruel and fanatical. A moral reason or even an elaborated theory can always be found that permits one's side any action or policy in pursuit of a sup-posedly great good, and the good end washes away the incalculable suffering inflicted in its pursuit. The inner censor of the people cannot bear to hear the truth about the policy's real causes, which though multiple are only contin-gently or arbitrarily related to one another, not by any thematic necessity, and are each of them sufficient and no single one of them necessary to pro-duce the policy; so the official speakers and writers go through distortions that hide the truth, not only by remote approximations to it or gross simpli-fications of it or by misattribution to others of one's own intentions, but above all by substituting for the truth those stories that best satisfy the people's self-conception and therefore help the elite to keep their balance and thus be able to persist in their endeavor. The elite's overdetermined rhet-oric is experienced by the people as an overdetermined dream.

Yet the dream is one's own; it is projected out of oneself; it comes from oneself, one's needs in turmoil, not from outside oneself. But often in a dream, one is hiding from oneself, with "eyes wide shut." I deceive myself in the form of unconsciously wanting and permitting unmastered forces to de-ceive me. A complex psychological process, albeit unconscious, is needed to achieve the unconsciously desired simplification, which is a gratifying dis-tortion. So, in some respects, the masters give the people the several forms of untruth about imperialism that the people need if they are to live with themselves, if they are not to be shocked repeatedly by truth. The people are constantly indicating that they want—should we say only half-want?—all the kinds of untruth that they are told. President Obama's Nobel Peace Prize acceptance speech is a model of comforting dream-like untruth about U.S. foreign policy: the entire record from the end of World War II to the present is celebrated as one continuous struggle to make the world freer and better off. The premise is that the enemies (whether actual or designated) of the United States never have grievances against it, only motiveless malignity; resistance to U.S. initiatives is always shameful or sinister. The speech gives in concentrated form what establishment media disseminate constantly and what people want to hear: reassurance, whenever U.S. foreign policy is discussed and whatever the policy is; reassurance, and also absolution and delusional hope. A dream-like story, which is worse than any series of outright lies, gives life by making it livable, but rains death on others. *My country is always right* is far worse than *my country right or wrong*.

There is, however, an important dis-analogy between a dream and the rhetoric of imperialism, which is that dreams must represent and can only misrepresent the unconscious because the unconscious cannot represent itself. The unconscious is without words in its origins and has to struggle to emerge in a medium (a compound of hallucination-like words and images) that is not its own, and can emerge only obliquely. In contrast, there is a more truthful verbal alternative to the rhetoric of imperialism—an alternative, however, that in its greater truth would damage the elite and demoralize the people. The people are dreaming, while the elite often appears lost in grandiose dreams and immersed in policies that partake of dream-like unreality in their confusion and remoteness, and in their ill-defined and often overwhelming quality.

***

I would like now to propose a general characterization of the attitudes and dispositions that take hold in those who make foreign policy and that therefore facilitate the loss of transparency and the dissemination of untruth. As I have said, the repertory of untruth includes lies of denial or affirmation, secrets or the withholding of knowledge, propaganda, exaggeration and other kinds of distortion, simplification, and construction of incidental stories and sweeping narratives. But we must not omit another cause of untruth, which is self-deception, and which indicates that sometimes those who begin by disseminating untruth knowingly and deliberately come to believe what they are saying, at least some of the time. The repeated sound of their own voice produces a conviction of the truth of their convenient rationalizations, but occasionally the truth forces its way back into their minds, only to be forced out again. The making of foreign policy—especially when it is activist or imperialist—enlists, elicits, or fortifies various attitudes and dispositions in the makers and those around them, and prompts them to have recourse to untruth. I will direct my attention to imperialism, though what I say can, with sufficient allowance, apply to the foreign policy of any country. I use three categories to give an abstract characterization of the mentality of an imperialist foreign policy elite: affinity to criminality (violence and coercion for collectively selfish ends); corruption by responsibility (preservation of the means at the expense of the ends); and immersion in unreality (forgetfulness of reality in the name of realism). These categories cover some of the salient tendencies that significantly diminish the transparency of foreign policy.

Let me say just in passing that when any foreign policy elite possesses nuclear weapons, each of these categories is intensified beyond the intensification that imperialism and adventurism already effect.

Criminality. Imperialism underscores the essential criminality inherent in foreign policy; it gives a heightened force to the general similarities of political action to criminality. Augustine refers to a kingdom as a large band of thieves (and a band of thieves as a small kingdom), but all that thieves want is wealth. Political societies, on the other hand, want to be as safe as possible, and they want respect from other political societies. But an imperialist power makes all general motives to policy active, indeed, hyperactive. Imperialism is always busily redefining safety or security as permanently imperiled, even if some danger has to be coaxed into existence to justify an activist policy of security. Danger must be sought in order to be overcome; the invited fear must be felt as if it were inflicted solely from the outside. Imperialism's material interests are as wide as its ambitions. And an imperialist power wants more than respect: it wants admiration, it wants to be glorified, held in awe; and in its own eyes, it is elevated above common humanity and it craves recognition of that special stature. Many political societies also want to dominate other ones in order to feel the pleasure of domination; an imperialist power carries that pervasive international tendency as far as it can be carried.

In every case, the foreign policy elite experience such emotions and passions as jealousy, envy, vengeance, suspicion, paranoid fear, and grandiose ambition—not for themselves as individuals, but as personifications or embodiments of their society. They experience the metaphor of the superperson from the inside, from inside the brain of the beast. They are small creatures inhabiting and mechanically moving from within some enormous entity; their personal feelings have nothing to do with the stage emotions and passions they must act and that they think appropriate to impute to the enormous entity, as enhanced power reinforces a sense of enhanced vulnerability. Imagined fear, interest, and glory lead to action on a grand scale. The mentality is nothing personal, it is only person-like, and as such, is able to achieve release from normal moral inhibition. The elite act immorally for the sake of the enormous entity. Belief in the imagined superperson is not confined to those in the general population who invest themselves in group identity; elites have the same belief, but hold it as team leaders and players, not merely as fans. To hold this belief with any seriousness is to be possessed by it.

Let us notice, however, that elites involved in foreign policy would not have the situation otherwise; they do not pine for a condition in which they could practice moderation and with it, morality or at least less immorality. They have no reluctance to perform their great deeds of immorality because the project of greatness dwarfs morality. The release from morality is usually associated with organized crime, but what is activist foreign policy, what is imperialist policy, except a kind of criminality in aims and methods? Any foreign policy, even if it is unambitious, verges on criminality. Yet criminals in a society realize that they are criminals, and that they break the law, even if they are quite capable of normalizing their activities, day in and day out, and act as if there were nothing abnormal in what they do. In contrast, the release from morality experienced by foreign policy elites is rationalized in various ways, all of which are conducive to an easy conscience—as easy a conscience as among professional soldiers. They all think that law (moral, constitutional, or statutory) does not apply to them, except incidentally, and that they are above the law because their work cannot be encompassed by the law. Idealism or ideology also helps to effect release from morality, but after a while, neither is required to keep the participants going, no matter how useful it may be to keep the people in line. But there must always be some justification handy.

All the forms of untruth I mentioned above are useful in the enterprise of rationalization. They are useful because a mass audience must have a story that puts all the activities into a coherent picture, just as the dream work strains for coherence. If the principals have a strategy that unifies much of their activities, it is best not stated candidly; it must be dressed in attractive clothing, perhaps especially garb that is moral in nature (but also realist for the semi-initiated). Imperialism cannot be called imperialism. After all, imperialism is using violence and intimidation in taking what is not yours, taking what you do not need, taking for the sake of taking, taking for the sake of feeling big and playing a big role on the world stage. The affinity to criminality is close. Perhaps some in the elite, some of the time, can be candid among themselves, but even they cannot handle a steady diet of the truth. If the elite hides from itself, it cannot dare to give a transparent account of what it does and why. Most people would not want it to do so anyway.

Responsibility. What I am about to say applies to all foreign policy elites, but it applies with greater force to those in imperialist societies. In "Politics as a Vocation" (1919), Max Weber famously speaks of the ethic of responsibility in contrast to the ethic of ultimate ends (usually morally pure ends). According to the ethic of responsibility, officials are responsible for the welfare of others, those whom they govern, not responsible only for care of their own individual selves and consciences. A feeling of responsibility will necessitate commission of acts that one wishes one didn't have to perform, and that if done for one's own benefit would be condemnable as immoral. What officials do may indeed be immoral, but they must do it out of a sense of responsibility. Their inwardness is not sullied by immorality when it is impersonal and is in any event justified, morally justified, as necessary. What is involved in this ethic is a more subtle form of corruption than a facilitated disposition to act immorally; officials are corrupted by the not completely hypocritical conviction of entrusted responsibility to which they sacrifice their personal integrity, but of course without being able to feel with any steadiness that they have in fact been corrupted.

What establishes the necessity to act immorally? Presumably, it is having responsibility for the welfare of others in a world of competition for scarce goods and honors. But there is another kind of responsibility, and it is prior. Not only is it prior, it is unexamined by officials, and unexamined by all except for a few observers. Its foundation is the metaphor of the superperson. I refer to an almost unconscious feeling that possesses strength all the greater for being unexamined, and if somehow brought to anyone's attention, would appear so obviously right that it would be impertinent to examine it. This feeling makes the first commitment to the preservation of the system or framework—that is, to the continued existence of the politically organized society. The deepest reason is not that without the state organization the people would lapse into anarchy and suffer all the ills of such a condition. No: the society, an artificial entity, is regarded as a fact of nature.

In the name of the society's self-preservation, anything goes, just as an ordinary person may without immorality prefer his own preservation to that of another. This means that numerous persons in the society or in adversarial societies can be sacrificed to preserve the entity. It matters, of course, that war may devastate one's own country and reduce it to partial anarchy or worse, but what matters above all is that the country has been weakened in its struggle. Nor does the historical acknowledgment matter that political forms change over time or that societies may lose their political independence. The fight is to keep the entity intact. Is that entity the state? The tendency might be to think so. Let us say rather that the agonistic entity is the whole society, but conceived as one society in a world of societies. Each society must be represented in its imputed unity by the state at its head, as its head. Thus, as a necessary consequence of the commitment to preserve the system or framework, high officials have the further responsibility to preserve the relative autonomy of the state vis-à-vis the people, and to preserve the territorial integrity of the country against regional secession.

One consequence of this nearly unconscious commitment to territorial integrity of the state is that the political society exists to preserve itself so that it can become a power base for struggles against enemies. I have already referred to the game-like or agonistic quality that foreign policy takes on in the minds of foreign policy elites. But the game can go on only as long as enemies exist; enemies are required for one's own entity to exist and be defined as not-the-other. Actual cultural differences matter much less to this mentality, as exemplified by, say, Carl Schmitt. The greens need the blues for a fight; perhaps they need each other, but the intensity of the will to fight is circumstantial and not always equal. But what Schmitt is really doing is underscoring Weber's idea. The commitment to the preservation of the political entity at any cost is the core of Weber's ethic of responsibility. As he says at one point, the "political element consists, above all, in the task of . . . maintaining the existing power relations."

In "Civil Disobedience" Thoreau writes, "Statesmen and legislators, standing so completely within the institution, never distinctly and nakedly behold it. They . . . have no resting place without [sc. outside] it . . . Webster never goes behind government, and so cannot speak with authority about it." Certainly a version of this unexamined and nearly unconscious feeling is found in the people in the form of patriotism, and it sustains officials in their ethic of responsibility. (Everyday experiences in any organization or institution make this feeling instantly familiar.) The preservation of the society, but with the state personifying it as an abstract entity to the world, becomes the end, and the population becomes the means to preserve the life of the abstraction. This is a kind of political perversion, and it is a parody and betrayal of the perfectly acceptable idea, sometimes associated with Hannah Arendt, that the content of politics is politics. One of her meanings is that the highest aim of political endeavor is to preserve a good constitution, which is understood as always in danger of sliding away from its principles. Weber and Schmitt, on the other hand, unlike Arendt, are pure formalists, as are many officials and citizens everywhere.

Imperialism intensifies the ethic of responsibility. Preservation of the political entity is inflated to include augmentation of the power or wealth or honor of the entity as essential to its preservation. The superperson becomes a giant, with no foreseeable limits on its growth, and no limits on its appetite to struggle for augmentation. But safety or security, other terms for preservation, is regularly risked in struggles to achieve this purpose. The thrill of risk raises the value of success, which, however, can never be certain, let alone final. Safety is a pretext for augmentation; augmentation is joined to the spirit of adventure. The delight of the game is open-ended, without end and without ends. Obviously, officials cannot speak of their various satisfactions in playing the game. They must hide their motives and profess to be pursuing the common interest. And though the people are naturally sympathetic to patriotism and delight in victory, there are nevertheless narrow limits on how much public rationalization of policy can ever avow the feelings and attitudes that make the running of foreign policy so intoxicating, one could say, metaphysically or spiritually intoxicating. The public discourse must be moralistic and secondarily, it must also be realistic. People must be appealed to with reasons that invoke high moral ideals or appeal to tangible material interests, as if, however, there could not be any conflict between ideals and interests. All the elements in the repertory of untruth are mobilized to cover over barely hidden passions in the elite and the cruder versions of them in the people.

Unreality. In this paper, I have several times referred to the abstractedness involved when the foreign policy elite think about foreign policy; all the more so when the policy is imperialist. That is a large part of the unreality they inhabit. But there are other elements. Of course I am trying to think my way into the elite mentality, and am doing so on the basis of analogous miniature experiences that I have had. All persons have their imperialist moments or tendencies in everyday life. I mean to deny the view that the elite make another reality that must be taken on its own terms ("a form of life"), just as, say, art and literature do. These self-described realists imagine that they experience a more intense and genuine form of reality only because they exercise an often fantastically powerful will. They lose that sense of proportion— another term is moderation—that a true realism requires.

No one member of the elite in foreign affairs, not even the few at the very top, can know completely what goes on when a given policy is executed. Members may know the basic strategy, but this knowledge is abstract and hardly stable. On the other hand, a strategy or a general purpose that is pursued is made up of countless specific actions over a wide geographic area. In a strict sense, the elite don't know what they are doing. How could they then speak truthfully of it? How could the people begin to comprehend what is happening, even if they wished to? There is too much to absorb. The course of activity in a whole foreign policy or the course of a war in its numerous or countless actions does not unfold like the plot of a novel. There is no official who can resemble the author of a novel who controls the events, arranges them into a pattern, and understands the motives and purposes of the characters. What is remarkable is that a few novelists, such as Henry James and Marcel Proust, write novels in which the narrator is often uncertain about what happens and why; there is no omniscient narrator; indeed, the author is a residual skeptic about the motives of his characters and leaves the reader in a degree of doubt. Even so, the novels of James and Proust provide no model for the comprehension of war and foreign policy, which usually frustrate the ambition of a master narrative, let alone omniscience. What these novels do provide is luminous examples of fiction in which the supposition of omniscience is shaken. In this way, too, they educate the reader.

But I am not suggesting an epistemological exoneration of anyone at any level in an imperialist society. The thought that there is too much to absorb, to take in what is happening, gives way rather easily to the idea that the very effort to absorb should be abandoned. Since you can't absorb everything, then absorb nothing, and replace reality with a grand abstraction or a glorious picture or a beautiful story. It is true, nevertheless, that it is harder for foreign policy officials to tell the truth about what they do, if they wanted to tell it, than it is in domestic policy. Much of foreign policy action is at a distance, invisible, and must seem unreal. High officials are often too remote from the consequences to experience them and would be overwhelmed by detailed accounts of more than a few of them. Yet there is little popular pressure on the elite to tell the truth to the extent that it can be told.

Then, too, the unreality that resists adequate utterance also derives from the feeling that what is happening is so vast in the scope of its terrible effects that it can't really be happening. It can't be real. We couldn't be capable of inflicting so much harm on others or extorting such a cost from our own people. So, it's not happening; it's not real. We have no truth to tell about it, there is no truth to tell that we are capable of telling. Repression of the truth thus takes over; the self-repressed persons must of course talk about their policies in distorted ways or withhold, wherever possible, those facts that at least some of the people would find abhorrent. How could a president truly face the fact that there is no sane connection between, say, prolonging a war year after year with all its death and destruction, and his motive of not wanting to be accused by the political opposition of weakness (Lyndon Johnson) or the motive of not wanting to surrender to domestic opposition to the war (Richard Nixon). Personal agonism turns pathological. Yet again, naturally, some in the elite and in the people exult in destruction.

If the elite could literally see the corpse of every soldier or civilian on their own side or their enemy's, if they could see the wounded, if they could see the impoverishment caused by war, if they could see the impoverishment caused by sanctions, if they could see the dispossession and displacement, if they could see the disruptions in everyday life in places affected by war, they would find it harder to go on; some of the elite could not go on. But I suppose many others in the elite could go on. The military profession does go on. No one can see a whole war in its physicality; few imaginations are intense and capacious enough to begin to provide a substitute for literal vision or compensate for its selectivity. I speak mostly of war because I speak here mostly of imperialism. But the same holds for every war-making power.

I have said that the foreign policy elite, especially in an augmentative or adventurous imperialist society, does not know what it is doing. In thinking from a height, they see what their moral blindness puts before them. The last kind of unreality I would mention is that they don't know what they are doing because they don't know themselves. They don't know their own motives; in a dark or stricken moment they can't believe that their motives are base or cowardly or so confused. They are unfamiliar with the worst about themselves, which is the bitter fruit of self-examination. They are masters of policy and make no attempt to master themselves; this is a lesson as old as philosophy, as old as the lessons of Socrates on the nature of tyranny, whether it is the tyrant in a city or a tyrannical city dominating other cities. There is often a failure to sort out and grasp the variety of motives that might be in play at the initiation or maintenance of an overall strategy or of particular policies. We are often at a loss to understand why wars are initiated; this is perhaps paradigmatic.

Leaders speak untruth to the people; they mislead themselves. They conceive of their deeds as those of the country, not those of a few persons. How could a whole country, imagined as one person that is ontologically superior to a real person, be motivated by any but the loftiest motives or the grimmest necessities? That persons in power are only persons, and that a country is millions of persons, and that the adversaries of the country are also millions of persons—all that realization is crowded out. And when critics try to awaken remembrance of these facts, they are called naïve or said to be concerned only with their own clean hands. The people at large are ready to endure real costs and inflict them on others, while they submit to the rule of unreality; and they submit because they support its tenets.The unreality inherent in the experience of political action in general stamps it as inferior reality: inferior because it rests on remoteness from correctly perceived actuality. Political realism is underlain by fantasies and metaphors that political participants don't recognize as such. Political action is not in the realm of real feelings that sponsor commensurate actions, feelings that emerge from the psyche immersed in reality close to hand. Yes, unreality descends on much of private life, too, but private life can sometimes recover from its pathologies. Political policies and strategies, especially when violence is involved, often set in motion lengthy chains of terribly real consequences— real in a way that the purposes behind them often aren't—that cannot be repaired or undone.

***

In an activist or adventurist foreign policy, public officials have many reasons not to tell the truth, and there are many causes for not being able to tell the truth (including the tangled nature of the process of policy formation amid constantly changing circumstances, and the elusive nature of the psyches of the participants). Transparency is both undesirable and difficult for those who hold power.

On the other hand, people have many reasons for not wanting the truth, and many causes for not being able to take it in, including the complex and confusing nature of the effects of public policy as well as the nature of the individual psyche. Where does that leave the observer or the conscientious and attentive citizen? If we are not at sea, then at least we are always puzzling over the course of political events. What happened? What is happening? What are the true costs in destruction and waste? What motives and purposes are in play? The given answers to any of these questions rarely provide the full and exact truth. Yet even with a sincere wish to speak the truth and a sincere wish to hear it, transparency would still be imperfect and intermittent; untruth would be prevalent. But the actual prevalence of untruth is owed largely to either the deliberate or the unconscious avoidance of transparency by officials and citizens alike. This avoidance seems to dominate foreign policy especially, and all the more when that policy is activist to the point of imperialism. In the face of these obstacles how can we ever know? How can we achieve more transparency for ourselves, even though others don't share our concern? Can our powers of inference be strengthened?

Suppose we mistrust philosophies of history, even the greatest one, which is Hegel's. We want to know, if possible, how it really was, how it really is, not what it supposedly had to be apart from human intention. We want to cut through the lies, the distortions, the exaggerations, especially in foreign policy, especially in wars and their causes. We also know that there are always crucial secrets; often we cannot know what we most want to know: the motives or purposes served by a policy or a war. Secrets make up perhaps the greatest barrier between the truth and us. No intuition or inference can make good the deficiencies of knowledge; no powers of detection can replace the kind of knowledge that emerges when the relevant secrets of motives and purposes are disclosed. I grant, however, that even if all secrets were disclosed, uncertainty would remain. Not even those at the top, as I have tried to suggest, have adequate self-knowledge (let alone knowledge of the totality of either the effects of a policy or the details of a long train of an indefinite number of events). Irremediable uncertainty joins deliberate, not quite deliberate, and helplessly undeliberate untruth as a serious impediment to our understanding. A large dose of powerless skepticism toward official rhetoric about foreign policy appears to be right.

Have I seriously overstated the difficulties that face the observer who is intent on understanding foreign policy? Isn't there usually enough to go on, if you work with a basic understanding of politics? Can't the repertory of untruth, no matter how skillfully exploited, be seen through, at least up to a certain far point? Haven't I come too close to skepticism and for insufficient reason? An anti-skeptic can say that the psychology of the political stratum, whether in foreign policy or any other area of policy, is *political* psychology, which is comparatively simple and does not reach into the depths of the psyche. Political action doesn't grow from personal psychology; it doesn't use the whole psyche; it typically doesn't involve the inner life and thus avoids the incessant interplay between the inner life and overt conduct that dominates everyday life. Let us notice, for example, what a small range of motivation is found in the analyses of Thucydides, Machiavelli, or Hobbes. It is reasonable to believe that these three writers are among the greatest political analysts of power holders in all areas of public policy. If any of them had a philosophy of history, we could make our way around it and try to come up with some fundamental elements of understanding that would apply throughout history.

Fear, interest, and honor make up the trio of constitutive motives or purposes these three writers impute to the political stratum, when the stratum acts in the name of and officially on behalf of the country, which is imagined in the likeness of a single person with the characteristics of a single person—a single person, however, that is reified and enlarged and that coexists with other such entities that lack a superior power above them all. This trio of motives is certainly thought to govern the conduct of foreign policy. I myself have employed these motives as the best shortcut to explaining foreign policy. Then these writers throw in love of power for its own sake. That complicates matters, especially because it is the only motive that is reluctantly avowed; it rarely lends itself to any utterance, let alone frank utterance. But this complication need not impede analysis. The other motives, especially fear (for security), may be declared, even matter-of-factly, but many times falsely or exaggeratedly. To be sure, the Athenians, on more than one occasion, avow this love of power but don't try to explain it; they just assume that all people have it, whatever they say or fail to say about themselves. When the conduct of foreign policy is under indictment by those who have been attacked, the general refrain of the aggressors is, "What do you expect? You would do the same if you were as strong as we are, and from the same causes that impel us."

Furthermore, advocates of the anti-skeptical line can go on to suggest that if the observer's inference concerning motive and purpose is difficult; that is, if the political situation seems to be opaque, then the causes lie in hypocrisy, lying, and secrets, not in obscurity of motivation. But the opacity can be more or less dispelled because the range of possible motives or purposes is narrow; therefore, hypocrisy, lying, and even secrets may present no insurmountable obstacles to analysis. Tactics can be complex and create surprises; a long-term strategy may temporarily resist being understood; but the motives and purposes are comparatively simple. Furthermore, if political analysis is difficult, the reason is not that political psychology is difficult, but that events are often too vast or confused or unclear even in outline to be described accurately. To be sure, analysis of motives and purposes in foreign policy is difficult in a way that analysis of moves in a competitive game is not. After all, what motive is there in a game but to win, and to do all that is allowed within the rules to win? No spectator worries about the personal motives that players have for playing. A game is a structurally confined activity; in contrast, foreign policy radiates outward to indefinite and often incalculable consequences that reach to every aspect of the lives of countless individuals. But the anti-skeptic can say that to emphasize the significance and open-endedness of foreign policy is nonetheless not to think that there are supposedly great puzzles in the inquiry to determine why a strategy or course of action has been adopted.

Before attempting to rebut this anti-skeptical line, which I think has many truthful points, I wish to reinforce it by reinforcing the contrast between political psychology and the personal psychology of everyday life. Isn't it the case that only in our endlessly diverse and multifaceted relations and transactions in society, can the developed individual psyche display itself in its fullness, while at the same time being subject to the hold of the unconscious and the subconscious? There, human beings often remain opaque to one another. To be sure, some of the work of analysis can be done if the trio of political motives is extended from the personified state back to real persons, together with the love of power for its own sake. But seeing everyday psychology by means of the categories of political psychology does not come close to adequacy when we try to think about why people are doing what they do in leading their private lives and pursuing their aims, despite the fact that we can attribute to everyone certain basic needs and desires. The range of motives in everyday psychology is as extensive as the range of feelings, emotions, passions, and drives, and includes love and affection, remorse and atonement, yearning and despair, the wish to conform and the will to deviate, gregariousness and misanthropy. All these and many others are missing from political psychology.

The complexity of mores and manners and the diversity of institutional arrangements allow for or demand a corresponding psychological complexity, and help to make it possible, while the vicissitudes of the inner life—conscious, barely conscious, or altogether out of the reach of consciousness—mingle with rules and conventions to produce a complexity of unpredictable conduct. Personal motives and purposes can be subtle or inchoate, impulsive or cold-blooded, self-aware or subconscious. Literature often draws out the meaning and implications of these countless, often unforeseeable, and, hence, surprising aspects of the psyche in private everyday life. Analysis of everyday life must not only be complex, but to be adequate to the complexity it analyzes, it must also be subtle, as, say, Henry James and Proust are subtle. Such subtlety, to be adequate to the truth, must be more consciously subtle than the subtle conduct it analyzes. This is not to deny that political psychology might have some subtleties of its own that are not reducible to tactical or strategic considerations, but what matters for analysis is the fundamental simplicity of basic motives and purposes. This means that political events are not nearly as psychologically interesting as everyday experience, just because political psychology is simpler than everyday personal psychology, which as literature attests, is inexhaustibly worthy of thinking about in its elusiveness.

Now, I grant to the anti-skeptics that political psychology must be in some major respects discontinuous from the not fully mappable psychology of everyday life, just as the conduct of public policy, foreign and domestic, is all broad strokes in its scale of endeavor, scope of consequences, and degree of abstraction, and thus discontinuous from the intricate complexity of the entanglements, pursuits, and transactions of everyday life. Although infinite details make execution of public policy enormously complex, this complexity is distinct from psychological complexity. To put it mildly, there is a categorical difference between a real person and the crudely fictional one of the personified society or state. In short, I am willing to grant the comparative simplicity of political psychology at its most apparently complex, and even to accept the centrality of the trio of motives I have referred to, together with the love of power for the sake of power. The elite will be of one mind on the basic orientation: to act for the country from the motives of political psychology, despite different weightings of motives, shadings of emphasis, and tactical disagreements. The theorists of political psychology—Thucydides, Machiavelli, and Hobbes, among many others—can indeed strengthen our powers of inference and guide us to a measure of greater transparence than officials give or citizens want, than officials are able to give or citizens are able to want. A main thing we must avoid, however, is thinking that political psychology is a complete picture of human psychology and is therefore adequate to analyzing the psychological complexity of everyday life. If we take a part for the whole, we produce a profoundly misleading reduction. At times in their texts, the most profitable theorists of political psychology are guilty of such a reduction, and their influence can tend to encourage narrow-mindedness or specious scientism in others not nearly as gifted as themselves.

But my concessions to the anti-skeptics stop when a fundamental fact asserts its claims: political life unleashes, in the psychology of the political stratum, the sense of possibility, which is most deeply entrenched in imperialist foreign policy. That sense is a standing challenge to analysts who confine themselves to a more complex yet still basically simple political psychology in every case they analyze. Concentrated power in the hands of any elite, even in a democracy, is a standing temptation to adventures or even to the disposition to engage in adventurism. Fear, interest, and honor, joined to love of power for the sake of power, do not exhaust the range of political motives and purposes. A sense of possibility is, in other terms, a sense of indefinite freedom in which imagination plays the key role. Strange motives may come to dominate. The more power in the hands of the elite, the more their imagination roams, and the more ill-defined their ambitions. Not only does unpredictability enter the situation, but also the difficulty of catching up with the action and deciphering it.

The imagination of possibility is often entwined with the passion of gambling. The game-like quality of politics turns into the search for big wins despite the risk of big losses. There is a thrill in submitting to luck and perhaps winning far more than could ever be earned or, failing that, losing worse than tragedy would demand.

At its worst, adventurism approaches being motiveless, a cruel parody of Kant's "purposiveness without purpose." It is hard, perhaps impossible, for members of the elite to recognize, formulate, and confess this passion (but it wasn't for Alcibiades). The force of the passion exceeds criminality, overpowers responsibility, and deepens unreality by investing it with magic. The passion is an effort to break out of standard motivation and into what is unprecedented (the spirit of Dante's Ulysses, in Canto 26 of the *Inferno*, urging his men to transgress limits, to sail through the forbidding landmarks of Hercules [what we call the straits of Gibraltar]). Adventurism is a flight from unreality to a greater unreality, from the self-imposed yoke of ordinary determinism, though not to freedom, but rather to the embrace of chance and fate. Explaining this mutation of political psychology is not easy and leaves political action, especially in the foreign policy of a great and imperialist power, largely untransparent and hence unaccountable. It goes on over our heads and behind our backs, and then when it hits home, it leaves us stunned or wondering. Of course, everyday life can show personal equivalents to the political sublime—another term for adventurism—but the political sublime affects us all. Citizens dreamily partake of it and endure its frequently terrible consequences, with either enthusiasm or resignation. We observers must make the effort to penetrate it, even though nothing we do as citizens could ever promise to tame it.

Yes, the elite's sense of possibility is a permanent obstacle to our clear understanding of their actions, most acutely in the field of foreign policy. I would mention one more obstacle, one that is shown in the numerous times when personal psychology inserts itself into the motivation of political leaders, whether the leader merges his or her psyche with that of the personified state or remains aware of the distance and difference between them. I have already referred to the anxieties of U.S. presidents who cannot tolerate the thought of the damage that losing a war either to the enemy or to the domestic opposition would do to their personal interests or self-image. This motive is made difficult to take in just because it is either so ill defined or meanly sordid. But suppose the use of power is driven in part by more obscure motives, not quite shabby, but immensely self-centered or vainglorious, and some of them subconscious or unconscious? As examples we can mention the wish to compensate for personal weakness or avenge personal humiliation, or being moved by Oedipal reasons or sibling competitiveness. How can the analyst estimate definitively the importance of such elements of personal psychology and thus dispel political untruth?

Or suppose that leaders are functionally pathological: obsessive, avaricious, personally sadistic, paranoid, infinitely vengeful, or ideologically crazy, and from one or more of these traits, they manage to get their following, who are more or less sane, to enact the leaders' personal pathology? Do we know how to *analyze* these occurrences, and not merely repeat phrases that might be correct but do not explain?

In sum, the sense of possibility (on the one hand) and the interjection of the personal into the political (on the other) will recurrently test the analyst's powers of inference to the limits of capacity and sometimes beyond.

Every analytic effort for the sake of understanding past or present will be hard, and in many cases impossible. But in making that effort for this event or that, this war or that, the analyst is performing one of the best—I mean, one of the most moral—acts of citizenship. In this way, the analyst rises, at least in aspiration, above the elite and the people, and reaches for an outlook that compels a fight against untruth. The analyst's true craving is transparence for its own sake, even apart from the democratic and constitutional political passion for accountability. Truth, in fragments, struggles to appear, and does appear, if only barely, and only to be ignored.

This essay first appeared in *Raritan*, A Quarterly Review (Winter 2012).

Fact-Checking and Truth-Telling in an Age of Alternative Facts

Linda M.G. Zerilli

01110100 01101000 01100101 00100000 01110000 01100101 01110010 01101001 01101100 01110011 00100000 01101111 01100110 00100000 01101001 01110110 01110110 01100101 01110110 01110110 01101001 01110100 01101001 01101111 01101110

The Contemporary Problem of Post Truth

In a now infamous NBC *Meet the Press* interview on January 22 of 2017, U. S. Councilor to the President Kellyanne Conway defended former Press Secretary Sean Spicer's false statement about the number of people who attended Donald Trump's inauguration. The ceremony, claimed Spicer, had drawn the "largest audience to ever witness an inauguration—period—both in person and around the globe." When asked by the interviewer Chuck Todd how Spicer could "utter a provable falsehood," Conway replied that Spicer was giving "alternative facts." To this Todd responded, "Look, alternative facts are not facts. They're falsehoods."

Conway's use of the phrase "alternative facts" to describe demonstrable falsehoods was widely mocked on social media and sharply criticized by journalists and media organizations in the US and abroad. The phrase was described as Orwellian. Within four days of the interview, sales of Orwell's *1984* had skyrocketed and reached Number 1 on Amazon's bestseller list. "Many Americans have become accustomed to President Trump's lies," cautioned *The New York Times*. "But as regular as they have become, the country should not numb itself to them." The President's daily deluge of fabrications, deceptions, shams, pretenses, untruths, deceits, mendacities, and "demonstrable falsehoods," observes Mary Dietz, have been tallied, fact-checked, parsed, characterized, and catalogued on the websites Politi-Fact and FactCheck.org and by the country's newspapers of record, including an interactive enumeration in *The New York Times*. As of September 13, the *Washington Post* reported more than 5,000 "false or misleading claims" made by Trump.[1] The number grew exponentially with the recent mid-term elections and an equally dizzying attempt on the part of the critical press to keep count.

Valuable though they are, journalistic and related practices of fact-checking can leave us wondering what democratic citizens might do with the exposure of alternative facts as falsehoods. How can we avoid becoming numb to them? Revelations that the President lied are increasingly met with a shrug of the shoulders: "so what else is new?" That the lies are brazen and easily countered by basic forms of evidence (e.g., National Park Service tallies or photographs of the crowds at presidential inaugurations) may well be the lynchpin for understanding what is new in the age-old game of lying and politics. This game has been characterized in the past by use of the deliberate lie on the part of previous administrations to justify or conceal their political interests and actions; it reached its U.S apogee with Watergate, The Pentagon Papers, and the resignation of Richard Nixon in 1974. With Trumpism, however, we seem to be moving from the register of the deliberate lie into another register. As Hannah Arendt will show us, in this new register the lie is not so much put forward and taken for truth. Rather, the very distinction between true and false ceases to exist—with consequences far more corrosive of democratic politics than anything cooked up by inveterate liars such as Nixon.

In the register of the deliberate lie it may be a strange comfort to believe that when Conway or Spicer or any Trump supporter actually *looks* at the images comparing the crowds at Trump's and Obama's respective inaugurations, they see what I see. But they consciously refuse to acknowledge what we both see as having any real political consequence for the liar. "Trump exaggerates, even lies—so what? He's got our back." 'Having one's back' could mean putting conservatives on the Supreme Court, ending NAFTA, putting tariffs on Chinese Steel, making Europeans pay "their fair share" for NATO, or keeping the "wrong kind" of immigrant out of the United States. On this view of the problem of so-called post-truth democracies, people *know* they are being lied to, but they refuse to *acknowledge* it. They refuse to accord the lie any public significance, because buying into the lie pays, so to speak. Accordingly, material interests outweigh fidelity to truth, but truth itself remains in principle knowable. It assumes that citizens are poised to recognize what is right before their eyes, if only their material interests could be properly aligned with what is real. It is a view of mystification and deception familiar to anyone who has worked on the classic question of ideology, where how things appear is a distortion of what really is, but a distortion in which subjects are invested because it aligns with what they take their interests to be. Understood as ideological mystification, this account of post-truth suggests that reality is there to be seen by all those who have an interest in seeing it and are conscious of what that interest is.

Though she did not subscribe to an interest-based theory of ideology, Hannah Arendt's trenchant critique of the Nixon administration and its hand-

is concerned with the question of when and how truth can matter for politics and accordingly critical of the assumption, inherited from the Western philosophical tradition, that truth simply does matter for politics and that all political thinking is by definition a search for truth. This way of conceptualizing the problem of truth and politics brings her remarkably close to the work of the late Foucault, as we shall see. Further, Arendt is deeply concerned with the fate of factual truths, which "constitute the very texture of the political realm."[7] Factual truths are inherently contingent; they could have been otherwise. Related to human action, they "have no conclusive reason whatever for being what they are."[8] That Germany invaded Belgium in August 1914 is a factual and hence contingent truth and in some important sense one among those "brutally elementary data . . . whose indestructibility has been taken for granted even by the most extreme and most sophisticated believers in historicism."[9] But Arendt herself gives innumerable examples that belie this intrinsic resilience of factual truths: the complete erasure of a man named Trotsky from official Soviet history, the Nazis' successful use of anti-Semitic tales, such as *The Protocols of the Elders of Zion*, that had already been fact-checked as false by journalistic authorities of the time, and the whole web of conspiracy theories that sustained totalitarian rule by terror. Whatever resilience factual truths may have ultimately depends on the continual testimony of human beings, who in their ordinary speech and action affirm a world that they have in common, reality as shared. Infinitely fragile because of this dependency, "once they [factual truths] are lost, no rational effort will ever bring them back."[10]

Alternative facts are not just more lies (or falsehoods) or better lies (or falsehoods); they speak to some significant shift in the shared factual reality that we take for granted when engaging in politics. Their corrosive force consists in the turning of fact into *mere* opinion, that is, opinion in the merely subjective sense: an "it seems to me" that remains indifferent to how it seems to plural others. Accordingly, the alternative fact that more people attended Trump's inauguration than Obama's is merely another opinion in the merely subjective sense of what is true *for* me. It can be a mere opinion, just as the number that attended Obama's inauguration is held to be a mere opinion, because there is no shared object on which to have an opinion. What we are debating, in other words, is not why more (or less) people attended one or the other inauguration; what we are debating is not what was said or done in the public space. We are not debating *anything* in fact. We are simply registering opinions that are "merely subjective," no different from the opinion that I like coffee and you like tea. What could there be to dispute?

Following Arendt, this transformation of fact into mere opinion destroys the common world about which to exchange opinions and form judgments. Yet Arendt, to the dismay of her cognitivist critics, refuses to oppose opinion to truth. In her Socratic view, there is truth in opinion, and the speaking and acting with plural others in the public realm is the practice of freedom that factual truth needs to survive, to be acknowledged in the politically significant way I mentioned earlier. Facts cut loose from this practice cannot survive and in some important way, therefore, remain irreducibly intertwined with the opinions that can also displace them as facts, namely, the "it seems to me" that is indifferent to how it seems to plural others.

The "it seems to me" can land in radical subjectivism, but it is also the irreducible basis of that which appears to us as objective. For Arendt, who thinks about objectivity as that which is given not through the transcendence of human perspective, as the Western philosophical tradition has held, but through its multiplication in the public space, "the *dokei moi* ('it seems to me')," cannot be gotten around or left behind in the search for truth.[11] The idea that it not only *can* but *must* be gotten around characterizes the rational or philosophic truth that she characterized as anti-political. Truth is not deduced (from first principles) but disclosed (in relation to plural others). In that case, fact-checking tends to lead not to the disclosure of truth but right back into the jaws of positivism, the tenacious idea that facts speak for themselves, that they do not rest on opinion or the "it-seems-to-me."

To sum up my argument thus far: The problem of alternative facts is not a problem of the deliberate lie, that is, a falsehood that is consciously deployed as a tool of political power. That was the argument I took from Mary Dietz. But neither is the problem of alternative facts one of relativism, where all perspectives are equal and no one perspective is any better than any other in its ability to reveal how things actually stand in the world. This would assume that there is a shared object about which to have different views and what is missing is only the means of adjudication: which view is correct? If that were the situation in which we now find ourselves, then checking the facts might well be a way of bringing these otherwise competing perspectives into the relation with each other that they now lack. Ordinary language can guide us here. We speak not of alternative *perspectives* but of alternative *facts*—this difference in phrasing should caution us against formulating our problem, as have many commentators on Trumpism, as a familiar one of relativism. Alternative facts are not incommensurable perspectives on a shared object; they are what remains in the absence of such an object and thus in the absence of the common world in which the object can appear as shared. If this is right, and the problem is not relativism but the loss of the common world, then we need to ask whether checking the facts can restore an object that has been lost or, better, that was not given as shared in the first place. I will now argue that it most likely cannot and, consequently, that we need to refigure the problem of truth, indeed the whole problem of post-truth politics, from a problem of fact-checking to a problem of truth-telling.

From Fact-Checking to Truth-Telling

What could this be? Isn't the truth-teller a fact-checker? Characteristically figured as the lone and courageous individual who speaks truth to power or who sees through the delusions that captivate her fellow citizens, the truth-teller stands at the center of Michel Foucault's late work on the Greek notion of parrhesia or frank speech.[12] As a "historian of thought" rather than "ideas," Foucault is concerned to outline a genealogy of what we could call the critical attitude in our society. Most of the time, the historians of ideas are interested in the problem of 'ideologies,' or in the problem of relationships between society and representation, in order to decipher how far social structures or social processes help or prevent the discovery of truth. I think there is another problem about the relationships between truth and society. This is not the problem of society's relation to truth through ideologies, it is the problem of what we could call the truth-teller, the *Wahrsager*.[13]

The study of parrhesia brings to light a crucial distinction between thinking about the problem of truth as being able to determine whether a statement is true, on the one hand, and being able to discern "who is able to tell the truth and why [we] should . . . tell the truth," on the other.[14] These related but different abilities represent the "two sides, two major aspects" of what Foucault calls "the problematization of truth" as it originated in ancient Greek society.[15] "One [side] is concerned with the question of how to make sure that a statement is true, that its reasoning is correct, and that we are able to get access to truth. And the other [side] is concerned with the question of the importance for individuals, for the community, for the city, for society of telling the truth and of recognizing which people are able to tell the truth."[16] The side that is concerned with determining whether a statement is true is what Foucault calls "the analytics of truth," and it can be traced back to the "great tradition in Western philosophy."[17] The side that is concerned with the importance of telling the truth is "the tradition of the question," which is "at the root, at the foundation of what we could call the critical tradition of philosophy in our society."[18]

To theorists of post-truth politics both Arendt and Foucault press us to ask: how are you problematizing truth? If you think of the problem of truth as a problem of correct reasoning, you will likely focus on practices of fact-checking. Important though those practices can be, if you neglect the other way of problematizing truth, namely, as a practice of truth-telling, you may miss the ways in which correct reasoning can operate and yet the truth not be told—or, if told, not heard. More precisely, you may miss how the truth might not appear as something that we acknowledge as having political significance for us. The Downing Street memo, recall, could not really appear in the U.S. context in the way it could in the British and, to the extent that it did appear at all, it was dismissed not as an act of truth telling but merely as fact checking:

facts that everyone already knows and accepts, merely old news. Furthermore, if you do not think about how you are problematizing truth, you may mistake an alternative fact for a deliberate lie and so, busily engaged in fact-checking, you may miss what is new in our political situation.

Truth-telling, as it bears on democratic politics, is not first and foremost a problem that can be addressed by means of what Foucault calls the "analytics of truth." Truth-telling is not correct reasoning. Truth-telling is a critical practice that involves attending to and caring for the worldly conditions in which correct reasoning can so much as get off the ground and those who tell the truth will be heard. What these worldly conditions are needs to be the focus of our critical attention when we discuss the situation of post-truth politics, not truth as such. The critical tradition that Foucault associates with truth-telling does not assume that we should be concerned with the truth as such because it does not assume that the truth is a good in itself. Instead, the critical tradition, he clarifies, is concerned with the question: "What is of importance for individuals, for the community, for society of telling the truth and of having people telling the truth and of recognizing which people are able to tell the truth?"[19] As critics of post-truth we should not simply assume that truth is a good in itself and that it presupposes an ability to determine the correctness of statements. We need a clearer sense of why truth matters for democratic politics, of how to determine who is telling the truth, and of cultivating democratic practices that make citizens receptive to those individuals who take the risk of telling the truth in political contexts where truth is at odds with power.

Foucault's account of parrhesia not only raises the problem of truth as one that is different from correct reasoning and the ability to assess the correctness of statements through practices such as fact-checking. It also provides a genealogical account of the deep skepticism with which we hold the very possibility of truth-telling in democracies, which can be traced back to the complex entanglement of parrhesia and democracy. The key turning point for the Western tradition, he argues, occurred with the Greek recognition that, though every citizen has the right to parrhesia, not everyone when speaking frankly will tell the truth. There can be "bad parrhesia."[20]

We could say that Athens, at the end of the fifth century, experienced this parrhesia-crisis at the intersection between an interrogation about democracy and an interrogation about truth. On the one hand, democracy as an institutional system of equality is not able by itself to determine who should have the right and the aptitude for telling the truth. On the other hand, parrhesia as a verbal activity through which one says frankly and courageously what he has in mind, this parrhesia as pure frankness is not sufficient to disclose the truth. That is, I think, the new problematization of parrhesia.[21]

This new problematization, which arises as a consequence of the "deterioration of the relations between parrhesia and democracy," Foucault goes on to show, gives rise to a *philosophical* idea of parrhesia.[22] Based on "care for the self" and modelled in his view by Socrates, such parrhesia takes its distance from the political realm and pursues truth as an ethical good. Democracy and the demos come to be seen as that which must be left behind in the search for truth and the truth-teller. Although this "problem . . . sounds to us rather familiar," observes Foucault, it represents a fundamental moment of discovery—discovery of "the necessary antinomy between parrhesia, freedom of speech, the relation to truth and democratic institutions"—that continues to influence our thinking about the possibilities of truth-telling today.[23]

Philosophical parrhesia as care of the self has been deeply attractive for readers of Foucault looking to loosen the hold of modern disciplinary and bio-power, whose locus is often enough a political realm characterized by rampant mendacity—by "bad parrhesia." But the deep skepticism towards democratic politics that Foucault described as being so familiar to us is a problem to be confronted, not avoided. As Arendt recognized, the disdain with which the Western philosophical tradition has regarded the realm of human affairs led Plato to seek truth wholly undisturbed by the contingency of politics. Preferring the enlightened company of the few over the opinions of the many, Plato would have the philosopher withdraw wholly into the Academy, which then becomes the model space for free speech.[24] This "new concept of freedom," argues Arendt, is hostile to plurality as a feature of political life and as such intended as "as fully valid substitute for the marketplace, the agora, the central space for freedom in the polis."[25] In her view, however, this new freedom is illusory, for the "few, whenever they have tried to isolate themselves from the many—be it in the form of academic indifference or oligarchic rule—have manifestly ended up depending on the many, particularly in all those matters of communal life requiring concrete action."[26] Is this not the situation we face today?

Although Foucault's account of philosophical parrhesia and especially of Socrates seems to endorse the truth-teller's turn away from politics, Foucault recognizes that the withdrawal of the philosopher from the political realm is bought at the price of complicity in autocracy. Freedom of speech and the right to speak across hierarchies as friends rather than equal citizens who enjoy shared constitutional rights seems to leave subjects alone to care for themselves and pursue truth undisturbed by politics.[27] The imbrication of parrhesia with power and thus with politics in Foucault's account, as Lida Maxwell argues, throws into relief readings of his late work that celebrate truth-telling as a strictly ethical practice of freedom.[28] I agree with Maxwell that Foucault's account is far more critical and nuanced on the relationship between politics and ethics than this reception of his late work makes it seem. However, because he was deeply attracted to the philosophical idea of parrhesia as care of the self in a way that remains foreign to Arendt, it is easy to lose track of the importance of *political* parrhesia for Foucault. Can there be on his account an enduring *philosophical* parrhesia (even for the few) in the absence not only of shared constitutional rights, as in autocracy, but of genuine *political* parrhesia: that is, a *public* practice of speaking frankly and freely that does not amount to "bad parrhesia" but instead tells the truth?

"For there to be democracy there must be parrhesia; for there to be parrhesia there must be democracy,' writes Foucault.[29] The imbrication of parrhesia and democracy in Foucault's view is not something to be rejected. Rather, one must "disentangle" a relationship characterized by a "fundamental circularity," he remarks.[30] The circularity blinds us not to an irreducible antagonism between parrhesia and democracy, as if democracy were by its very nature at odds with telling the truth. Rather, such circularity makes it difficult for us to think through something that we already know: parrhesia does not *always* involve speaking the truth. To blame democracy for "bad parrhesia" represents a failure to think through the complex and fraught relationship of democratic societies to their truth-tellers—a problem that Arendt will also address. That there can be democracy and thus the parrhesia secured by constitutional rights but no actual truth-telling leads us—when we fail to think it through—to a deep distrust of democracy and the opinions of the many. It leads at best to the pursuit of truth and care of the self in the company of the few.

Captivated by the problematization of truth as correct reasoning bequeathed by the strand of the Western philosophical tradition that Foucault calls "the analytics of truth," we have lost track of the other "critical" strand of "the question" that is concerned with the broader problem of truth-telling. The problem is broader because truth-telling can never solely involve the single individual as correct reasoner or even as truth-teller; it must always depend on the ability and willingness of citizens to listen and hear the truth that is told. Convinced that the truth-teller would be killed, Plato abandoned this side of the tradition that he also helped to found. But, if Arendt is right, the self-appointed guardians of truth who have rejected political parrhesia for the philosophical pursuit of truth are not secure: they inevitably find themselves at the mercy of the many, whose opinions have been discarded by the few as cognitively worthless from the standpoint of philosophical truth. Under an anti-democratic regime such as autocracy, good parrhesia, even for the few, will be short lived. It can deny but never escape the radical entanglement of parrhesia and democracy.

Foucault's description of the "crisis of parrhesia," which sets truth-telling at odds with democracy, then, does not endorse the separation of truth-telling from democracy, let alone celebrate autocracy, as Plato did. But Foucault's account of parrhesia as truth-telling fails to respond to the more fundamental question posed by his own genealogical account: namely, why and how do some people come to be accepted as truthtellers while others do not? Any plausible answer must be critically alert to the uneven reception that different people and groups receive as speakers of truth. By defining the new problem discovered by the Greeks as general skepticism towards democratic citizens and political parrhesia as such—however correct that may be in certain respects—Foucault does not go on to attend, as he might have, to what Maxwell calls "the problem of the hierarchy of truth in which some people . . . are assumed to be truthful while others . . . are not."[31] An attempt to shift our focus from truth as a problem of correct reasoning to truth as a problem of truthtelling, as Foucault has valuably done, must come to terms with the social, racial, and gender hierarchies that authorize received understandings of who is authorized to tell the truth and who counts as a truth teller.

The problem today is clearly not that democratic citizens think that those who have walled themselves off in their modern version of the Platonic Academy are truth-tellers—on the contrary, they are viewed as elites who have nothing true to say. The problem, rather, is that we are far less likely to accord credibility to the speech of historically disenfranchised individuals and groups. The truth is being told (by some), but many of us are not listening. This is the irreducibly dialogic problem of parrhesia that both Arendt and Foucault bring to light. Any successful effort to relocate the discussion of post-truth from the "analytics of truth," where it is a problem of correct reasoning, to the "critical tradition," where it is a problem of truth-telling, must confront the problem of the hierarchy of truth, lest it lose track of the central question of power that Foucault's analysis otherwise usefully tracks.

The Truth-Teller

"Truthfulness has never been counted among the political virtues," writes Arendt, "because it has little indeed to contribute to that change of the world and of circumstances which is among the most legitimate political activities."[32] This is less the Arendt who cautions against the antipolitical character of truth than the Arendt who calls our attention to when and how truth can matter in politics. To state what is the case, as she sees it, is to utter words that are in some sense invisible and powerless in their ordinariness. And yet Arendt herself has also shown us that the speaking of ordinary words in the form of factual truths—Germany invaded Belgium in August of 1914—when engaging in politics is what holds together our sense of sharing a common world. In her account, it is not the facts that hold up our common world; it is we who hold up the facts and so our common world—or not.

When, then, is telling the truth more than stating a fact in this ordinary sense? "Only where a community has embarked upon organized lying on principle, and not only with respect to particulars, can truthfulness as such, unsupported by the distorting forces of power and interest, become a political factor of the first order. Where everybody lies about everything of importance, the truth-teller, whether he knows it or not, has begun to act; he, too, has engaged himself in political business, for, in the unlikely event that he survives, he has made a start toward changing the world."[33] The truth-teller, then, may be a fact-checker, but he or she is above all an actor who cannot go it alone.

Thinking about truth-telling as a form of action and thus of politics, Arendt invites us in ways left unremarked by Foucault to refigure what we think of as fact-checking, which we tend to equate with telling the truth: to check a fact is not to point—not simply—to what already exists, to what is past, but to what could have been otherwise and so to what could be otherwise, to the future. That revisionism lurks as a danger in every reference to the contingency of the past is for Arendt the price of freedom, of truth-telling as action. As a practice of freedom through which we are reminded of the contingency of what has happened and cannot be changed, truth-telling is crucial to what can be changed. That is what most current forms of fact-checking tend to conceal or deny.

Understandably worried about historical revisionism and the political manipulation of factual truths, fact-checkers are driven more and more into the position occupied by their opponents. When factual truths are stated in the manner of rational truths—that is, truths that do not rely on the "it seems to me" but attempt to derive their validity in opposition to opinion and by the force of their intrinsic logicality—they do not recover but undo the common world. Arendt can help us understand why. One of her most intriguing insights is that both the truth-teller in a context of pervasive lying and the liar are engaged in forms of action: their speech brings something new into the world. Reminding us of "the contingent character of facts, which could always have been otherwise, and which therefore possess by themselves no trace of self-evidence or plausibility for the human mind," Arendt goes on to argue that it is the liar who has the advantage in the game of truth.[34] "Since the liar is free to fashion his "facts" to fit the profit and pleasure, or even the mere expectations, of his audience, the chances are that he will be more persuasive than the truth-teller. Indeed, he will usually have plausibility on his side; his exposition will sound more logical, as it were, since the element of unexpectedness—one of the outstanding characteristics of all events—has mercifully disappeared."[35] Arendt's key insight here is that the liar, though engaged in action, is also engaged in the denial of action's central feature: contingency.

Truth-telling and any related practice of checking the facts, then, needs to be part of a larger effort to recover contingency and with it a sense of futurity in critical thinking and practice. It is not that by calling forth the contingency of what is, the truth-teller has the advantage over the liar. On the contrary, the liar who denies contingency may well have the upper hand. This is a practical political dilemma to be sure. But there is also the potentially transformative world-building character of truth-telling that is inherent to it as a practice of action. To get at that point I want to close by placing Arendtian truth-telling in a larger discussion of what goes under the name of prefigurative politics.

Truth-Telling as Prefiguration

By prefigurative politics I mean to draw on a line of thinking about the character of social protest that tries to create in lived action and behavior the desired society. Coined by Carl Boggs and later developed in the writings of scholars working on everything from the historical debate between Marxists and anarchists, the emergence of the new left and the new social movements of the 60s and 70s, Occupy, the Zapatistas in Chiapas, Mexico and the Indignados in Spain, the shared idea behind prefigurative politics is the insistence that political action should enact or model the very freedom towards which it strives. Freedom is not a future state but something that we create now in our everyday modes of making decisions and acting collectively. Freedom is not that which is to come in an ideal future but takes the form of the present way of being in common.

Prefigurative politics is often contrasted with so-called strategic politics, aimed at bringing about a desired end through political means. Without entering the highly contested terrain of the debates that follow upon that distinction, I would argue that truth-telling, to be a prefigurative practice of world-building, has to be distinguished from fact-checking as a means to an end. We should still check facts; that checking facts matters was never in dispute. But checking facts has to be part of a larger political practice of prefiguration: to enact in the present those forms of relating to each other and to the past that are enabling for the future. Fact-checking that insists on factual truths in a manner that denies their contingency also denies the *dokei moi* or "it-seems-to-me," the opinion, from which the common world is built. Forms of fact checking that repeat the philosophical gesture seeking truth regardless of what human beings think or say won't save truth in an age of alternative facts. On the contrary, such checking will more likely accelerate the very corrosion of reality that it seeks to contest.

Writing about totalitarianism Arendt said that what it calls for is not so much explanation but understanding, and that no addition of facts or grasp of causes could produce understanding. Understanding is distinct from having correct information or scientific knowledge. Truth-telling, though it surely states facts, reminds us that it could have been otherwise: that prior to the crystallized structure of any event, things could have been different. Germany could not have invaded Belgium in August of 1914—but it did. To "tell a story" of what is, she observes, "is to eliminate from the real happening the 'accidental' elements, a faithful enumeration of which may be impossible anyhow, even for a computerized brain."[36] The denial of contingency seems to be the price of coherence, of stating what is in a way that does not reduce to "mere opinion." And yet losing track of those accidental elements, of contingency, of the "it could have been otherwise," might produce knowledge but not (political) understanding: facts without meaning, perhaps alternative facts.

When seen in light of what Arendt says about the difference between explanation and understanding, truth-telling is not fact-checking but a practice of understanding or relating to what is in ways that are democratically enabling in the here and now. To tell the truth is to prefigure in our speech and action what it means to understand.

Where does this leave us? Less with an answer to the problem of post-truth politics than a cautionary note. As Foucault reminds us, certain ways of problematizing truth and politics can lead us to chase after an ideal of correct reasoning and factual truth without gaining a clear idea of why we, democratic citizens, should care about truth. Further, there are ways of caring for the truth that lose sight of what Arendt would say is the only reason for democratic citizens to care for the truth, namely, care for the world. The real danger in failing to grasp the historical and irreducible entanglement of parrhesia and democracy is what Arendt diagnosed as a turning away from politics as Plato did the polis, "an *a-politea*, so to speak, or indifference to politics."[37] To the extent that we don't turn away, many of us have become so enthralled by practices of fact-checking that we have wholly bypassed the problem of truth as both Foucault and Arendt would have us see it: as a problem of truth-telling that involves at once the dialogic relationship between those who tell the truth and those who are able to recognize them—a relationship that is not static but dynamic and at odds with the idea of a permanent class of truth-tellers. On the contrary, to see the problem anew—or better—to return to the critical tradition to which truth-telling belongs, we shall need to attend to the often unarticulated but nonetheless decisive criteria by which we decide who is capable of telling the truth. A politics of truth as a practice of prefiguration would seek to alter the inherited hierarchies that shape who can count as a truth-teller.

Bibliography

Arendt, Hannah. "Lying in Politics." In *Crises of the Republic*, 1-48. New York: Harcourt Brace & Co., 1969.

Arendt, Hannah. *The Life of the Mind*, ed. By Mary McCarthy. One-volume edition. Vol. 2, *Willing*. New York: Harcourt Brace & Co., 1974.

Arendt, Hannah. *The Origins of Totalitarianism*. New York: Harcourt Brace & Co., 1976.

Arendt, Hannah. "Truth and Politics." In *Between Past and Future: Eight Exercises in Political Thought*, 227-264. New York: Penguin, 1993.

Dietz, Mary. "Lying as Politics in the Age of Trump: What Hannah Arendt Does, and Does Not, Anticipate under a Deeply Vicious Presidency."*Public Seminar*, October 23, 2018. http://www.publicseminar.org/2018/10/lying-as-politics-in-the-age-of-trump/.

Foucault, Michel. *The Government of Self and Others: Lectures at the Collège de France, 1982-1983*. Trans. By Graham Burchell. New York: Picador, 2011.

Foucault, Michel. "Discourse and Truth." In *Discourse and Truth and Parresia*. Ed. By Henri-Paul Fruchaud and Daniele Lorenzini, 39-228. Chicago: University of Chicago Press, 2019.

Maxwell, Lida. "The Politics and Gender of Truth-Telling in Foucault's Lectures on Parrhesia," *Contemporary Political Theory* 18, no. 1, 22-42, 2018.

Zerilli, Linda M. G. "Objectivity, Judgment, and Freedom: Rereading Arendt's 'Truth and Politics'." In *A Democratic Theory of Judgment*, 117-142. Chicago, IL: University of Chicago Press, 2016.

Zerilli, Linda M. G. "Critique as a Political Practice of Freedom." In *A Time for Critique.* Ed. By Didier Fassin and Bernard E. Harcourt, 36-51. New York: Columbia University Press, 2019).

Endnotes

1 Mary Dietz, "Lying as Politics in the Age of Trump: What Hannah Arendt Does, and Does Not, Anticipate under a Deeply Vicious Presidency," Public Seminar, October 23, 2018, http://www.publicseminar.org/2018/10/lying-as-politics-in-the-age-of-trump/.

2 Hannah Arendt, "Lying in Politics," in *Crises of the Republic* (New York: Harcourt Brace & Co., 1969), 44.

3 Linda M. G. Zerilli, "Objectivity, Judgment, and Freedom: Rereading Arendt's 'Truth and Politics'," *A Democratic Theory of Judgment*, ch. 4 (Chicago: University of Chicago Press, 2016), 117-142.

4 Dietz, "Lying as Politics in the Age of Trump."

5 Hannah Arendt, *The Origins of Totalitarianism* (New York: Harcourt Brace & Co., 1976), 474.

6 Hannah Arendt, "Truth and Politics," in *Between Past and Future: Eight Exercises in Political Thought* (New York: Penguin, 1993), 257.

7 Arendt, "Truth and Politics," 231.

8 Arendt, "Truth and Politics," 242.

9 Arendt, "Truth and Politics," 239.

10 Arendt, "Truth and Politics," 231.

11 Arendt, "Truth and Politics," 237.

12 See Michel Foucault, *The Government of Self and Others: Lectures at the Collège de France, 1982-1983*, trans. Graham Burchell (New York: Picador, 2011); Michel Foucault, "Discourse and Truth," *Discourse and Truth and Parresia*, ed. Henri-Paul Fruchaud and Daniele Lorenzini (Chicago: University of Chicago Press, 2019).

13 Foucault, *Discourse and Truth*, 63.

14 Ibid., 223.

15 Ibid., 223.

16 Ibid., 224.

17 Ibid.

18 Ibid.

19 Ibid., 224.

20 Ibid., 124; Foucault, *The Government of Self*, 168.

21 Ibid., 114.

22 Foucault, *The Government of Self*, 173.

23 Ibid., 124.

24 See Hannah Arendt, "Introduction into Politics," in *The Promise of Politics*, ed. Jerome Kohn (New York: Shocken, 2005), 93-200. I have discussed Arendt's view on the Academy and the transformed idea of free speech that it represented in Linda M. G. Zerilli, "Critique as a Political Practice of Freedom," in *A Time for Critique*, ed. Didier Fassin and Bernard E. Harcourt (New York: Columbia University Press, 2019).

25 Arendt, "Introduction into Politics," 131.

26 Arendt, "Introduction into Politics," 133.

27 Commenting on Plato's description of the empire of Cyrus in *The Laws*, Foucault writes:

> *Parrhesia is the most manifest form of an entire process which, according to Plato, guarantees the good functioning of the empire, namely that the hierarchical differences that may exist between the sovereign and the others, between his entourage and the rest of the citizens, between officers and soldiers, and between victors and vanquished, are in a way attenuated or compensated for by the formation of relationships which are designated throughout the text as relationships of friendship. . . . In this way, the text says, the entire empire will be able to function and work according to the principles of 'eleutheria' (a freedom), not in the constitutional form of shared political rights, but in the form of freedom of speech. . . . This freedom of speech, this parrhesia is therefore the concrete form of freedom in autocracy. It is a freedom which founds friendship—friendship between different hierarchical levels of the State—and the collaboration—the koinonia which ensures the unity of the entire empire.*

Foucault, *The Government of Self*, 203-204.

28 Lida Maxwell, "The Politics and Gender of Truth-Telling in Foucault's Lectures on Parrhesia," Contemporary Political Theory 18, no. 1, (2018), 22-42, esp. 26. Examples of the ethical reading include Nancy Luxon, "Truth, Risk, and Trust in Foucault's Late Lectures," *Inquiry* 47 (2004), 464-489 and "Ethics and Subjectivity," *Political Theory* 36, no. 3 (2008), 377-402; David Owen and Claire Woodford, "Foucault, Cavell, and the Government of Self and Others,"*Iridie: filosofia e discussion*

pubblica 25, no. 2 (2012), 299-316; Sergie Prozorov, "Foucault's Affirmative Biopolitics: Cynic Parrhesia and the Biopower of the Powerless," *Political Theory*, https//doi.org/10.1177/0090591715609171715609963.

29 Foucault, *The Government of Self*, 155.

30 Foucault, *The Government of the Self*, 155.

31 Lida Maxwell, "The Politics and Gender of Truth-Telling in Foucault's Lectures on Parrhesia," *Contemporary Political Theory* 18, no. 1, (2018), 23.

32 Arendt, "Truth and Politics," 251.

33 Arendt, "Truth and Politics," 251.

34 Arendt, "Truth and Politics," 251.

35 Arendt, "Truth and Politics," 251.

36 Hannah Arendt, *The Life of the Mind*, ed. Mary McCarthy, Vol. 2, *Willing*, (Harcourt Brace & Co., 1974), 140.

37 Arendt, "Introduction Into Politics," 131.

When Words Cease to Matter

Marianne Constable

01110100 01101000 01100101 00100000 01110000 01100101 01110010 01101001 01101100 01110011 00100000 01101111 01100110 00100000 01101001 01101110 01110110 01100101 01101110 01110100 01101001 01101111 01101110

November 17, 2016

As we struggle to understand the shock of the 2016 Presidential election, we realize how deeply language, on which productive debate depends, has been abused. Words matter. As so aptly and ironically put in Melania Trump's plagiarized words at the Republican national convention, "your word is your bond." The gravest problem at this moment then lies not in the hate and fear-mongering racism and misogyny that critics accuse the Republican candidate of engaging in, although these are indeed frightening for many. It lies in the willingness of the President-elect himself and of others to disregard things he has actually said. Such disregard of language goes beyond lying and giving offense. It ruptures the possibility of a meaningful political sphere. Dialogue and discussion, including civil disagreement, depend on words. All become impossible when words cease to matter.

Deliberate disregard of language poses a worse danger to political discussion and to the public realm than do ignorance and lies. Ignorance can be met with education. Falsehood and deception can be called out as illusion; they can be challenged in the name of what actually appears to be. Even insults can be acknowledged and addressed. When, by contrast, speakers and hearers routinely disavow or neglect the utterances that they hear or make, they cast words adrift, and language no longer shows us a shared or common world in which to take our bearings.

Such indeed is the situation in the U.S. in the days of disorientation, unease, and unrest following the election of Donald Trump as President. Regardless of what kind of president Trump turns out to be, or of the policies he puts in place, the rhetoric of this election season has shaken our faith in the possibility of meaningful public exchange. This is not because persons are afraid to speak, although some will be. Nor is it because mainstream media has missed or mischaracterized the story, although it has. Our faith is shaken because to deny one's words is to disregard what is. When this disregard coincides with more talk than ever before, the upshot is a mistrust in the possibility of genuine public exchange.

✱✱✱

Trump's factual misstatements are legion, as fact-checkers have been quick to point out. But the difficulties with Trump's utterances involve more than the occasional lie. Hannah Arendt reminds us that lies are no stranger to politics: lying is a form of action and politics is the realm of speech and action. Catastrophe comes when lying becomes routine and fact can no longer be distinguished from falsehood. When this happens, what words say no longer matters. Whether or not Trump's lies are any more responsible for the current catastrophe than are the lies of others, his words leave us at sea.

Even if Trump's platform, as the most charitable account would have it, can be understood as an "opening bid" for negotiations, we are left wondering just what this bid is. What are his opinions? Which, if any, of his slogans and sound bites matter? How do his claims—of tax cuts and growing infrastructure—cohere? What are his plans to make the United States—clearly not the two continents of "America"—great again? How do all sides sift through the conflicting utterances around his campaign to find the answer? Why is it that now, in the aftermath of the election, so many of us are trying to do so?

What are Trump's views about the environment, for instance? Would he really do away with the Environmental Protection Agency? How does he plan to create jobs? Exactly what health care policies will he pursue? What are his foreign relations priorities? What is his position on women's rights? Websites, from the right and the left, offer quotations left and right. From these can be gleaned no more than some possible policies favoring business and an animus against Washington D.C. (Check out the non-partisan www.ontheissues.org.) In 1999, Trump declared himself to be "pro-choice." In 2011, he proclaimed himself "pro-life," attributing his flip to stories he had heard. After beginning his run for president, he admitted that he had changed his mind for the purpose of the nomination. He has shifted from claiming that women should be punished for abortions, to announcing that their doctors should be punished for carrying them out, to maintaining that after he appoints a pro-life Supreme Court justice, *Roe v Wade* would be overturned and the issue would be left to individual States.

These inconsistencies and many other arguably premature or unthought public announcements—on Obama's nationality, immigration, government reform, gun laws, and the Middle East—indicate that one cannot trust him to mean what he says. Public disorientation—and perhaps even Trump's own—at the result of the election cannot be blamed entirely on the press or its polling data then. Television and newspapers have studiously relayed and glossed only his own mixed messages, including his enthusiastic and contradictory tweets for attention.

At least some Trump supporters (Muslims for Trump, Women for Trump) have asserted that one cannot take issue with some of Trump's more offensive remarks precisely because he doesn't really mean what he says. Some of these supporters claim to be victimized by being identified, by opponents, with the offensive views articulated in or implied by his statements. Such ostensible defenses hardly restore confidence in public discourse.

Other supporters, and Trump himself, deny the very fact that he has said things which we have heard him say. When Trump says "X" and later adds not only "I never meant X," but also "I never said 'X'," fact-checkers work over the issue of whether Trump actually said "X." His disavowal of having said "X" raises a more crucial issue than what was or was not said though. When what one hears is denied, and the denials continue no matter the facts, the issue becomes one of disregard and not simply disavowal. One can no longer believe one's ears. No wonder that at least half of the country is reeling. We have entered very shaky ground when we cannot rely on our hearing and speech.

Trump's readiness to dismiss what words say in favor of what they do only makes things worse. Asked whether he regrets any of the incendiary rhetoric of his campaign, he retorted, "No, I won." It appears that for him utterances, which are ostensibly "speech acts," no longer speak, but only act. Unmoored from what they say, they serve as instruments with which to bulldoze his way through the game.

The public dismissal both of what words say and of any commitment to words as saying, leaves us speechless. Literally. At a time when more is being said through a greater variety of media than ever before, it appears that anything can be said and everything can be unsaid. Hence nothing that is said matters. Or perhaps it is only that one cannot tell the difference between what matters and what doesn't. No matter. The point is that one cannot debate opinions with a person who disregards the very fact of their own statements of opinion. One never knows what further undermining of speech awaits. In such tenuous terrain, words cannot bind. We are deprived of the capacity for political speech with those—or as those—to whom words do not matter.

***

Upon his victory, Trump mouthed the words that it was time to set divisions aside. It is time for him to put his money where his mouth is. He tells the public, those who can no longer believe their ears, that the week's protests against him are occurring "because they don't know me." Perhaps so. But it is precisely his words and their failure to distinguish fact from falsehood that have made him impossible to know as a political figure, as a speaker and actor in public. His disregard for his own words has contributed to making public speech impossible to trust.

This week's protests manifest the queasiness in which the evacuation of meaning from speech throws us all. Trump's challenge now is to show, through his deeds, what he has not shown through his speech—indeed what his utterances have completely thrown into question—that his word is his bond. The task confronting the next leader of the United States must be to affirm that we share—and that he shares with us—a common world in which are respected the conventions of language that make mutual hearing and speech possible. The alternative is a frightening void in which there is no room to say, in words that one can count on to be heard, "I disagree."

When at the 2016 convention, Melania Trump claimed, in stolen words, that her parents had "impressed on me the values that you work hard for what you want in life; that your word is your bond and you do what you say and keep your promise; that you treat people with respect," she referred only to herself and she left out two important phrases. She did not steal enough. When Michelle Obama spoke during the 2008 Democratic national convention, she had explained that "we," she and Barack, were raised with certain values: "that you work hard for what you want in life; that your word is your bond and you do what you say you're going to do; that you treat people with dignity and respect." She had also added, "even if you don't know them, and even if you don't agree with them." Let us hope that the Donald Trump whom we don't know finds a way to agree and to commit to a world in which words matter.

Supplement to *When Words Cease to Matter*
October 8, 2020

The Promise and the Threat

Almost four years ago, I argued in "When Words Cease to Matter" that we were in danger of losing the promise of truth that accompanies language. The then-incoming administration's lies about words portended the complete loss of this admittedly often-unfulfilled promise. The repercussions of the loss of the truth of words, I argued, correspond with the dismantling of the public sphere as a place of discussion and exchange. Completely bereft of its promise of truth, speech—properly speaking—is impossible.

Words are still uttered, of course. But, as many have noted, speech has been transformed during the last four years. As racism and violence have become more manifest, the promise of language has given way to the threat of words. The mockery of truth that marks much of today's public political speech accompanies a growing culture of threats and verbal offenses.

Recall that promises and threats act differently; they do different things. Promises freely grant something that is presumed to be good for their beneficiary; threats create a Catch-22. They force their addressees onto the horns of a particular dilemma, that of having to choose between two evils: the evil of undesirable cooperation and that of harm. A promise expresses a commitment; it instantiates the word that is "our bond." A threat reveals a will to dominate. It renders impotent those who fail to obey or to conform to the will of the speaker by "promising" harm.

The conflation of promise and threat was manifest before the election. In discussing his word in *Crippled America: How to Make America Great Again* (2015), now-President Donald J. Trump writes, "The most important lesson is this—*Stand behind your word, and make sure your word stands up.*" His next paragraph begins, "I don't make promises I can't keep." Trump seems to align his word with his "promises" here, but he immediately follows "I don't make promises I can't keep" with "I don't make threats without following through. Don't ever make the mistake of thinking you can bully me. My business partners and employees know that my word is as good as any contract—and that better go for the other side's word as well" (138).

The "word" that "stands up" and "behind" which Trump stands is a weapon of defense against bullying. It is also a threat by "me" (Trump) against "you" should your word turn out not to be, like Trump's word, "as good as any contract." Even if Trump does not explicitly invoke the slang usage of "contract" (i.e., hiring an assassin to kill someone), he "follow[s] through" on his threats against "the other side," whose word had "better" be as good as his.

The slippage between promise and threat here and elsewhere may explain some of the world's confusion surrounding U.S. foreign and domestic policy: is the President peddling in promises or in threats when he deals with particular nations or agreements? And is there a difference? In a house divided, is a US-Mexico wall a promise to some and a threat to others? Are Trump's many executive orders commitments or do they constitute bullying in the face of imagined or actual slights? Trump's performance in the September 29, 2020, presidential debate against Joe Biden simultaneously revealed his breach of a promise to the agreed-to terms of debate—and the ways that his words bully.

Not only speakers, but all manner of hearers today experience words as weapons and threats. Hate speech has long been an issue. Persons who have historically been on the receiving end of threats, domination, and violence, as well as others, call out microaggressions. The outcry against offensive words now joins with protest against the physical violence that images of police brutality bring to the fore. Media concerns over "cancel culture"— whether referring to the withdrawal of attention, approval and support for celebrity figures, companies and their messages or to broader silencing and erasures of persons and groups—recognize the harm that words can do. Even the powerful, it seems, now encounter speech not simply as privilege and right, but as a destructive initiative launched from the mouths and pens (and posts) of others. Words ricochet like bullets to which all are susceptible, masked and unmasked, online and off, in parking lot altercations and in remote-classroom zoom bombings.

High and low, public speech discharges its words as barbs. In a stirring speech on the opening night of the physically-distanced, made-for-television, 2020 Democratic National Convention, Michelle Obama repeated, in an apparent rebuke, Donald Trump's words about the coronavirus death toll in the United States: "It is what it is." Again her words are telling; they may be what they are, but speech at least is no longer what it is, nor even what it says. Words today—hers, his, those of our language—matter less for the truths that they promise than for the damage they do.

When words become weapons, that is, our word is not our bond. The threats of speech instead give rise to fear and domination. Fear and domination accompany threats. "As a principle of public-political action," as Hannah Arendt again so aptly points out, fear "has a close connection with the fundamental experience of powerlessness that we all know from situations in which, for whatever reasons, we are unable to act." Powerless to act, we are unable to engage in politics as a realm of common action. Unable to speak or to hear without injury, we cannot listen: we watch with bated breath as cameras zoom in on the fly on the Vice President's head!

Show Me the Birth Certificate!
How America's Internet-Enabled
Conspiracist Media Culture
Is Destroying American Politics

Jonathan Kay

01110100 01101000 01100101 00100000 01110000 01100101 01110010 01101001 01101100 01110011 00100000 01101111 01100110 00100000 01101001 01110110 01110110 01100101 01110110 01110100 01101001 01101111 01101110

L ewis Lapham, who spoke from this podium earlier in the day, said something interesting. He said, "The truth doesn't have a big fan base. It's not a popular product." That really echoed for me because that is exactly what I heard from certain publishers when I pitched my book about conspiracy theories. At first they were excited: "Oh, you're writing a book about conspiracy theories. Great! You believe the lizards are taking over . . . or maybe some kind of zombie apocalypse?" I said, "No, no, no, this is a book against conspiracy theories—a book about how we all have to be more rational." The publishers became much less excited. They said, "Well, it sounds a little dry." But then, Adam Bellow, an editor at Harper Collins, took a chance on me. And for that, I am grateful. The result was my book *Among the Truthers: A Journey Through America's Growing Conspiracist Underground*, which came out in 2011.

I think it is important to talk about this subject at a conference such as this, dedicated to "truthtelling," because conspiracy theories are both a symptom and a cause of a media culture and an Internet culture that promotes nonsense, for reasons I'm going to explain.

Before I get into the theory, I'd like to give you a case study, which involves something that happened after my book was published. The case study involves Anders Breivik, who killed dozens of people in Norway in July 2011. At the time, I was on a book tour. One night I instinctively went back to a lot of the conspiracy theory websites that I had used to research my book, because I was curious as to what the conspiracy theorists were saying about this horrible mass slaughter. Of course, we all know the truth of it. The killer composed a turgid 1,400-page manifesto explaining his dark motives—no mystery there. Still, I was interested in what the conspiracy theorists were saying about what they imagined the real story was.

What was interesting to me was that the conspiracy theories about the Norway killings broke down into three different subgenres; I'm going to go briefly through them. The first conspiracy theory was that the Norway shootings were actually a clever plot by Muslims to discredit cultural conservatives in Europe. The lead on this particular conspiracy theory was taken by a website that some of you may know, called WorldNetDaily. It has become infamous as the clearinghouse for Barack Obama Birther conspiracy theories, but they also dabble in other conspiracies. Following is what appeared a day or two after the Norway shooting.

"This has all the appearances of a cover-up," radio host Michael Savitch told WorldNetDaily.

> *"They created their Reichstag fire, they found their Timothy Mc-Veigh, they created their Jack Ruby. How could one man have blown up downtown Oslo and then raced to the island to kill those teenagers? This is likely a fabrication of the Norwegian labor party, which needs to hold onto power to enforce their multiculturalist Muslim favoring antinationalist views."*

That was the first conspiracy theory—that it was Muslims and multilateralists who were trying to discredit conservatives.

The second Norway conspiracy theory was that the attacks were actually part of a "New World Order" plot to create fear and anxiety in Europe, so that the "globalists" could ram a collectivist banking agenda down Europe's throat. A fellow named Alex Jones took the lead on this one. I'm not sure if people in this room know who Jones is. He has a popular radio show, and he is a particular hero among libertarians. Here is the way Jones reported the Norway shootings.

> *"They are now pulling out all the stops in an effort to crush resistance to endless bailouts, designed to crash local economies and destroy national sovereignty. It is no mistake the corporate media is comparing Anders Breivik to Timothy McVeigh. Hours after the terrorist attack Norway public broadcasters said the attack resembled the bombing of the federal building in Oklahoma, which, as we all know, was a false-flag event used to roll out draconian aspects of the American police state in the 1990's. Breivik is obviously just a patsy for those seeking to destroy political opposition to the world's neoliberal bankers."*

So, the first conspiracy theory is that it was Muslims and multiculturalists. The second conspiracy theory is that it was the world's bankers.

The third conspiracy theory was that Anders Breivik was actually a stooge of the Israelis, purportedly because Israel wanted to punish Norway's pro-Palestinian politicians. The lead on this one was taken by a 9/11 conspiracy theorist by the name of Kevin Barrett, who lives in Wisconsin. He said, "Friday's bloodbath in progressive Norway bears the markings of an Israeli Mossad false flag terror attack. No Western country has supported the Palestinian cause more than the Norwegians."

So, there you have it. Anders Breivik was a tool of the bankers, the Jews, or the Muslims. Take your pick.

Of course, we know all of this is nonsense, but it's representative nonsense. It's representative of the millions of conspiracy theories that you're going to find on the Internet. Because, first of all, what are conspiracy theories? They are theories of evil—evil such as the mass-murdering kind that Breivik epitomizes. Such theories answer the question: Why do bad things happen to good people? This is a question that used to be answered through religion. But for many people, we now live in a post-religious world. As a result, we have to make up new narratives that attempt to make sense of horrible things.

Second, my three Norway examples show—and this is something I didn't know, going into the project—that all conspiracy theories are essentially exchangeable.

Originally, I thought I would have to spend 10 years researching my book, because there are so many conspiracy theories out there. Yet it turns out that conspiracy theories are remarkably similar. They all follow the same structure. The structure is this: there is evil in the world—terrorist attacks, depressions, wars—but all of these evil acts are perpetrated by a small group of conspiring men (it is always men, not women) in a smoke-filled room, somewhere in the world, trying to further some kind of evil agenda. What is interesting is that, for purposes of this narrative, the actual identity of the evil-doer—Jew, Muslim, banker—is fairly interchangeable.

In one chapter of my book, I talk about *The Protocols of the Elders of Zion*, a notorious anti-Semitic hoax published in the early part of the 20th century alleging that the Jews of the world were conspiring to produce revolutions, wars, depressions, all manner of evil, to further their sinister Jewish agenda. What I found was that if you take the *Protocols* as your starting point, and then you replace the word *Jew* with the word *Muslim*, you actually wind up with something that closely resembles a lot of the stuff that appears on militant right-wing websites today. Or you can replace the word *Jew* with *Bilderberger*, or *New World Order follower.* Or you can replace *Jew* with *Catholic*, and get a Dan Brown novel.

The point is that the structure of conspiracy theories is remarkably consistent, which is why I urge the readers of my book to read *The Protocols of the Elders of Zion*. Not because the *Protocols* are true, obviously, but because that book is a blueprint for so much of the conspiracism and nonsense that we see on the Internet today. Ancient conspiracism helps us understand modern conspiracism.

When I started analyzing these conspiracy theories, I ended up reading a lot of manifestos that were very similar to the *Protocols*. I also went out and started interviewing conspiracy theorists. This seems like a fairly obvious thing to do when you are writing a book about conspiracy theories. But it turns out that not many authors have done it. Most books about conspiracy theories are either promoting conspiracy theories (these sell very well—the bookstores are full of them), or they're making fun of conspiracy theories, which is very easy to do, since many of these theories are ridiculous. But very few people have actually sat down with conspiracy theorists and asked them what they think.

When I sat down with these people, I had two questions for them. The first was: "What do you believe?" The second was: "When did you start believing it?"

If you ask a 9/11 conspiracy theorist, "What do you believe happened on 9/11?" they'll start telling you that first Dick Cheney's CIA minions put the bombs in the Twin Towers. Then his friends at NORAD shut down the entire flight defense system over North America. I'm a former engineer, a nerd, I like video games and sci-fi, and at first I was interested in this technical Tom Clancy–type stuff. But, after a couple of months of hearing this sci-fi fantasy, I got bored with the details. I realized I was hearing the same details over and over and over.

What was much more interesting was asking my interviewees the second question—*when* did they starting believing conspiracy theories.

As I said before, conspiracy theories are narratives about why bad things happen, about why evil exists in the world. But, they are also narratives of distrust. The people who believe in conspiracy theories obviously don't trust the government, or the media, or any public institutions. (When I told my interviewees I was an editor for the *National Post* in Canada, they just took it for granted that I was a professional liar who got his marching orders every week from George Soros or the Zionists or whoever they imagined was the ultimate paymaster.) And so when you ask a conspiracy theorist, "When did you start believing that 9/11 was an inside job?" you're asking them a very personal question. You are essentially asking them the question: "When did your world fall apart? When did you start believing that every-body was lying to you?" That is a very personal question, and I got some very interesting answers.

What I found was that different people had their own, very different, very personalized points of entry into the world of conspiracy. But once they went down that rabbit hole, once the trust was broken, they became vulnerable to every conspiracy theory under the sun. You very rarely run into someone who believes only one conspiracy theory. Typically, what happens is that at first they'll buy into one conspiracy theory, then they'll get on the Internet, they'll get on a few websites, they'll start watching some videos, and before you know it, they believe dozens of conspiracy theories.

When does this distrust start? Where is the point of entry?

For a lot of liberal 9/11 conspiracy theorists, distrust didn't start right after 9/11, but rather in 2003, when they found out there were no weapons of mass destruction in Iraq. The first question they asked was: What *else* is the government lying about? When you ask that question, the extrapolation of it can lead you into some very dark areas, and you start believing that the government is lying about *everything*, from which vaccines to get to whether cigarettes are bad for you, to whether there are UFOs in Colorado, to who destroyed the Twin Towers. After all, that was the event that ultimately led to the Iraq War, right?

One guy I interviewed for the book is a former NFL football player. He played defensive end for the New York Jets, and he's now a successful investment banker in Toronto. He is Serbian by ancestry and he became radicalized during the Kosovo conflict in 1999. He started to believe, with some justification (there's always a grain of truth behind these things), that NATO wasn't telling us the full story about the Balkans. He believed there was a campaign of lies against Serbia. He told me that he thought that the videos showing the brutalization of Kosovar Albanians had been doctored in a studio.

Once that trust had been broken for this guy, he started to see everything through the same distrustful lens. So, two years after the Kosovo conflict, when 9/11 happened, he saw those terrible events through the same lens and became a 9/11 conspiracy theorist.

In some cases, the source of the distrust is something very personal. I interviewed some people whose children had autism and they had become convinced that their children's condition was a result of vaccines given to the children, in particular the MMR vaccine. Believing that, they also came to believe that the pharmaceutical companies and the government, the FDA in particular, were lying to them about tests they had conducted on these vaccines. If the FDA was lying to them about the vaccines, and the government was lying to protect the FDA . . . what else was the government lying about? From then on, they started believing all sorts of things.

No matter the reason that brings a person into the world of conspiracy, bringing them out again is very difficult. Rarely could you get a conspiracy theorist to "recover." Once their trust is broken with the powers that be, it is like a broken relationship—it is very hard to build the trust back.

In the last chapter of my book I confess that I've never won an argument with a conspiracy theorist. I spent three years working on the book, speaking with conspiracy theorists, and never once was I able to convince any of these people that . . . you know, maybe it was al-Qaeda behind 9/11, or maybe Barack Obama was actually born in Hawaii. That's because, for the people who adopt these theories, they become a worldview. The theory becomes a form of religion. And like all religions, the theory becomes very precious to these people, because it is an explanation for evil. They hang onto it, as a sort of security blanket to explain why bad things happen.

Unlike real religions, conspiracy theories do not supply gods, but they do supply something that might be even more important than gods for some people—they supply demons. They supply a singular address for evil upon which you can blame everything.

And, in some cases, they provide literal demons. Many of the extreme Obama birthers you talk to actually do believe that Barack Obama is either the Antichrist or the false prophet from the Book of Revelation. The political conspiracy theory becomes a secularized version of the religious conspiracy theory that is embedded in the last book of the New Testament.

Because conspiracy theories are an explanation for evil, they always flourish in the aftermath of terrible, evil, historical events. In the modern era, the first great conspiracy theories emerged in the aftermath of the French Revolution. We now look back at the French Revolution and focus on some of the positive ideological principles that came out of it. But at the time, thousands of people were dying; you had blood running in the streets; you had "The Terror." A lot of people became convinced that the French Revolution must have been a plot by the Jews, for instance. More than a century later, *The Protocols of the Elders of Zion* became popular in the aftermath of the Russian Revolution and World War I, when all of Europe was aflame. You also had conspiracy theories after JFK's assassination, after 9/11, and after the 2008 financial crisis, as I explain in my book.

But conspiracy theories also have a political function, not just a psychological or quasi-spiritual function: for militant political movements, conspiracy theories act as a bridge between political ideology and reality.

Take Barack Obama Birthers, for instance. Let's say you spent your entire political life believing that America is a right-wing country, and that it would never elect a left-wing Harvard type like Barack Obama—a community organizer from Chicago, no less. And then along comes the 2008 election, and this is exactly what America does. This shatters your view of the world. It is comforting to think that somehow that historical episode never happened, that it is illegitimate, that it is a hoax, that somehow if you do enough investigation, and if you count enough pixels on a PDF of Barack

Obama's electronic birth certificate, you can somehow discover "the truth." You can roll back presidential history in God's eyes, and you can show the world that this episode never really happened. You can erase Obama's presidency, and thereby bring the real world into compliance with the world that exists in your ideology.

This fetish for using conspiracy theories as a tool to change history—to make history align with some militant ideology—exists on both sides of the political spectrum. Many 9/11 conspiracy theorists that I interviewed, for instance, were left-wing ideologues. They had convinced themselves that America was the epicenter and font of all true evil in the world, and this became their mantra. When 9/11 happened, and they were forced to see a truly despicable act of evil happen in their own backyard, perpetrated by America's *enemies*, it did not compute. A cognitive dissonance arose between their ideology, which was anti-American, and the reality, which was that America's enemies had perpetrated this epic, signature act of evil. They were able to bring ideology and reality into a unified whole only by creating a theory that somehow this act of terrorism had been inflicted on America by its own leaders. The theory protects them from cognitive dissonance. It is a bridge between ideology and reality.

A common question I get about the book is, "Are there real conspiracies out there?" And the answer is, of course: Iran-Contra, Watergate, Teapot Dome. In Canada, we had something called the Sponsorship Scandal, which no one here has heard of. It involved the Liberal Party and their fund-raising irregularities. Real conspiracies do happen. They tend to be small, they tend to be grubby, and they tend to be about money or sex. They don't tend to be about taking over the planet in the name of the Vatican, or the Bilderbergers. That's the way you can tell a real conspiracy from a bogus conspiracy theory.

I was on the Diane Rehm show on NPR, and a lot of people who phoned in said, "You know, I lived through the JFK era. That conspiracy-theory stuff is nothing new. We had our own conspiracy theories back in the day. This is exactly what we went through 50 years ago." And there is truth in that. But, there is a huge difference between then and now. That difference, in a word, is the Internet.

Back in the era of JFK, if you were a conspiracy theorist and you wanted to get the word out about your far-out theory, it was hard. You couldn't go to an editor of a mainstream newspaper or a magazine. Most would say, "Forget it, I'm not publishing your nonsense." There were gatekeepers to the media. So, you went around wearing a sandwich board, or you called into radio stations, or you handed out leaflets on the street. You know, we make fun of these things, but if you're a conspiracy theorist, this was the only option you had back then. You may have had community access television at two o'clock in the morning. Otherwise, you didn't have many other options, because the media had real gatekeepers.

These days, there is a difference. Take me: I'm the editor of the op-ed page at the *National Post* (Canada's *Wall Street Journal*, as I like to think of it). I walk around very puffed up. I'm a gatekeeper; I get to decide which opinions get disseminated in my pages.

But these days, conspiracy theorists have no time for someone like me. Their attitude is, "Forget that guy, I'll just put it on a blog! I'll make a YouTube video. I'll cut out the media middleman." Thanks to online technology, these folks can completely get around people like me, something that was impossible in the JFK era. That's why, in my book, I argue that conspiracism has been transformed by the Internet, as much as social media or pornography. Ninety-nine-point-nine percent of conspiracism now takes place on the Internet. They barely even have conferences anymore. What is the point when you can just create a website or a YouTube video?

And then there's the rise of cheap digital video, something that obviously did not exist in 1963. How many people here have seen the 9/11 conspiracist film *Loose Change*? Often, I'm on college campuses and some guy in a 9/11 Truth T-shirt is giving it out for free. This is a really slick video purporting to explain why 9/11 was an inside job. The thing was made on a shoestring. All told, the ease of entry into the media market by conspiracy theorists has gone down by several orders of magnitude since the JFK era.

But the Internet has had another effect, which in some ways is more disturbing because it affects not only conspiracy theorists, but also mainstream media consumers. That effect is the segmentation of media markets into silos.

Fifty years ago, it didn't matter if you were a conspiracy theorist. In order to get the news, you had to read the paper, listen to the radio, or watch TV. That was the only way you were going to get the news. It didn't matter how crazy you were; chances were, if you lived in New York, you read the *New York Times* or some other major newspaper. There was no other way of getting the news. These days, the people I interviewed for this book didn't read a newspaper. Nor did they listen to the radio. (NPR? God forbid.) Nor did they watch TV. In some cases, they didn't even look at websites. Instead, when they woke up in the morning, right there in their inbox, they would have 50 messages from various conspiracist pals from around the world, giving them updates on news items they were following. This was their news source.

This is a really scary thing. And I see it all the time, even among colleagues in the mainstream media. They'll tell me something, and I'll ask where they heard it, and they say, "Oh, it's all over my discussion group." I say, "Well, you should check that out, it sounds kind of bogus—like something I should put in my book."

A lot of times, I find that middle-aged people are the most vulnerable to conspiracy theorists. This is a very interesting phenomenon. When I was in university, and I was surrounded by anarchists and Trotskyites and people clutching copies of Ayn Rand's books and Scientologists, I couldn't wait until I grew up and met people who were more "normal." Well, I grew up. And now Fox News has turned our grandpas into raving conspiracy maniacs who think George Soros is taking over the world. (I went to Jon Stewart's Rally to Restore Sanity in Washington in October [2010]; there were all these hilarious signs, and the funniest said, "Glen Beck, stop scaring my Dad!")

The reason for this, once again, has to do with the Internet. I notice there are a few young people in the crowd, and these people know how to use the Internet. If someone sends them a crackpot story, they search for it on Wikipedia, or on snopes.com, or on some other quasi-reputable site where they can see if something is nonsense. The people I interviewed who were 50, 60, 70, even 80, were different: hip enough to use the Internet, but not hip enough to use it properly. So when their brother-in-law sent them a link to something about how Barack Obama wasn't a U.S. citizen, they just forwarded it to their whole address book. (When I wrote an article entitled "Who Taught Bubba and Zadie How to Use the Internet?" I got hate mail in Yiddish, which was a first for me.)

Then you get to a fundamental question: Does all of this hurt America? This is a question I'm often asked. People say, "Oh, come on, these crackpots are having their fun on the Internet—who cares? This is just a hobby for these people. It's harmless."

And yes, for many people, it is just a hobby. I want to emphasize that I am not against the *X-Files*, I'm not against Thomas Pynchon, I'm not against Dan Brown (whose novels I've read, I'll confess. I thought the movie was terrible but the book was fun.) I'm not against conspiracy theories being used for entertainment. They are fun and they're titillating. That is the main reason that radio producers decided to put me on their show to promote my book. People are interested in conspiracies. However, when people make conspiracy theories their worldview, it becomes impossible to have any kind of public discourse. The example I give is: How are you supposed to have an intelligent argument or discussion with someone if that person thinks that Obamacare is a secret plot to put Grandma before a death panel? What if Grandma herself thinks it's a plot to put her before a death panel? Likewise, you can't have a discussion about the legitimacy of Barack Obama's presidency or his policies with someone who thinks he is an illegal alien. You can't have a discussion about antiterrorist policy or foreign affairs or security with someone who thinks that 9/11 was an inside job. It is just impossible. They live in different realities. You can't span those realities with rationalism.

The question is: What can we do about this? Obviously, Hannah Arendt supplies inspiration because she shows that being a truthteller is a noble thing. Even if the truth is difficult to accept, even if it might take a lot of time and attention to process, even if it may be boring at times, the truth is important. But I think we also have to accept the fact that the truth can be really difficult. That's why people like Hannah Arendt are such heroes, telling the truth and accepting the truth when it is very difficult. Writing this book showed me how difficult the truth is for ordinary people. It's easy for wealthy, well-educated people with brilliant children and grandchildren to accept the world as it is sometimes, because the world for these people is a very sunny place.

Many of the people I interviewed for the book weren't in that place. They were confronting circumstances in their life—failed businesses, medical situations—that perhaps drove them into the arms of conspiracism. You have to appreciate that. For those people, it is really difficult to accept the truth. I confronted it right here in upstate New York. I flew in from Toronto last night. I ate by myself at a pizza restaurant. I was the only guy in the place. I was sipping my coffee, and the waitress came to talk to me. This being America, and 2011, it took her about eight seconds to talk about how horrible Obama is. It was very sad. She told me she had a mother who was 52 with two degrees and can't find a job. She herself was working for what I assume was a very low wage in a pizza restaurant. She has a three-year-old and very little hope for the future. So it didn't surprise me that she hated Obama and thought Obama was responsible for all of her problems.

Ten minutes later, she started talking about immigrants. She talked about a successful immigrant family she knew who were running not one, but two restaurants now, and had three cars. She claimed—falsely, I think—that they were receiving all kinds of government support because they were Mexican. What she was saying began to creep into what was approaching a conspiracy theory. I thought it was implausible, but I listened to her. I realized that for people like her and for tens of millions of other people around the United States, it is really hard to accept a reality in which the United States is a second-rate power compared to China, a place where you're in danger of losing not one but two wars, in Iraq and Afghanistan, where the economy is a mess, where people's mortgages are under water. I realize that a lot of this may not apply to people in this room; but for people to whom it does apply, it is much easier to find one single person or group of people to blame for all their problems than it is to analyze the extremely complex subject of, for instance, mortgage-backed Wall Street securities, which most people can't understand. So, you blame taxes, or you blame Obamacare or you blame Obama himself.

The good news, I think, for fighting conspiracy theories, is that the United States, for all of its problems now, is actually a wonderful place in one great respect—something that as a Canadian I've always admired—and that is its capacity for intellectual self-awareness and change. When you look back at the civil rights struggle, you don't look at Canada or Europe, you look at the United States. In the space of just a generation or two, the United States succeeded in stigmatizing racism, sexism, homophobia, all different pathological forms of discrimination, basically removing them from the polite discourse of politics and even dinner-party conversation. All of this was done in the space of basically 30 or 40 years—an unbelievable achievement in the history of human sociology.

If the United States can do this, if the United States can get rid of these other toxic 'isms' from its intellectual discourse, maybe it can do the same with conspiracism. I think one step, obviously, is to engage in conferences like this, which is why it was such a delight for me to come here and attend. Another is to read my book. But a third step is to recognize the problem as a serious problem and not just make fun of people who seem to have odd theories about the way the world works. It's fun to make fun of Tea Party types, or 9/11 truthers, or the people handing you leaflets on the street. But they are a symptom of a serious problem, and I think you have to take the problem seriously. It is what I've tried to do in my research and I urge other people to do the same in theirs.

Why Are We So Matter of Fact About the Facts?

Peg Birmingham

01110100 01101000 01100101 00100000 01110000 01100101 01110010 01101001 01101100 01110011 00100000 01101111 01100110 00100000 01101001 01101110 01110110 01100101 01101110 01110100 01101001 01101111 01101110

Underneath the infamous photo of President George W. Bush standing on the Air Force carrier in front of a large banner proclaiming "Mission Accomplished," the headline states in bold block letters, "So false it must be true." This article in the German newspaper goes on to say that opponents of George W. Bush still believe in facts and that this is their weakness; by contrast, the Bush Presidency is "post-reality," that is, beyond the traditional belief in an objective reality with its claim of factual truths. The article suggests that Bush's refusal to acknowledge the existence of factual truth makes him the first postmodern U.S. President, insofar as for both Bush and postmodernism, reality is performative, that is, constituted from out of speech and deed. Indeed, the article quotes a Bush adviser: "We are an Empire and when we act we create our own reality . . . We are the actors of history, and we can therefore do whatever we want."[1]

Reading this in the Berlin airport in 2006 at the end of a three-day celebration of Hannah Arendt's 100th birthday, I found it disturbing to see the Bush Presidency linked with postmodernism, with which I had more than a few shared commitments, most notably, its critique of the notion of an already constituted objective reality that demanded that human thinking be adequate to it. At the same time, I began to reflect upon the adviser's claim that the administration con-

So falsch, dass es wahr sein muss

sidered itself actors, involved with the task of beginning something new. Was this not very close to Hannah Arendt's own celebration of political action rooted in our capacity for new beginnings? And, furthermore, were not the glorious deeds of these actors, however opposed I might be to them, an Arendtian example of acting for the sake of political immortality that delivers the actors from obscurity into the light of the public realm?

Of course, as the headline suggests, the proclamation "Mission Accomplished"—indeed, the entire premise of going to war with Iraq—turned out to be political action based on a lie, a lie "so false that it must be true." The question I want to take up here is why the lies were so easily accepted by the American public. Why did the facts not matter either in the initial invasion of Iraq or in the events that followed? It would be comforting to suggest that the American public was simply deluded, gullible, taken in by the images and the spectacle because it did not have access to what was really going on.

I would like to suggest, however, that the American citizenry was not so much deluded or taken in by the images and the lies (although there was certainly some of that) as much as it was the case that the facts simply did not matter. And what I want to explore in these remarks is the question, "Why not?" Why is the American public so matter of fact about the facts?

I want to begin by noting a striking difference in the English language in the meaning of the phrase *matter-of-fact*. On the one hand, we say "matter of fact" when we want to correct whatever it is that is being claimed, such as when my colleague suggests that we should be patient with a graduate student having trouble finishing his dissertation because he is, after all, just in the preliminary stages. I reply, "As a matter of fact, he has been working on the thesis for six years now." Here my use of *matter of fact* is an assertion of what is actually the case and a correction of my colleague's view of just how long the student has been working on his dissertation. We also say *matter-of-fact* to denote a manner of indifference or off-handedness concerning a person's attitude toward a situation or state of affairs. I might say of this same student, "He is matter-of-fact about the whole thing," thereby indicating that the student conveys indifference and a lack of concern about the time it is taking him to finish the dissertation. In the case of the lies surrounding the invasion of Iraq and its aftermath, the attitude of the U.S. citizenry is in my view characterized by this second sense of *matter-of-fact*. The citizenry conveyed a lack of concern, an apathy or even antipathy, toward matters of fact. Again, why is it that in the case of the Iraq War and its aftermath, the American public was simply indifferent to the facts? Why did the facts not seem to matter? Or to say it differently, why was the U.S. citizenry so matter-of-fact about lying in politics?

My hypothesis, and it is counter-intuitive, is that the facts don't matter because the U.S. democratic space is founded on a moral vision in which history and matters of fact play, at best, a subordinate role. To say it more forcefully: from the "city on the hill" to "manifest destiny" to "American exceptionalism," there has been in American politics from the beginning a depoliticization of the political by an ahistorical ethical vision. Here we need only to recall Francis Fukuyama's well-known claim of the "end of history"—from his book *The End of History and the Last Man.* After the fall of the Berlin Wall and the supposed victory of democracy over communism, Fukuyama's claim can be made only if democracy is an ahistorical project linked to the progress and the moral perfectibility of human beings. Most recently, this view of American democracy as embodying a moral or ethical vision was articulated in President Barack Obama's acceptance speech upon receiving the Nobel Peace Prize, in which he said:

> *Yet the world must remember that it was not simply international institutions—not just treaties and declarations—that brought stability to a post-World War II world. Whatever mistakes we have made, the plain fact is this: the United States of America has helped underwrite global security for more than six decades with the blood of our citizens and the strength of our arms . . . We have borne this burden not because we seek to impose our will, but because we seek a better future for our children and grandchildren, and we believe that their lives will be better if other peoples' children and grandchildren can live in freedom and prosperity.*[2]

Here we see again the moral vision that underwrites all political action: not strength or force, but a moral vision for the future has underwritten global security. Obama refers to the Iraq war only as a "war that is winding down," a war in which the United States bore the moral burden of making the future possible for "its children and grandchildren," with no mention made of the thousands of "other peoples' children and grandchildren" that have been killed in that war. This kind of historical forgetfulness is noted by Susan Sontag at the conclusion of her book *Regarding the Pain of Others,* in which she points out that the United States has a Holocaust museum and is breaking ground on a museum dedicated to the remembrance of the Armenian genocide but yet has no equivalent national museum of slavery or the genocide of the Native Americans.[3] Again, I want to suggest that this forgetfulness of history—this lack of concern for matters of fact—is made possible by an ethical rather than a political vision of democracy.

To grasp the significance of this for the political lie, we need to recall Arendt's distinction between the moral and the political. For Arendt, the moral sphere is characterized chiefly as a concern with the self. For her, the moral concern is that of individual conscience that tells the individual not to ". . . do anything that you will not be able to live with."[4] Therefore, from the ethical perspective there may be times in which lying may not much trouble our conscience and, indeed, may be justified for a variety of good reasons, for instance, furthering a moral end. This last is Rousseau's claim that I suggest is taken up wholesale by the Bush administration: for the sake of justice, we can lie. In *Reveries of a Solitary Walker*, Rousseau makes a distinction between "moral truth" and "factual truth," arguing that when there is a conflict between the two types of truth, moral truth is "far superior."[5] He states, "It follows from all these reflections that my professed truthfulness is based more on feelings of integrity and justice than on factual truth, and that I have been guided in practice more by the moral dictates of my conscience than by abstract notions of truth and falsehood."[6] Moral justice may require the lie at the expense of factual truth. The adage *Fiat justicia et pereat mundus* (Let justice be done even if the world perishes) expresses this moral perspective on the world: acting justly trumps the existence of the world itself.

By contrast, Arendt argues that politics is not concerned with the self and its moral conscience, but instead, with the world:

> . . . *conscience is unpolitical. It is not primarily interested in the world where the wrong is committed or in the consequences that the wrong will have for the future course of the world. It does not say, with Jefferson, 'I tremble for my country when I reflect that God is just; that His justice cannot sleep forever,' because it trembles for the individual self and its integrity.*[7]

Jefferson's concern is the injustice and harm slavery does to the country, not to his individual soul. Arendt goes on to give the example of Lincoln, for whom the paramount concern was the nation:

> *This does not mean that Lincoln was unaware of '"the monstrous" injustice of slavery itself,' as he had called it eight years earlier; it means that he was also aware of the distinction between his 'official duty' and his 'personal wish that all men everywhere could be free.' And this distinction . . . is ultimately the same as Machiavelli's when he said, "I love my native city more than my own soul."*[8]

For Arendt, a political wrong harms the public space itself. Thus the adage *let justice be done though the world perish* is devastating from the political point of view. An enduring world is the concern of politics. From the political perspective, to act in such a way that the world perishes in the name of justice is to act in the most profoundly unjust manner possible. The *political* lie, therefore, harms the world, not the self. Thus it is misguided to ask, "Are there legitimate ends that could be served by the political lies?" For Arendt, the political lie can serve no legitimate political ends because the political lie destroys the political space itself. In other words, the political lie destroys the very ground upon which political action is possible.

It is important to note that for Arendt lying is a form of action. The deliberate denial of factual truth—the ability to lie—and the capacity to begin something new—the ability to act—are interconnected; they owe their existence to the same source, namely, human freedom rooted in the capacity to imagine a reality different from what it is. For example, we are free to say it is raining when the sun is shining, but more important:

> *We are free to change the world and to start something new in it. Without the freedom to deny or affirm existence, to say "yes" or "no"—not just to statements or propositions in order to express agreement or disagreement, but to things as they are given beyond agreement or disagreement, to our organs of perception and cognition—no action would be possible; and action is of course the very stuff that politics is made of.*[9]

With her claim that lying is a form of action, it is clear that Arendt does not unconditionally celebrate our capacity to act. Instead, she claims that action itself has become for the contemporary world the political problem par excellence. Not only is it the source of the totalitarian lie, but also it is the source of what she calls world alienation and quite possibly the source of the annihilation of the world itself. In her essay "The Concept of History" she writes, "The world we have now come to live in, however, is much more determined by man acting into nature, creating natural processes and directing them into the human artifice and the realm of human affairs, than by building and preserving the human artifice as a relatively permanent entity."[10]

Contrary to those who seek the remedy for totalitarianism in Arendt's notion of action, a key element of totalitarianism for her was precisely that "the human capacity for action dominated all other human capabilities, the capacity for wonder and thought in contemplation no less than the capacities of *homo faber* and the human *animal laborans*."[11]

For Arendt, confronting totalitarianism involves confronting its key condition, namely, the radical lie. At the very outset of *Origins of Totalitarianism*, she raises the issue of deception, considering the difference between ancient and modern sophists and their relation to truth and reality:

> *Plato, in his famous fight against the ancient Sophists, discovered that their 'universal art of changing the mind by arguments' (Phaedrus 261) had nothing to do with truth, but aimed at opinions which by their nature are changing, and which are valid only 'at the time of the agreement and as long as the agreement lasts,' (Theatetus 172) . . . The most striking difference between the ancient and modern sophists is that the ancients were satisfied with a passing victory of the argument at the expense of truth, whereas the moderns want a more lasting victory at the expense of reality.*[12]

In these early pages of *Origins,* Arendt claims that the characteristic that sets totalitarianism apart from tyrannical and dictatorial regimes is precisely the victory of the lie at the expense of reality, which, she argues, institutes a "lying world order."[13]

In "The Concept of History," her first essay published after *Origins,* Arendt explores further the totalitarian lie, connecting it to a certain conception of history. In this essay Arendt claims that there is a paradoxical relationship between a certain conception of history and the totalitarian lie as the erasure of history. The paradox for Arendt is that the totalitarian lie is rooted in the modern conception of history that allows for the total erasure of history. The modern concept of history that allows for this erasure of itself emerges from the rise of the secular, that is, the separation of religion and politics. For Arendt, this was not to deny the existence of the gods, but to ". . . discover in the secular realm an independent, immanent meaning which even God could not alter."[14] The most important consequence of the rise of the secular was that human immortality "lost its politically binding force."[15]

By contrast, for the Greeks and Romans, "the foundation of a body politic was brought about by man's need to overcome the mortality of human life and the futility of human deeds."[16] Politics for the Greeks and Romans was understood as the *activity* of immortalizing: "The word [immortality] designated an activity and not a belief, and what the activity required was an imperishable space guaranteeing that 'immortalizing' would not be in vain."[17] The modern rise of secularization meant that life and the world "had become perishable, mortal, and futile."[18] According to Arendt, the modern concept of history offers redemption from this unbearable human futility by claiming that history, like nature, is a process without beginning or end; it reaches infinitely into the past and infinitely into the future. While individual acts have no meaning, they can become meaningful as part of a process that will bestow "earthly immortality" on human affairs. In Arendt's reading, this status is no longer achieved in action as it was for the Greeks, but simply by living in the historical process itself.

According to Arendt, this modern concept of historical process, with its emphasis on "earthly immortality" coupled with the modern scientific conviction that we know only what we make, sets the stage for the totalitarian lie with its complete disregard for factuality, the givenness of reality, and the actual deeds and incidents of history:

> . . . *The perplexity is that the particular incident, the observable fact, or single occurrence of nature, or the reported deed and event of history, have ceased to make sense without a universal process in which they are supposedly embedded; yet the moment man approaches this process in order to escape the haphazard character*

*of the particular, in order to find meaning . . .his effort is rebutted
by the answer from all sides: Any order, any necessity, any meaning
you wish to impose will do.*[19]

In other words, the modern concept of history allows for the totalitarian
move from "everything is permitted" to "everything is possible." Action can
be based on any premise, and in the course of the action, the hypothesis will
become true. Consistent action can be as mad as it likes; it will always end
up producing the facts that are "objectively true." We are back to the Bush
administration and its claim that it can produce the reality that it likes. Ironically, the modern concept of history that gives birth to the boundlessness of
action and the totalitarian lie has led to the loss of both history (through the
destruction of factual truth) and nature (as action now involves the changing
of natural processes at will). At the same time, Arendt suggests that with the
emergence of the boundlessness of action, action has lost the condition of its
possibility. In other words, she claims that without the historian and the concern for establishing factual truth, political action is impossible: "We lose
our capacity to act if we lose the capacity of factual truth-telling."[20] Without
the capacity of truthtelling, she argues, we are left with "the constant shifting
and shuffling in utter instability." Shifting and shuffling, the political actors
are not able to find their feet, a necessary condition for acting in concert for
the sake of beginning something new. Speaking of the joy and gratification
of acting together and appearing in public, Arendt concludes her essay
"Truth and Politics" by claiming:

*However, what I meant to show here is that this whole sphere, its
greatness notwithstanding, is limited—that it does not encompass
the whole of man's and the world's existence. It is limited by those
things that men cannot change at will. And it is only by respecting
its own borders that this realm, where we are free to act and to
change, can remain intact, preserving its integrity and keeping its
promises. Conceptually, we may call [factual] truth what we cannot change; metaphorically, it is the ground on which we stand and
the sky that stretches above us.*[21]

Arendt argues that the historian not only establishes the border between
factual truth and *doxa*, but at the same time establishes the ground for
worldly being-in-common, which, in turn, allows for our capacity to act in
concert with others. Arendt often uses the metaphor of a table to illuminate
what she means by a "common world or a public realm." The common
world, she argues, is like a table "that gathers human beings together and
relates them to each other." And it is essential to note that the common world
that relates and separates us is established *not* by action, but instead by the
historian. In her essay "Understanding and Politics," Arendt argues that it is

the historian and the historical imagination that bridge differences, bring the distance closer, and put the proximate in perspective.[22]

If the political depends upon a common world, as Arendt suggests that it does, then here too we see that action, the capacity to begin something new, has its conditions in factual truth. Without an enduring common world established by the historian, who collects and assembles the stories that establish factual truth, the public space loses the condition of its possibility. Thus, Arendt writes, "In such a world, the first task is . . . to bear witness to the givenness of factual truth, to recall evidence and give testimony to what has happened, to undertake the work and discipline of facing up to and bearing reality." We must do what Arendt says Herodotus was the first to do, namely, say what is:

> No human world destined to outlast the short life span of mortals within it will ever be able to survive without men willing to do what Herodotus was the first to undertake consciously—namely, legein ta onta, to say what is. No permanence, no perseverance in existence, can even be conceived of without men willing to testify to what is and appears to them because it is.[23]

Arendt's concern for an enduring world that outlasts the onslaught of boundless action leads her to rethink the modern concept of history. This last point must be emphasized. While it is certainly the case that in "The Concept of History" and in the *Origins of Totalitarianism*'s critique of the "law of history" at work in totalitarian terror, she is extremely critical both of the modern concept of history as process and the missed opportunity that occurs when the modern concept of history replaces the possibility of a concept of the political, it is not the case that Arendt has no concept of history at work in her political thought. On the contrary, Arendt is as concerned for an immortal world established by the historian as she is for the new beginnings made possible through a plurality of actors.

What, then, is Arendt's conception of history? How do we bear witness to the past in a way that allows for an enduring world? And, perhaps most important, how do we say what is (*legein ta onta*)? To answer these questions, I submit that we must examine Arendt's immense debt to Walter Benjamin's "Theses on the Philosophy of History," in particular his critique of historicism and conformism in Thesis XIII and his notion of *crystallization* in Thesis XVII.

Given the central importance that Arendt gives to factual truth as the condition of possibility for political action, what must be asked is how Arendt understands "the givenness of factual truth." On the face of it, she seems here to be very close to a positivist conception of factual truth, as if it were nothing more than something to be grasped in a kind of presence-of-hand by the witness who testifies to it. Certainly this is Derrida's claim in "History of the Lie," an essay largely devoted to Arendt, wherein he raises the suspicion of whether in her formulation of factual truths, Arendt appeals to something like an objective reality as the bulwark against deception:

> *This suspicion can touch on everything that exceeds, in more than one direction, the determination of truth as objectivity, as the theme of a constative utterance, or even as adequation; at the limit it touches on any consideration of performative utterances. In other words, the same suspicion would be aimed at any problematic that delimits questions and a fortiori deconstructs the authority of truth as objectivity.*[24]

I would like to suggest, however, that Arendt is far from positing some sort of notion of objective reality upon which she grounds her understanding of factual truth. Instead, Arendt's conception of history and the status of factual truth are deeply indebted to Walter Benjamin, whose essay "Theses on the Philosophy of History" she carried with her to New York. My suggestion is that from the very beginning of *The Origins of Totalitarianism*, Arendt understands herself as writing history and therein the establishing factual truths very much within what we can call the "Benjaminian conception of history." Arendt's first explicit mention of Benjamin occurs in *The Origins of Totalitarianism* in her analysis of the concept of history at work in imperialism. Here Arendt explicitly links the imperialistic, endless accumulation of power with "the endless process of history." She writes:

> *Hobbes's insistence on power as the motor of all things human and divine . . . sprang from the theoretically indisputable proposition that a never-ending accumulation of property must be based on a never-ending accumulation of power. The philosophical correlative of the inherent instability of a community founded on power is the image of an endless process of history which, in order to be consistent with the constant growth of power, inexorably catches up with individuals, peoples, and finally all mankind.*[25]

Arendt is explicit that a certain conception of political power is inseparable from a certain conception of history. Analyzing this endless process of history, which was "ready to sacrifice everything and everybody to supposedly super-human laws of history," Arendt cites Benjamin: "What we call progress is the wind . . . [that] drives [the angel of history] irresistibly into the future to which he turns his back while the pile of ruins before him towers to the skies."[26]

Important to note is the footnote to this citation: "Walter Benjamin, 'Uber den Begriff der Geschichte,' *Institut fur Sozialforschung*, New York, 1942, mimeographed."[27] It is evident from this footnote that Arendt has the mimeographed copy of Benjamin's essay, not yet published, on her desk as she is writing *Origins,* an endeavor that she began almost immediately upon arriving in New York in 1941, and whose methodology, I submit, was guided throughout by her friend's conception of history.

In his essay on the concept of history, Benjamin is clear that the notion of historical progress is what causes the rubble heap of destruction that the angel of history faces but cannot offer any remedy for, insofar as the force of progress is such that it is blown into a future. Benjamin elaborates on this destructive force of progress in Thesis XIII:

> *Social Democratic theory, and even more its practice, has been formed by a conception of progress which did not adhere to reality but made dogmatic claims. Progress as pictured in the minds of Social Democrats was, first of all, the progress of mankind . . . Secondly, it was something boundless, in keeping with the infinite perfectibility of mankind. Thirdly, progress was regarded as irresistible, something that automatically pursued a straight or spiral course . . . The concept of the historical progress of mankind cannot be sundered from the concept of its progression through a homogeneous, empty time. A critique of the concept of such a progression must be the basis of any criticism of the concept of progress itself.*[28]

In Thesis XIII Benjamin is deeply engaged with a critique of historicism, with its claim of progress as empty, homogenous time, its belief in the irreversibility of time, and its belief in boundless human perfectibility. In earlier theses, Benjamin has pointed to the conformism that is part and parcel with historicism and which prizes nothing more than "keeping up with the current." As Arendt explicitly saw in her analyses of historicism in *Origins,* the danger of historicism is its understanding of time as continuous, one moment automatically following another, uniformly and in linear succession toward some pre-given political ideal to which everyone conforms. For the attainment of this ideal, everybody and everything, including factual truth, can be sacrificed. Conversely, then, what is needed is a concept of history that blasts apart the historical continuum. Time must come to a standstill.

This is precisely how we must understand the notion of "historical crystallization" in Benjamin's concept of history, a notion that Arendt imports wholesale into the preface to the first edition of *Origins* as well as in her reply to Eric Voegelin in an attempt to describe her methodology. I turn first to Benjamin, who introduces the notion of historical crystallization in Thesis XVII:

> *Materialist historiography, on the other hand, is based on a constructive principle. Thinking involves not only the movement of thoughts, but their arrest as well. Where thinking suddenly comes*

to a stop in a constellation saturated with tensions, it gives that constellation a shock, through which thinking crystallizes itself into a monad. The historical materialist approaches a historical object only where it confronts him as a monad. In this structure he recognizes the sign of a messianic arrest of happening or, to put it differently, a revolutionary change in the fight for the oppressed past.[29]

The historical materialist bears the shock of a crystallizing moment in which time has come to a stop. The present is no longer a transitional moment to the future but instead it stands still, breaking off the course of history. Still further, the present is a "constellation . . . that establishes a conception of the present as the 'time of the now' which is shot through chips of Messianic time."[30] The Messiah ceases the happening of historicism in order for there to be "a revolutionary chance in the fight for the oppressed past." In Thesis XII, Benjamin argues that the historical materialism is concerned with "our enslaved ancestors" rather than our "liberated grandchildren."[31]

It is instructive at this point to turn to the 1950 preface to the first edition of *Origins*, wherein Arendt is concerned with the question of how to comprehend this unprecedented event of totalitarianism. She states:

Comprehension does not mean denying the outrageous, deducing the unprecedented from the precedents, or explaining phenomena by such analogies and generalities that the impact of reality and the shock of experience are no longer felt . . . Comprehension, in short, means the unpremeditated, attentive facing up to, and resisting of, reality—whatever it may be.[32]

Later, in the preface to Part One entitled "Anti-Semitism," Arendt goes further, claiming that the book addresses those elements "that later crystallized in the novel totalitarian phenomenon; they had hardly been noticed by either learned or public opinion because they belonged to a subterranean stream of European history where, hidden from the light of the public . . . they had been able to gather an entirely unexpected virulence."[33] She goes on to say that the book is concerned with "the final crystallizing catastrophe." Comprehension, she insists, must face up to this impact of reality and the shock of experience.

In writing a "history" of totalitarianism, Arendt therefore stands entirely in the present, facing up to the shock of reality and this crystallizing event. And this is precisely the language she uses in her reply to Eric Voegelin when she reflects on her methodology in *Origins*: "The book, therefore, does not really deal with the 'origins' of totalitarianism . . . but gives a historical account of the elements which crystallized into totalitarianism."[34] Drawing together these passages, it is clear that Arendt is drawing heavily from Benjamin's "Concept of History" as a frame for her own work. And I want to suggest that this frame provides us with a way of grasping Arendt's conception of "factual truth" as the task of the historical witness.

It must be noted that Arendt's notion of factual truth seems to put her squarely at odds with Benjamin insofar as the latter is clear in Thesis VI that "Articulating the past historically does not mean to recognize it 'the way it really was.' It means appropriating a memory as it flashes up at a moment of danger. . . . Every age must strive anew to wrest tradition away from the conformism that is working to overpower it."[35] It would seem, then, that Benjamin has no truck with anything like "factual truth." However, this is not his position. Instead, Benjamin is claiming that history is never ". . . revealed in the naked and manifest existence of the factual; its rhythm is apparent only to a dual insight. On the one hand, it needs to be recognized as a process of restoration and re-establishment, but on the other hand, and precisely because of this, as something imperfect and incomplete."[36] It is clear in the passage just noted that Benjamin is not dismissing factual truth altogether; instead, he is dismissing the self-evidence of factual truth. In other words, and in opposition to the historicist Ranke, who argues that facts are self-evident, Benjamin claims that the "facts themselves" must be wrested from history, a wresting that is always incomplete and ongoing. Against Ranke, Benjamin claims that the factual truth of what happened, especially what happened to the victims, is often purposely hidden away in the subterranean stream of history. Thus the historian works as a witness to testify to this subterranean stream. This is precisely the language Arendt uses in her conclusion in the Preface to the First Edition of *Origins*:

> *The subterranean stream of Western history has finally come to the surface.*
>
> *. . . This is the reality in which we live. And this is why all efforts to escape from the grimness of the present into nostalgia for a still intact past, or into the anticipated oblivion of a better future, are in vain.*[37]

For both Benjamin and Arendt, the site of history is the site of the present, the moment of discontinuity that requires the activity of collecting and assembling. Benjamin calls the historian the "chronicler," one who is involved with "construction of history" and who "stands at the summit of a materialist historiography." It is he who "recites events without distinguishing between major or minor ones" and "acts according to the following truth: nothing that has ever happened should be regarded as lost to history."[38] The chronicler is the truthteller. Here Benjamin is making a distinction between the one who explains history (the historian proper) and the one who narrates it (the chronicler). The chronicler is the "witness" who does not explain, but simply narrates what happened and what did not happen. The historian proper, the one who interprets and explains history, relies on the chronicler as the one who establishes factual truth. This is why Benjamin argues that the chronicler stands at the summit of a materialist historiography. In his essay "The Storyteller," Benjamin calls Herodotus the "first storyteller of the Greeks" because Herodotus "offers no explanations. His report is the driest."[39]

Certainly, the chronicler could also be the judge and vice versa, but Benjamin cautions not to conflate the difference between the two.

The notion of the historian as the chronicler who testifies to the events of history—its failures as well as its possibilities, its victors and its vanquished— is also at work in Arendt's understanding of the witness who bears testimony to factual truth. As we saw above, Arendt follows Benjamin in turning to Herodotus as a chronicler who is willing to testify to what is. Moreover, this work of the historian as chronicler characterizes Arendt herself, a chronicler who speaks of the victor and the vanquished—those who carried out the Shoah, those who were complicitous, and those who were truly innocent. Arendt as chronicler creates the firestorm around the publication of *Eichmann in Jerusalem*. "Truth and Politics" is her explicit response to those who dammed her for speaking of the role of the Jewish leadership. In fact, we cannot understand *Eichmann in Jerusalem* unless we grasp Arendt's debt to Benjamin, especially his reading of Herodotus; she is the chronicler who must collect and assemble all the stories that make up the event. To do otherwise, as she had stated much earlier to Voegelin regarding *Origins*, is not to write history but instead to offer an apologetics.

Certainly Benjamin's figures of the *flaneur* and the pearl diver, and Arendt's profound interest in both, would have to be brought into this discussion of the "construction of history" and the establishing of factual truth. Suffice it to say here that for Arendt, following Benjamin, factual truth is neither a forensic nor a positivist notion. There is nothing simple or self-evident about it. Instead, the establishment of factual truth occurs at the site of the present, the site of the crystallizing historical event. This requires the laborious work of the historian, specifically the chronicler, who bears witness to the truth of what happened, and in doing so rescues the past and the present from the destruction of historical progress and establishes an enduring, immortal world.

Let me conclude by returning to the problem of action and the question that is often posed to Arendt's political thought: Just what is it that actors do in the public space? What do they talk about and what are their concerns? To answer this, we must again recall Arendt's insistence that action, our capacity to begin something new with a plurality of others, has its ground in history. Arendt argues that the historian works in the light of the event that brings the past into being in the crystallization of the present. This crystallization must be understood as a suspension between past and future, a break in the time continuum, a break with all conformism and all notions of progress. For Arendt, this means that the present is not a transition to another futural point, but rather always a crystallizing moment in which the failures and possibilities of the past are contracted and fixed. Thus, the light of history provides the illumination for action in the public space. The actors, therefore, must also have their back to the future. Contrary to President Obama's *moral* and *ahistorical* invocation of acting for the liberation of our future children and grandchildren, Arendt, following Benjamin, suggests that we must act politically for the liberation of our ancestors. Illuminated by the light of history that gives them their material, political actors must act for the sake of beginning something new that saves the world from ruination by taking up and bearing the failures, possibilities, and demands of the past in its present crystallization. This is both action's limitation and its redemptive possibility.

Redemption, in other words, is only possible on the condition of worldly immortality established by our concern for history and factual truth. Returning to the beginning of my remarks and the question of a democratic politics today: a notion of political redemption rooted in history and a deep and abiding concern for factual truth must replace the current notion of political redemption rooted in a moral vision of the world, a vision where we can be matter-of-fact about the facts.

Endnotes

1. *Frankfurter Allgemeine Sonntagszeitug*, 8 oktober 2006, Nr. 40.

2. Barack Obama, "A Just and Lasting Peace," Nobel Prize acceptance speech, December 10, 2009.

3. Susan Sontag, *Regarding the Pain of Others,* (New York: Picador, 2003).

4. Hannah Arendt, "Civil Disobedience," *Crises of the Republic* (New York: Harcourt, Brace and World, 1969), 64.

5. Rousseau, *Reveries of a Solitary Walker*, trans. Peter France, (New York: Penguin, 1979 (1782)), 71 (Fourth Walk).

6. Ibid., 79.

7. Arendt, "Civil Disobedience," 60–61.

8. Ibid., 61.

9. Hannah Arendt, "Lying in Politics" *Crises of the Republic,* 5–6.

10. Hannah Arendt, "The Concept of History," *Between Past and Future* (New York: Penguin, 1968), 59.

11. Ibid., 62.

12. Hannah Arendt, *The Origins of Totalitarianism* (New York: Harcourt, Brace and Company, 1951), 9.

13. Ibid.

14. Arendt, "The Concept of History, " *Between Past and Future,* 70.

15. Ibid.

16. Ibid., 71.

17. Ibid.

18. Ibid., 74.

19. Ibid., 88–89.

20. Hannah Arendt, "Truth and Politics, " *Between Past and Future*, 258.

21. Ibid., 263–264.

22. Hannah Arendt, *Essays in Understanding*, ed. Jerome Kohn (New York: Harcourt Brace Jovanovich, 1994), 322.

23. Arendt, "Truth and Politics," *Between Past and Future*, 229.

24. Jacques Derrida, "History of the Lie," *Without Alibi*, ed., trans., introduction, Peggy Kamuf, (Stanford: Stanford University Press, 2002), 159.

25. Arendt, *Origins of Totalitarianism*, 143.

26. Ibid.

27. Ibid., 143, footnote.

28. Walter Benjamin, "Theses on a Philosophy of History," *Illuminations,* ed., introduction, Hannah Arendt, (New York: Schocken Books, 1969), 260 (Thesis XIII).

29. Ibid., 262–263 (Thesis XVII).

30. Ibid., 263 (Thesis XVIII, A).

31. Ibid., 260 (Thesis XII).

32. Arendt, "Preface to the First Edition, " *Origins of Totalitarianism*, viii.

33. Ibid., "Preface to Part One, Anti-Semitism, " *Origins of Totalitarianism*, xv.

34. Arendt, *Essays in Understanding*, 403.

35. Benjamin, "Theses on a Philosophy of History," *Illuminations*, 255 (Thesis VI).

36. Walter Benjamin, *Origin of German Tragic Drama*, trans. John Osborne, (London: Verso Press, 1985), 45.

37. Arendt, "Preface to the First Edition, " *Origins of Totalitarianism*, ix.

38. Benjamin, "Theses on a Philosophy of History, " *Illuminations*, 254 (Thesis III).

39. Benjamin, "The Storyteller," *Illuminations*, 89–90.

Is Lying a Political Virtue?

Uday Singh Mehta

01110100 01101000 01100101 00100000 01110000 01100101 01110010 01101001 01101100 01110011 01110011 00100000 01101111 01100110 00100000 01101001 01101110 01110110 01100101 01101110 01110100 01101001 01101111 01101110

In her review of the Pentagon Papers in 1971, Hannah Arendt claimed that "Truthfulness has never been counted among political virtues, and lies have always been regarded as justifiable tools in political dealings."[1] Writing in the context of the Cold War and the war in Vietnam, and with an awareness of the history of totalitarianism, Arendt felt a deep ambivalence in affirming this troubling postulate of political thought and long-standing political practice—but affirm it she did. Her words capture an important idea with a long pedigree, namely, that the justification of political ends trumps truthfulness, so that lying, when it is politically warranted, becomes justified. The link between "truth and politics," as discussed by Arendt with characteristic insight and erudition in her earlier essay with that title, was as old as philosophy and politics themselves. In its original stipulation in Plato, truth's relationship to politics was doubly compromised: first, in the philosophic claim that even in the ideal polity, truth would have to be mingled with noble lies to meet the imperatives of politics; and second, in the fact that the embodiment of truth, Socrates, could only have survived the whims of the Athenian electors by reneging on the truth. What the Athenian citizens represented was not the inescapable pressure and presence of lies in sustaining the polis, but rather a disposition for being governed by mere opinions, ignorance, and a susceptibility to images. As Arendt put it, they had a "perverse love for deception and falsehood."[2]

In ancient political thought and with redoubled emphasis in modern thought, the very sort of human existence that political life offered was one in which the role of truth would be, at best, secondary to that form of existence. But unlike Plato's *Republic*, in which the love of falsehood does not stem from any fear of enemies or threat to the community, in the modern tradition it is precisely this fear and threat, along with the way they disseminate themselves into the governing norms of the domestic community and the perception of those outside of it, that have served as the main ground for the latitude that political society has given to lies and, as it turns out, also to violence.

In this paper I want to do two things: first, to consider the question of what it is about political ends and the form of existence that politics offers, or at least promises, that allow it to justifiably overwhelm the insistence and even the expectation of truthfulness, so that the moral and epistemic qualities of truth become secondary to that form of existence; and second, to reflect on what politics would have to be if it *were* the sort of activity that was constrained by the truth, rather than being in a position always to overwhelm it.

The first question elaborates on Arendt's idea that truth is not, and in her view has never been, a political virtue, the second on the conditions under which it could or might be such a virtue. I should make clear that in this context my conception of a virtue is simply something one endorses unconditionally without regard to the harm or benefits that may stem from it. It is what Kant calls a duty. Precisely because Arendt takes the position that she does regarding the first question, she does not engage the second. This is not to say that she affirms falsehood as a positive value—she certainly does not; nor does she believe that truthfulness is of limited importance as a value in itself. For on this too she was explicit; she could countenance a world in which justice and freedom were sacrificed, but not one in which truth was.[3] Despite that, truth could not, for Arendt, be a political virtue. There was something ultimately otherworldly about it because it inhibited the human desire to act in concert, to appear in public, to do great deeds and to change the world in light of our ideals—in brief, truth went contrary to our desires to be political actors bent on changing the world and "beginning something entirely new."[4]

The agon and flux of political life, which Arendt celebrated, existed, by her own admission, under a sky of unchanging verities. But in terms of everyday life, the rays of those verities were necessarily refracted as they entered the political domain. In this sense Arendt supported Plato in his account of the highest and transcendent ground of reality, which he associated with truth, while she sided with Aristotle on the priority of the middle ground of collective human existence. This latter space, she believed, was irredeemably political, and it is here that truth could not be a virtue because it would always be trumped by a political justification.

Both of the questions I wish to consider in this paper turn on justification. That is to say, what is it about the context of politics that justifies lies, so that truth cannot be a political virtue? And second, what would justify truth being of such an order that it could trump, rather than be subservient to, political rationality? In addressing the first of these questions I offer a rather abstract account of the basis of political society and political rationality in the modern tradition of political thinking to explain the relationship of politics and lying. The account I give is abstract because it must meet a correspondingly abstract challenge that truth cannot be a political virtue. The claim, after all, is not that it cannot be a virtue in patently deceitful regimes, but rather that truth loses its justification as an absolute value in political societies as such. The challenging and worrying aspect of Arendt's claim is precisely that it applies to the entire domain of politics and hence to the very mode of human life when lived in multitudes.

With regard to the second question, I focus on Gandhi. Gandhi plainly did not accept a subsidiary status for truth. The term *satyagraha,* which is the caption to his various forms of activism and to the form of existence he avowed, is best translated as steadfastly holding onto the truth. It was a steadfastness that he advocated in the contexts of numerous mass public actions, within the more sequestered domain of the ashram, and to individuals who sought his counsel on matters of personal and domestic reach. Whether the forms of activism that Gandhi endorsed should be thought of as political is an issue to which I will return in the conclusion. What I wish to consider are the implications of having a steadfast conception of the truth for the familiar view we have of political society and political action.

To anticipate the argument I will make, in the modern tradition of political thinking, the justificatory ground for lying and violence (and of course much else) is the professed security of the political community. This is in principal part because they are taken to be the best guarantor of the highest value, namely, human life. I say *professed* because neither lying nor violence may in fact, as a general matter, serve the end of securing the political community or human life. However, to the extent that a claim can be made to that effect, they meet the challenge of justification because they can be identified as serving the highest value of life. In this broad political orientation there is no foundational value attached to truth (which is not to say that there is *no* value placed on it). In contrast, Gandhi places a value on truth that is entirely independent of any form of existence. He associates truth with the metaphysical form of being, with God and with sacrifice, but not with the securing or enhancing of life in a quotidian or material sense of the term. For Gandhi, truth was an absolute, and hence no form of existence, whether individual or collective, could be an alibi for denying it.

I.

From the 17th century onward in Western political thought, one can identify at least three points of emphasis that persist into the contemporary era and that have retained their salience during the intervening three-and-a-half centuries. They constitute the main theoretical basis of political society as well as a principal feature of the rationality that courses through its functioning, that is to say, the mode of justification that modern politics advocates and on which it relies. The first point of emphasis is the idea that political society offers the only reasonable redress to the insecurity, fear, and prospect of violence that individuals, in its absence, have good reasons to expect. Second is that political society, once it is formed, must itself expect to be the object of competition and potentially of violence from other societies, forces, and domestic groups, and must therefore have the resources to contend with this insecure and permanent predicament. And third is that political societies must be unified in order to best deal with this predicament and with the other exigencies of politics, and thus there is something in the nature of a political imperative to cultivate that unity.

These three broad ideas do not, of course, constitute an exhaustive template of modern Western political thought. The emphases on freedom and equality, for example, which are also enduring and significant aspects of this political tradition, are not featured in any of the three points I refer to. But my purpose is not to be exhaustive, only to highlight those aspects that are relevant to the issue of truth as a political virtue and to those modes of thought that have played a foundational role in articulating the basis and functioning of political society.

The first idea that I pointed out recalls the state of nature, which Hobbes identified as a condition of extreme corporeal vulnerability and which neither moral regulation, social conventions, or individual volition could ameliorate. The decisive feature of this condition was not natural death along with the anxiety that it might engender, but rather unnatural death that was violent and painful—the product of fierce competition, scarcity, and distorted passions, and thus wholly tied to an existential and nonmetaphysical or transcendent context. The subjective analog of the prospect of such a death was a condition of universal and acute fear. One of Hobbes's many achievements was to normalize the expectation of such a death in an unregulated condition and to have correspondingly normalized the fear that was a permanent accompaniment to it. One might say that in Hobbes, death ceased to be natural; instead, like its political redress, it became something artificial. It was one of his achievements to have given corporeal life and its preservation a primacy and to have associated the redress of that unacceptable condition wholly with the benefits of political society. In Locke, notwithstanding the existence of a moral community of humankind anchored in natural law, natural rights like private property, and social institutions such as the family, the natural state was nevertheless still liable to unsettling forms of uncertainty and "inconvenience" that would lead to insecurity and, ultimately, akin to Hobbes, to a context in which fear and violence were endemic.

The second idea that has persisted is the pervasive view that even though political society is formed as a redressing response to the violence and the insecurity of the natural state, it cannot itself, at a foundational level, forgo the use of violence, because it is never freed from the predicament of insecurity for both external and domestic reasons. Moreover, it cannot forgo the use of violence because violence is an essential feature of the power through which political society secures domestic peace, administers justice, and furthers the public interest. Violence, like the fear of death that political society can only ameliorate, is hence constitutionally bound to politics as both its cause and its enduring instrument.

The third idea expresses the thought that whatever the social, ethnic, cultural, geographical, or other forms of diversity and unity that might characterize a collection of individuals, they must in addition be forged into a "people" with a distinctive political self-conception or collective identity. A central feature of that political identity—even if it involves as shared and founding an allegiance to certain "inalienable rights" and abstract normative principles as the American act of "separation" did—is an awareness that the people constitute "one body" with a shared vulnerability. Even in the American Declaration of Independence, in which the appeal to normative principles was so conspicuous, the forging of a distinct political identity explicitly stipulated the need "to provide new guards for their future security" and to "have full power to levy war, conclude peace, contract alliances, establish commerce, and to do all other acts and things which independent states may of right do." The Declaration did not just indicate a desire to defect from George III's empire; it was a document that professed the formation of something separate, singular, and unified—a people bound together in part by a shared insecurity along with the means to contend with that predicament. Hobbes signaled the significance of this metamorphosis of multiple individuals into "one body" by invoking the gravity of the biblical term *covenant*, thereby associating the formation of the Commonwealth with a new communion and a radically transformed ontological condition. Locke, though his language was less dramatic, was equally explicit, stating that "it is easy to discern, who are, and who are not, in political society together."[5] In brief, the unity and the diversity of the social, whether they be the bonds of family, religious orders, professional guilds, or territorial and functional forms of association such as towns and villages, could not serve as a substitute for the unity of the political.

This third idea concerning the importance of establishing a collective identity also anticipated a history in which the formation of modern political societies was linked, both as a cause and effect, with patriotism and the notion that each member was communally linked with every other member. The nature of this link was especially poignant because the issues of security, defense, and preservation of the corporate body of the people were always at stake. In this tradition, security and self-preservation literally become obsessions; no amount of attending to them ever fully assuages the anxiety that underlies and permanently fuels them. Even with thinkers like Rousseau, Kant, and Hegel, who endorsed a federative ideal, there was no relaxing on the importance of patriotism, notwithstanding the civic accent they placed on it.

Related to this third idea is the emphasis that political societies placed on territorial and other kinds of boundaries, which were to be rigid and not porous. Hegel was summarizing the broad orientation of modern political thought and practice when he wrote: "Individuality is awareness of one's existence as a unit in sharp distinction from others. It manifests itself here in the state as a relation to other states, each of which is autonomous *vis-a-vis* the others."[6] And finally, the third idea points to the thought that in political society there must be a central source of power, even if that power is limited or checked by contesting divisions and established norms for the transfer of power.

All three of these ideas are now commonplace. They give us, for one, an account in which the principal ground of politics is a sense of an acute physical vulnerability at both an individual and collective level. They tell us, furthermore, that the main motive for the formation of political society is fear and an overriding concern with self-preservation, again both individual and collective, and that politics can never fully assuage that fear but only manage and direct it. The fact that politics is also associated with other imperatives such as justice and enhanced material well-being—and, as in the democratic tradition, with the establishment of institutions that give expression to the ideas that individuals are free and equal, and that the power of the state should be limited and accountable—does not undermine the claim that an important tradition of modern political thought has been guided by Hobbes's rendering of the Latin expression *salus populi suprema lex esto,* in which *salus* no longer refers to salvation but rather to the safety of individuals and, more important, to the security of the political society as a whole.[7]

There are, of course, other traditions of modern political thinking in which the formation of political society is not rooted in the bellicosity of a natural condition; and there are traditions in which an imagined contractual agreement among individuals does not serve as the basis of exiting the state of nature through a contractual agreement upon the principles by which they are to be regulated thereafter. In Hegel, for example, there is neither a bellicose natural condition nor an appeal to the social contract as a regulating and constraining ideal for political society. Rather, it is the self-consciousness of freedom as the underlying destiny of human existence, not the enduring motive of fear, that spurs reason's long tutelage in history. Similarly, J. S. Mill, in the brief remarks he makes as the relevant preconditions for the application of the Principle of Liberty, offers an account in which the struggle against despotic power has finally brought Western civilization and its public culture to the point where it can be "improved by free and equal discussion."[8]

But even in Hegel and Mill, or for that matter Rousseau and Kant, political society, once it is formed, is wedded to the primacy of individual and collective security. In fact, Mill's capacious conception of individual liberty has its limit at the point where physical security is threatened. Even the contemporary emphasis on justice and rights recalls a concern with security in the ubiquity of the language of the "protection of rights." By way of contrast, it is worth recalling that fear and corporeal security play scarcely any role in articulating the motives for both forming and sustaining political society in the political thought of Plato and Aristotle and more generally in the ancient world—this despite the fact that Greek city-states were regularly embroiled in war and conflict. Fear and security acquire their salience as markers of the political only in the modern era.

At the risk of some overstatement and historical privileging, one might say that the trauma of the English Civil War; the attendant struggles between crown, court, and country; and the decades in the 16th and 17th centuries of internecine religious conflict in much of the expanse of Europe—all of which did so much to discredit the social as the ground of identity and as a self-subsistent order, and which, correspondingly, raised the need for a distinctively political society to the status of an imperative, anchored and spurred by fear and an obsessive concern with security—have cast a long shadow on the past three-and-a-half centuries. The resulting primacy of the political can be assessed not merely in the common claim that everything is political, but also in the fact that the determination of the nonpolitical falls exclusively within competence of the political. Hobbes may have been wrong to believe that only a singular and absolute sovereign with the awesome power to tame a generalized fear in the population could hold together a political society with the appropriate level of unity. But given the salience of fear and the high value placed on unity to political society over the last three centuries, he has been substantially vindicated, and through a range of very different political regimes at that.

In this abstract and no doubt overly simplified overview of the broad strokes of modern political thought, I have emphasized three things as characterizing both the cause and effect of political society and its rationale: fear, the concern with security, and the foundational value placed on unity. I have emphasized these because they constitute the basis for why truth has not been and cannot in this tradition be a political virtue. As John Mearsheimer has emphasized in his recent book *Why Leaders Lie* and as Sissela Bok did in *Lying: Moral Choice in Political and Private Life*, the most pervasive motive for lying in politics is a professed concern with the security and unity of the polity. Mearsheimer makes the related point that lies, even though they claim as a primary justification the presence of an eminent external threat, are really directed at a domestic citizenry, in whom the fear of political insecurity has been cultivated and with whom it has taken root (whereas lying generally tends not to take place between the leaders of various countries). Not surprisingly, such lies become the warrant for additional lies, as they did conspicuously in the war in Vietnam and as emerging evidence suggests they did in the recent wars in Iraq and Afghanistan. Here, in fact, was the working of a domino effect at the expense of truth in the public realm. Where security and the unity of political society are foundational values, lies, like violence, always have a conditional justification. Within this orientation is always some future eventuality with respect to which a lie can be politically justified. In asserting that truth had never been, and could not be, a political virtue, Arendt had in mind the sort of justification that is permissive of lies, which I have outlined, a justification that is alloyed at a foundational level with the rationale of politics.

II.

I now turn to the second question mentioned at the beginning of this paper. I want to reflect on what the implications might be if none of the three ideas with which I have associated modern politics were held to be valid or normatively creditable. I do this by considering Gandhi's thought and writings and, to a lesser extent, his actions.[9] There are ample reasons to believe that Gandhi did not subscribe to any of the three ideas. Regarding the first idea, he did not think that corporeal vulnerability was in need of redress. Human vulnerability was an ineradicable fact of life, subject to contingency and moral response. He embraced this fact and its contingency and made it the very ground of crafting a morally meaningful response to it. The central feature of this moral response was an unconditional endorsement of truth.

Gandhi emphasized that the etymology of the word *satya* (truth) came from *sat*, which referred to absolute being, hence to God. Truth called for a kind of devotion. He certainly did not believe that the only redress to the fact of human vulnerability and the fear of death was the formation of political society, with its conditional efforts toward peace and simultaneous retention of the means to deploy violence. Instead, he accepted the fear that came with vulnerability by transmuting it into the demand for courage—courage that entailed a permanent willingness to surrender or sacrifice one's life. In doing so he blunted the principal motive for the formation of and the submission to political society, namely, fear and the prospect of security. For Gandhi, the devotion to truth had its analog in the high value he placed on courage, both individual and collective. Courage was a quality for which no social or political artifact could serve as a substitute. As he said, "The path of truth is for the brave alone, never for a coward."[10]

Courage, while it blunts the motive for political society, also extends the ambit of moral action to everyday life. One must, according to Gandhi, always be prepared to sacrifice one's life for the sake of moral action. This is why the scene of battle—be it the fratricidal war at the heart of the *Mahabharata*, the Boer War, the First World War, or the Jewish predicament in the Second World War—constituted for Gandhi the ideal site for moral action. He was drawn to the battlefield because it exemplified something commonplace for him. It was the model of everyday life, not an exceptional predicament against which to construct a political refuge. It could serve as such a model because the facts of violence and insecurity were themselves facts of everyday life, not things that could be quarantined or pacified by political society or anything else. The very ubiquity of violence in the natural state, which for Hobbes served as the ground for a sequestration of the social from the political and a presumption in favor of the logic of the latter, serves for Gandhi as the basis for articulating the universality of ethics, the center of which is truth. Consider Gandhi's interpretation of Arjuna's dilemmas on the battlefield of Kurukshestra, when Arjuna's will to fight his kinsmen is deserting him:

> *Let us suppose that Arjuna flees the battlefield. Though his enemies are wicked people, are sinners, they are his relations and he cannot bring himself to kill them. If he leaves the field, what would happen to those vast numbers on his side? If Arjuna went away, leaving them behind, would the Kauravas have mercy on them? If he left the battle, the Pandava army would be simply annihilated. What, then, would be the plight of their wives and children? [. . .] If Arjuna had left the battlefield, the very calamities which he feared would have befallen them. Their families would have been ruined, and the traditional dharma of these families and the race would have been destroyed. Arjuna, therefore, had no choice but to fight.*[11]

Two points are significant here. First, Gandhi does not see Arjuna's actions or inactions as diminishing the fact of war and violence. In either response, war and violence persist. Neither nonviolence as a response nor Arjuna's necessarily violent actions in the battlefield intervene to quell or sequester the fact of violence. Second, in Gandhi's rendering, Arjuna has no choice but to fight because violence itself is written into the situation. The resolution of Arjuna's dilemmas does not lie in the exercise of choice in the ordinary sense, where ethics stems from an amplitude of alternative possibilities governed by some metric of external consequences, but rather in the moral meaning of his actions under conditions where such amplitude is precisely absent and where the relevant consequences are not external but instead turn on a steadfast vigilance to the truth of his own being. The crucial lynchpin that connects truth and morality is the personal comportment that backs the act. It cannot rely on any alibis external to these considerations. By invoking the effect that Arjuna's flight would have on the wives and children of the Pandavas, Gandhi associates morality not with a heroic condition but with the most commonplace facts of social life. It is striking that Gandhi should offer the mundane, almost banal social fact of Arjuna's being a brother-in-law and an uncle as being motivationally crucial to his decision in joining such a momentous battle, which had the imprimatur of the conflict between the forces of righteousness and those of evil. The truth of the self, which Gandhi sees in Krishna's guidance to Arjuna, is tied to these quotidian and arbitrary features of the self. They are meant to emphasize that the conditions of moral behavior reside in the mundane minutia of everyday existence.

Gandhi accepted the battlefield and the fact of violence as a quotidian thing that requires an exacting—and again quotidian—courage, while the tradition of Western politics identifies violence as an exceptional condition, but one to which it gives a permanent, albeit qualified, warrant. For Gandhi, the battlefield functions as the crystallization of a site that calls for fearlessness and courage, which for him were the essence of truthfulness and virtue. The demand for security is thus the demand of a deserter seeking to flee the battle, not prepared to sacrifice him or herself. It is important to recall that Gandhi reserved his highest admiration for sacrificial figures like King Harish Chandra, who was prepared to sacrifice his only, long-sought-after son to fulfill a promise made to the god who had facilitated the son's birth. Even Rama, the much-invoked king of Ayodhya, is celebrated as a quotidian figure, as a son, brother, father, and husband who was prepared to be banished and see his wife suffer and die in the name of duty. Gandhi seldom mentions the nature of Rama's rule as a king or the privileged location of Ayodhya, the capital of his realm and alleged place of his birth. But Ghandi always singles out the quality of Rama's sacrifice. As he made clear in his autobiography, Gandhi himself would have gladly assumed that role and would have allowed his own wife to die by denying the beef broth on which, according to the attending physician, her survival depended. Gandhi's life is replete with examples of his own willingness to die. Indeed, it has often been pointed out that by spurning the police security detail that was urged upon him in the fractious months of 1948, he all but invited the death that ultimately felled him.

In Gandhi's thought, the willingness to be sacrificed was paired with the requirement of absolute truthfulness, which Gandhi made of all *satyagrahis*. He stipulated that they had to be prepared to die without resorting to violence or killing. As Gandhi said in a speech on March 7, 1919:

> *Satyagraha was a harmless, but unfailing remedy. It presupposes a superior sort of courage in those who adopted it—not the courage of the fighter. The soldier was undoubtedly ever ready to die, but he also wanted to kill the enemy. A satyagrahi was ever ready to endure*

*suffering and ever lays down his life to demonstrate to the world the
integrity of his purpose and the justice of his demands. His weapon
was faith in God and he lived and worked in faith. In his faith, there
was no room for killing or violence and none for untruth.*[12]

But even in this supreme demand, Gandhi vouched for the ordinary.
After all, the *satyagrahis* were ordinary folk, yet Gandhi thought them capable of the ultimate sacrifice, fearlessness, and courage that truth entailed,
and that too without assuring them of even a hint of security. Hobbes in particular would have understood the full force and the contrary implications of
Gandhi's emphasis on courage. For Hobbes, courage was a passion that, because it inclined men to be indifferent to bodily wounds and violent death,
also inclined them to "unsettling the public peace."[13] The virtue of courage,
such as it was, was too deeply tied to the devoted integrity of the self for it to
be given anything other than a disdainful authorization by a thinker for
whom public order unity meant everything.

Nowhere was Gandhi's call to sacrifice more audacious and controversial than in what he said he would do were he a Jew in Germany faced with
the genocidal might of Hitler and the Nazis. Writing in November 1938 in
the journal *Harijan*, in response to letters that had sought his views on what
was happening in Germany and Palestine, Gandhi responded in words that
deserve to be quoted at length:

*The nobler cause would be to insist on a just treatment of the Jews
wherever they are born and bred. The Jews born in France are
French in precisely the same sense that Christians born in France
are French. If the Jews have no home but Palestine, will they relish
the idea of being forced to leave the other parts of the world in
which they are settled? Or do they want a double home where they
remain at will? This cry for the national home affords a colourable
justification for the German expulsion of Jews.*

*But the German persecution of Jews seems to have no parallel in
history. The tyrants of old never went so mad as Hitler seems to
have gone. And he is doing it with religious zeal. For, he is pro-
pounding a new religion of exclusive and militant nationalism in
the name of which any inhumanity becomes an act of humanity to
be rewarded here and hereafter. The crime of an obviously mad but
intrepid youth is being visited upon this whole race with unbelievable ferocity. If there ever could be a justifiable war in the name of
humanity, a war against Germany, to prevent the wanton persecution of a whole race, would be completely justified. But I do not
believe in any war. A discussion of the pros and cons of such a war
is, therefore, outside my horizon or province . . .*

Germany is showing to the world how efficiently violence can be worked when it is not hampered by any hypocrisy or weakness masquerading as humanitarianism. It is also showing how hideous, terrible and terrifying it looks in its nakedness. Can the Jews resist this organized and shameless persecution? Is there a way to preserve their self-respect and not to feel helpless, neglected and forlorn? I submit there is. If I were a Jew and were born in Germany and earned my livelihood there, I would claim Germany as my home even as the tallest gentile German might, and challenge him to shoot me or cast me in the dungeon; I would refuse to be expelled or to submit to discriminating treatment. And for doing this I should not wait for the fellow Jews to join me in civil resistance, but would have confidence that in the end the rest were bound to follow my example. If one Jew or all the Jews were to accept the prescription here offered, he or they cannot be worse off than now. And suffering voluntarily undergone will bring them an inner strength and joy which no number of resolutions of sympathy passed in the world outside Germany can. Indeed, even if Britain, France and America were to declare hostilities against Germany, they can bring no inner joy, no inner strength. The calculated violence of Hitler may even result in a general massacre of the Jews by way of his first answer to the declaration of such hostilities. But if the Jewish mind could be prepared for voluntary suffering, even the massacre I have imagined could be turned into a day of thanksgiving and joy that Jehovah had wrought deliverance of the race even at the hands of the tyrant.[14]

Not surprisingly, Gandhi's words provoked an uproar of controversy and, mainly, of condemnation. But they deserve to be considered carefully. There are two broad issues that Gandhi refers to in his statement: first, that of a Jewish national homeland in Palestine, and second, the German Jews' response to the barbarity of Hitler. For Gandhi the two issues are linked, but I will initially consider them separately.

Regarding the second issue, i.e., the Jewish response to the Nazi racial laws, Gandhi's suggestion was that if he were a Jew born, bred, and earning his livelihood in Germany—that is to say, if he were a German in the most mundane social sense of the term—he would defy the discriminatory racial laws at the risk of being imprisoned and killed. Gandhi's suggestion is implicit in the very question he asks. It is not how can German Jews survive in a corporeal sense, but rather how can they "preserve their self-respect and not to feel helpless, neglected and forlorn?" Gandhi would refuse to be expelled, that is, he would refuse to be forcibly made into a deserter from the scene of the battle for self-respect. He would stand up to the tallest German gentile by refusing to concede that race, religion, or law should define a homeland. He would act alone, but with the full confidence that his example would be followed by other Jews without his even advocating such concurrence; that is, he would refrain from transforming the singular moral act into a collective and strategic political act. He would even spurn the support of Britain, France, and America, knowing that such support would, at best, be for his security and not for the inner joy and strength that motivates and gives meaning to his action. Gandhi would act with a full measure of self-confidence knowing, as a religious man, that his god would not forsake him. And finally, as with his counsel to Arjuna, who had no choice but to fight, he would do all of this without believing that his actions would leave the Jews any better or worse off with respect to the violence that would be visited upon them.

Three years earlier, in 1935, while writing about the Italian invasion of Abyssinia, Gandhi had made a similar point. He associated the strength of the Abyssinians with their deciding against armed resistance to the invasion and in making "no appeal to the League [of Nations] or any other power for armed intervention." He went so far as to say that precisely by not offering armed resistance would the Abyssinians deny the Italians what they sought, which was not their land but their submission.In each of these instances, Gandhi's insistence upon self-sacrifice is free from the incalculable effects of its external implication. Self-sacrifice is literally an autonomous act (that is to say, self-legislated and indifferent to the world of appearances), though Gandhi would have resisted some of the Kantian connotations that tied it to a rationalistic absolutism. Like Arjuna, whose call to moral action was rooted in an everyday concern for the wives and children of his kinsmen, Gandhi, as a German Jew or an Abyssinian, would find his motivation for the ultimate bodily sacrifice in an inescapable and prosaic everyday reality.

There was, as George Orwell rightly noticed in his review of Gandhi's *Autobiography,* something profoundly democratic in his exacting moral standards. One can easily imagine Gandhi being deeply impressed by stories of knights in shining armor performing acts of great valor and thinking that they were written for people like himself who hardly wore any clothes and came from the most middling of backgrounds. As an aside, I think Orwell placed the accent in the wrong place in characterizing Gandhi's counsel to Jews living in Germany as a call to commit collective suicide. For Gandhi the difference between collective suicide and conscious individual self-sacrifice was nothing less than the former being a political and strategic act, while the latter was a moral act.

The other matter Gandhi refers to in his statement about the Jewish situation in prewar Germany is the issue of a homeland for the Jews in Palestine, but this captures his broader views on the sort of unity that a political homeland must evince. Gandhi was aware that in seeking a homeland in Palestine, the Jews were seeking a national state anchored in the exclusive particularity of their religion. For Gandhi, those claims were similar to the Muslim League in its advocacy for Pakistan. He was confirmed in this equivalence by the frequency with which Mohammad Ali Jinnah (leader of the Muslim League and later the first governor-general of Pakistan) and the Pakistani state invoked, without any sense of irony, Theodor Herzl's pamphlet *The Jewish State*. But more relevantly, for Gandhi the Jewish demand for their own state made the Jews analogous to Hitler and the Germans, whose ideology he identified as a form of exclusive religious nationalism. The demand for a Jewish state thus vindicated the exclusionary laws that mandated the expulsion of Jews from Germany or wherever they lived. The claim of exclusivity, when backed by a religious and national form, could not be squared with the idea of Jews being at home in many different places or wherever they happened to live. If the nation-state, with its assurance of security for its exclusive members, was the appropriate mode of existence for particular religious groups, then the demand for a Jewish state vindicated even the Nazi "inhumanity" that professed to be "an act of humanity." If the appropriate destiny of human beings was to be organized into political nation-states, then the inhumanity visited on them to achieve this would, at a minimum, have considerable normative and political credence.

That was precisely the form of life that Gandhi wished to challenge. It was the specifically political sort of unity, the making of one people as a body politic, that Gandhi viewed with deep suspicion because he saw in it a concern with corporeality that could never resolve itself into a fearlessness that truth required; it was from the very outset concerned with the preservation of life and security and not with the conditions of moral actions. To the extent that such unity valued sacrifice, it was garnered only through a contractual relationship with a group of people specifically chosen for that purpose, such as those in the army and the police.

It is worth noting that in Gandhi's statement regarding the formation of a Jewish state in Palestine he made no reference to the Palestinians who would be and were being displaced, though he knew this and in other contexts even wrote about it. It was not from a lack of sympathy for their plight that he did not mention them, but rather because that plight was extraneous to the main point he was making. To bring up the matter of the injustice of Palestinian displacement was itself to raise a political consideration, which the British were happy to consider in the context of the mandate in terms of some compromise or negotiated settlement. This was their preferred way of dealing with such matters, as the partition of Ireland had already proved, and as the later partitioning of India and the island of Cyprus were to confirm.

Gandhi's point here, as elsewhere, was different. It was to draw attention to a kind of specifically political unity, which by its emphasis on the collective security of an exclusive group and the rigidity of borders and territorial markers that singled out that group, disregards the everyday conditions of truthful moral action. For Gandhi those conditions belonged to the unity and the diversity of the social, to the given conditions that people found themselves in, and to the places where they were born and where they lived and worshiped: Jews living in France or in Germany, Muslims who had Hindu neighbors with different dietary taboos, or Indians living in South Africa but who, as Gandhi said, "lived as though they were living in India" and hence in their everyday lives were indifferent to the vast distance that separated them from their native land. He associated the social rather than the political with the conditions that made truth and therefore moral action possible. Nationalism, by vouching for a different kind of community, displaced the moral imperative nestled in the contingent particularities of everyday life with an imperative in which one was to kill and die for the political community.

III.

By way of conclusion, let me return briefly to Arendt and the question of truth and its relationship to politics, while keeping Gandhi in mind. At the end of her essay "Truth and Politics" Arendt considers what she calls the "standpoint outside of the political realm."[15] For her, that standpoint is associated with the philosopher, the scientist, the artist, the historian, the judge, the fact-finder, the witness, and the reporter. What they all shared, when described as such, was that they had no political commitment, no adherence to a political cause that involved human beings acting in concert in light of their ideals for a public purpose. Gandhi, I have been arguing, very self-consciously spurns a political orientation, but he does not, on account of that, recede from the public or from great public causes. Indeed, one might claim that he did more than any single individual in the 20th century, more than even Lenin and Mao, to bring the common man and woman into the fold of public life, on terms that were marked by a singular absence of hierarchy, prescriptive authority, and the condescension of political parties and elites. He did this while being deeply skeptical of the rationality that courses through modern politics—i.e., politics conceived in terms of the motive of fear and the redressing of corporeal insecurity through the medium of the unity of political power.

Just about everywhere that Arendt mentions Gandhi, she views him through the narrow lens of nationalism in its struggle with empire. In effect she politicizes Gandhi by association. In doing so, I think she misunderstands Gandhi by making him into an unusual version of something very familiar, namely a political actor—unusual only because he advocated nonviolent means. Arendt was of course right in conceiving of Gandhi as a profound critic of the British Empire, but she did not understand that this was because of the form of power that the empire exercised and not because he thought there was something wrong in the British being in India or elsewhere. He did not. He made that clear. The British were welcome to stay. As late as 1943 he told the viceroy, "This is as much your country as it mine, you live here too." In his book *The Atomic Bomb and the Future of Man*, Karl Jaspers has a slightly different and more capacious take on Gandhi than Arendt. Even though Jaspers also accepts the postulate that "the essence of politics is association with force employed for self-preservation," when faced with Gandhi's achievement, he demurs to the interrogative form. Speaking of Gandhi, he says, "He wanted the impossible: politics by non-violence. He had the greatest possible success: the liberation of India. Is the impossible possible, after all?"[16]

Nowhere, to the best of my knowledge, did Gandhi emphasize the importance of forging a unitary people obsessed with their individual and collective security. In all the ways that mattered to him, the conditions for meaningful moral action were ready at hand. As he said, "The opportunity [for virtuous behavior] comes to everyone almost everyday."[17] For Gandhi those conditions are diverse and mundane rather than exclusive, social and individual rather than national, attentive to the present rather than the future, and present in a space that is porous rather than well defined. They involve an individual tenacity, self-awareness, truthfulness, and courage rather than idealism on behalf of a unified collectivity. Under those conditions truth can indeed be a virtue, exemplified by large numbers of individuals, even acting in concert.

Endnotes

1. Hannah Arendt, "Lying in Politics: Reflections on the Pentagon Papers," *New York Review of Books*, November 18, 1971, 30-39.

2. Hannah Arendt, "Truth and Politics," *Between Past and Future* (New York: Penguin, 1985), 230.

3. Ibid, 229.

4. Ibid, 263.

5. John Locke, *Two Treatises of Government*, ed. Peter Laslett, 2nd ed. (London: Cambridge University Press, 1967), 367.

6. Georg Wilhelm Friedrich Hegel, *Hegel's Philosophy of Right*, trans. T. M. Knox (Oxford: The Clarendon Press, 1945), 208.

7. Thomas Hobbes, *Leviathan: With Selected Variants from the Latin Edition of 1668*, ed. E. M. Curley (Indianapolis: Hackett Publishing Co., 1994), 3.

8. J. S. Mill, *On Liberty* (New York: Penguin Classics, 1982), Introduction.

9. I deflate the role of Gandhi's actions because to understand them fully one would need to consider their surrounding historical context. That is neither appropriate to my competence nor to the specific purpose I have in mind. Gandhi deserves to be taken seriously as a thinker, because that is what he was; he engaged with ideas as ideas. But since he was also a figure of great historical importance, it can be quite dissatisfying to ignore his activist and historical role. The two perspectives often pull in different directions. I think the best to way to deal with this is to acknowledge the fact or the charge and move on.

10. Raghavan N. Iyer, *The Moral and Political Writings of Mahatma Gandhi* (New York: Oxford University Press, 1987), 222.

11. M. K. Gandhi, *The Bhagavad Gita* (New Delhi: Orient Paperbacks, 1980), 20.

12. *Collected Works of M. K. Gandhi*, Vol. 17, 324.

13. Hobbes, op.cit., 489.

14. M. K. Gandhi, *Non-Violence in Peace and War* (Ahmedabad: Navjivan Publishing House, 1942), Vol. II, 170–172.

15. Arendt, "Truth and Politics," 259.

16. Karl Jaspers, *The Atomic Bomb and the Future of Man* (Chicago: University of Chicago Press, 1963), 35.

17. Iyer, op. cit., 250.

When Telling the Truth Demands Courage

Wolfgang Heuer

01110100 01101000 01100101 00100000 01110000 01100101 01110010 01101001 01101100 01110011 00100000 01101111 01100110 00100000 01101001 01101110 01110110 01100101 01101110 01110100 01101001 01101111 01101110

Truthtelling is often very unpleasant when it contradicts the opinion of the majority. Telling the truth can easily lead to a minority position and exposes the truthteller to the pressure of the majority. To resist this pressure demands courage. Therefore, courage is not only the virtue of political action par excellence, but also quite evidently the virtue of truthtelling. To tell an inconvenient truth is not only a statement, but also an action.

To say what is—to oppose truth to lies or to corruption, dissent to conformism, a scandal to the silence of an indifferent or a hostile majority, transparency to censorship, and diversity to dictatorship—all that requires civic courage, which is interpreted as provocation or treason and does not find consent or admiration from the majority.

There are two ways to tell the truth of facts: first, by telling of the action of courageous men and women, in public or in politics; and second, through the reports of a spectator.

In what follows I will analyze these two forms of truthtelling. First, I will discuss the actor by presenting some examples of courageous truthtellers in dictatorship and democracy and asking after the source of their courage. Then I will discuss narrators by presenting two narratives about the same topic that are talking about the same reality, but in quite different ways, due to their different perspectives: Hannah Arendt's report about the Eichmann trial in Jerusalem, and Steven Spielberg's movie *Schindler's List*.

I. Telling the Truth

I would like to present some people who told the truth in different ways and who, by doing so, acted courageously: first, people under the conditions of dictatorship in Eastern Europe before 1989; second, a whistle-blower in the European Union administration in Brussels; and third, a politician fighting the Mafia in Italy.

1. To Live in the Truth

First, the people under the conditions of dictatorship. I will start with a fictitious person imagined in Vaclav Havel's exceptional manifesto, "The Power of the Powerless," written in 1978.[1] In German, the title translates as "An Attempt to Live in the Truth." This essay reflects the alienated life in "real socialism," a life lived from within the lie, as Havel calls it. At the same time, Havel offers a strategy to defy and overcome the reign of the lie. In his reflection, Havel chooses a new way beyond the usual categories of public and private life. It is about neither a political opposition, which runs the risk of operating according to the logic of its adversary, nor about the withdrawal from any political controversy into the niche of private life. It is instead about noncooperation, the refusal to conform.

Havel describes this strategy using the example of a greengrocer. Every year on May 1, the battle day of the international working class, this grocer has to put the slogan "Workers of the World, Unite!" in his window between the onions and the carrots. He does not (yet) believe in the content, but executes this action nonetheless, which, on closer examination, turns out to be nothing other than a symbolic act of submission. Despite the content of the slogan, this act is in fact the equivalent of saying, "I am afraid and therefore unquestioningly obedient" (Havel, 28). The greengrocer does something that he considers completely senseless, as he does not believe in the content of what he says. The meaning of this act consists simply in not getting into trouble with the authorities.

The same happens to those who order and control the showing of these slogans when they march in the May Day demonstrations. Only few of them, if any, care about the meaning of what they are doing, but all contribute so that this ritual occurs without a hitch. "They need not accept the lie. It is enough for them to have accepted their life with it and in it. For by this very fact, individuals confirm the system, fulfill the system, make the system, *are* the system," Havel writes (Havel, 31).

Now, this system is challenged by the "aims of life," that is, its essence to move "towards plurality, diversity, independent self-constitution and self-organization, in short the fulfillment of its own freedom" (Havel, 29). What happens when this greengrocer simply follows his own aims of life? When he does not display the slogan anymore, because he does not care to ingratiate himself with the authorities? When he does not participate anymore in elections because he knows that they do not present any real choice? Or when he says what he really thinks in assemblies and not what he does not believe? Then, Havel says, "the bill is not long in coming" (Havel, 39). But what is more important is that the greengrocer has broken the rules of the game and has finally "disrupted the game as such" (Havel, 40). He will have transformed himself from an anonymous part of the system, from a hanger of a slogan and an empty face in gray everyday life, into a personality with its own face, own voice, and own will. At work here is what Arendt calls the Socratic morality, the inner dialogue of the two-in-one, the dialogue of a man who wants to live together with himself and not with a liar. It is a "negative" morality, "only working . . . in borderline situations, that is, in times of crisis and emergency."[2]

2. To Say What Is

Havel's ideal-typical person represents the emergence of dissent and opposition as a cultural movement in Eastern Europe. I also found this search for the pure aims of life—plurality, diversity, and the fulfillment of freedom—in my research about the emergence of civic courage in oppositional people in the German Democratic Republic.[3] These civic dissenters not only refused to live a life in the lie but also told the truth, thereby provoking the disclosure and self-disclosure of the regime. Their main motives were not necessarily political in the sense of opposing the regime. Rather, they simply sought freedom of movement, freedom of speech, recognition, and justice. I will briefly present four examples of people who courageously opposed the GDR.

• A pupil, very active and rhetorically gifted, liked very much to organize the affairs of her class as a secretary of "Free German Youth" (FDJ), the communist youth organization. She dared, more than her classmates, to ask inconvenient questions in her "Citizens' Rights and Duties" class (Staatsbürgerkunde) and eventually faced the expectation of the class that she should ask all the critical questions. Growing up in an atheistic family, she joined the peace movement of the Protestant Church out of curiosity and increasingly got into trouble with the state.

• The manager of a little theater organized discussions about taboo topics in the GDR (e.g., anxiety and dying) and resisted the exigencies of censorship of his city's administration. In a similar way, he spoke about inconvenient topics as a member of the party in political assemblies. Other colleagues supported him, and he was sometimes asked to put forward their demands. During the communal election in 1989, he organized an observation of the polling places and made public the massive fraud. He always liked to be in the center of a big group of friends and people of the same opinion and to be supported by them. Recognition was of special importance to him.

• From the time of his schooling, an engineer was angry about the phrases used in the official party declarations and by

their representatives. Like Havel's greengrocer, the engineer reacted against the submission required by these declarations. In
1968 he worked as an assistant at his university and witnessed the
GDR invasion of Czechoslovakia. He disobeyed his duty to conduct surveillance of student homes to prevent any protest against
the invasion. Only later, as an engineer with a safe job, did he feel
strong enough to retaliate for all these humiliations. He studied
political topics thoroughly to unmask the stupidity of party func-
tionaries at employee assemblies. He also used legal means to
present non-party members in workers' council elections.

• A teacher of "Citizens' Rights and Duties" acted strongly
and altruistically when she refused to join the party, which was
extremely unusual for a teacher of this political topic. Instead, she
encouraged open debates among her pupils to make them "fit for
life," as she called it, and did not avoid inconvenient discussions
despite the hostility and control of her superiors. She acted according to her belief in freedom of opinion and criticism, resistance against humiliation, the search for recognition, and the
defense of the weak.

3. To Defend Professional Ethics

We find another form of acting justly and in accordance with oneself in the
second case, the action of whistle-blowers. Whistle-blowers make public the
illegal practices of or grievances against the companies for which they work.
Three whistle-blowers were nominated by *Time Magazine* for Persons of the
Year in 2002: Sharon Watkins, who discovered the falsification of the balance sheet at Enron; Cynthia Cooper, who discovered a similar deception at
WorldCom; and Coleen Rowley, who complained about the mismanagement
at the FBI before 9/11.

The motives for whistle-blowing are often similar to those of an employee of the EU administration in Brussels, the Dutch Paul van Buitenen.
Soon after he started his work as an accountant in 1995, he discovered immense corruption in the vocational training program Leonardo under the
commissioner Edith Cresson. His discovery began with a laptop lent to a
private company that was not returned to the department following the end
of an EU-financed research program. It continued with an increasing number
of documents proving deceptions concerning several billion euros, among
them the beneficial treatment of Mme. Cresson's dentist. The scandal was
aggravated by the fact that his superiors did not take seriously the complaints
of van Buitenen, who received more and more revealing documents from
colleagues in other departments. The corruption ended, finally, with the
resignation of the EU Commission after a long power struggle and a public

debate in the European parliament.Throughout the sequence of events, van Buitenen suffered repression, insecurity, and anxiety, public defamation by his superiors, a 50-percent reduction of his salary, the fear of the security company of the EU cooperating with neo-Nazi groups, the siege of his house by the media, etc. He sought advice from his friends and became a member of a Christian church in an effort to find consolation and the strength to steel himself against the power of the bureaucracy.[4]

Van Buitenen was an employee who took his work—the control of spending—seriously and did not tolerate corruption, as little as it may be. He was an inconvenient accountant, but not a cold bureaucrat, and least of all an unquestioning subordinate.

4. To Love the Public or Oneself

Finally, the third example: Leoluca Orlando, the former mayor of Palermo, who successfully managed in the 1990s to end the influence of the Mafia in his city. Its influence consisted of the control of politicians, public spending, contracts with companies handling garbage collection, water supply, and school buildings. The consequences were the disregard of public space, the ruin of the historical center, the closing of cultural institutions, public silencing, and a high number of killings. At the end of the Orlando administration's eight years, the public works were again in the hands of companies free of Mafia control, a part of the old city center was restored, the Massimo Theater reopened, and shootings had ceased. As in the former socialist countries, the inhabitants readopted the public space.

The reason for this astonishing change was not only the reestablishment of the public order, but above all the mobilization of the population. Orlando won the power struggle not only because he intensified the police response and criminal prosecution, but also because he fought against public support and toleration of the Mafia. He hardly would have reached such a quick success by focusing on criminal prosecution alone. He had to act among the city's inhabitants themselves, an act that was much riskier and required much more courage. He appealed to the pride of the Palermians for their city, created a system of godparenting to restore Palermo, and received, due to his fearless actions for the democratization of the city, so much acceptance and support that, for the Mafia, the fight against him became increasingly unwinnable. For Orlando, the fight was about the liberation of the cultural identity of the Sicilians from the hegemony of the Mafia.[5]

Leoluca Orlando is similar to the politicians praised by John F. Kennedy in the 1950s in his book *Profiles in Courage* as examples of political commonsense and independent judgment. Kennedy contrasts the persons whom he profiles to contemporary politicians, who, in his opinion, were responsible through their boundless populism for the decline of public politics. He describes eight senators in American history who distinguished themselves by their courageous behavior toward their own parties, factions, and electorate. Regardless of whether the senators' opinions were right or wrong, they had renewed their country's political life by fighting for their convictions and not acting out of opportunism.

Kennedy addresses his book to other politicians and to citizens, and asks them to assume their unavoidable responsibility. In a democracy, he writes, "every citizen, regardless of his interest in politics, holds office; every one of us is in a position of responsibility; and, in the final analysis, the kind of government we get depends upon how we fulfill those responsibilities."[6]

Where do these role models praised by Kennedy—and for that matter, where can we—get the power to act in this way? Kennedy answers:

> *It was not because they 'loved the public better than themselves' (John Adams, WH). On the contrary it was precisely because they did love themselves—because each one's need to maintain his own respect for himself was more important to him than his popularity with others—because his desire to win or maintain a reputation for integrity and courage was stronger than his desire to maintain his office—because his conscience, his personal standard of ethics, his integrity or morality, was stronger than the pressures of public disapproval.[7]*

The historian Allen Nivens, advising Kennedy, adds that a man without character occasionally may give fitful exhibitions of courage, but "moral courage is allied with the other traits which make up character: honesty, deep seriousness, a firm sense of principle, candor, resolution."[8]

So, the answer to the question of where to find the power to act courageously and truthfully: from love of oneself and one's conscience, which must be guided by a strong character and firm moral norms.

We have seen three different forms of truthtelling. Comparing them, we can see that keeping one's dignity rather than living a life in the lie under dictatorship, with its limitations and humiliations, resembles the whistleblowers' life in the truth. The latter do not want to be confidants of lying, corruption, fraud, and violation of law because it would contradict their dignity and, in the case of van Buitenen, their work ethic. Questions of conscience, moral criteria, or character are not mentioned, but rather the defense of oneself and one's relationship to others are invoked. The life in the truth is potentially a life shared with others. It is what Arendt calls the common world or the truth, with its diversity of perspectives resulting from the principle of human plurality.

The priority Kennedy gives to the love of oneself excludes this intersubjective perspective. His pleading for the duty of public responsibility and individual self-perfection is marked by a Christian, nonpolitical idea of man. In contrast, Arendt's intersubjectivity offers a standpoint that is neither the place of the liberal individual, nor the place from which John Adams says to love the public better than oneself. It is the place of a common judgment and common action, where we act as individuals and citizens, as spectators and actors. How much this place differs from our common concept of the lonely subject is demonstrated by Arendt's entry in her diary about reason and imagination:

> *Because it is not the self-bound reason but only the imagination which makes it possible to 'to think in the place of each other,' it is not the reason but the imagination forming the bond between men. Against the sense of oneself, the reason, living by the I think, stands the sense of the world, living from the others as common sense (passive) and as imagination (active).*[9]

Furthermore, action in Arendt's definition differs from that of Kennedy and Adams: for Arendt, action is not only about self-accordance and the plea for a higher esteem of the public, but also about the need to share the world with others through action. Arendt called this the sheer delight to act, which she discovered in men in local associations, councils, and similar spontaneous forms of organization. They correspond to what de Tocqueville saw with regard to the French Revolution:

> *That a genuine love of freedom is ever quickened by the prospect of material rewards . . . What has made so many men, since untold ages, stake their all on liberty is its intrinsic glamour, a fascination it has in itself, apart from all 'practical' considerations. For only in countries where it reigns can a man speak, live, and breathe freely, owing obedience to no authority save God and the laws of the land. The man who asks of freedom anything other than itself is born to be a slave.*[10]

When truthtelling is dominated by moral and religious criteria or interests, the truth is exploited and finally destroyed. Therefore, distrust toward courageously acting persons arises again and again: Aren't they dogmatic persons or serving unknown, secret interests? Is van Buitenen not a strangely fanatic person? And why did the Mafia not kill Orlando?

II. Telling the True Story

This leads us to the second part, the question of how to narrate the truth. In her essay "Truth and Politics," Arendt writes, "Who says what is . . . always tells a story, and in this story the particular facts lose their contingency and acquire some humanly comprehensible meaning."[11] In this sense, everyday life stories, reportage, historiography, and literature are very similar. There is no understanding without thinking about and judging truth and finding the right words for it.

Arendt's report *Eichmann in Jerusalem* possesses two characteristics: First, it is the product of a courageous thinking—what Arendt called "thinking without banisters"—that analyzes the specifically new phenomenon of bureaucratically organized totalitarian mass murder. Second, Arendt chose a corresponding form of narration that Leora Bilsky rightly called a "counter-narrative" in her essay "Between Justice and Politics: The Competition of Storytellers in the Eichmann Trial."[12] After the publication of Arendt's report, a storm of protest arose against its content and tone that reverberates even today. Arendt was aware of writing inconvenient truths, and the ensuing campaign against her demonstrated that she had hit upon the truth exactly.

1. Eichmann in Jerusalem—Arendt's "Heartlessness"

For Arendt, the trial of Adolf Eichmann "offers the most striking insight into the totality of the moral collapse the Nazis caused in respectable European society—not only in Germany but in almost all countries, not only among the persecutors but also among the victims."[13] As Leora Bilsky explains, everyone involved in the trial situated Eichmann's deeds within different narrative contexts. While the chief prosecutor, Gideon Hausner, wanted only to tell the classical Jewish history by concentrating on the stories of the victims in order to underscore the importance of the State of Israel, Arendt concentrated on a story based on the facts in their entirety. She wanted to prevent the emergence of holes resulting from concealment or self-deception in the collective memory. Arendt did not aim at "a final judgment" that would master the events once and for all. Her book "was not meant to produce consensus but to set in motion a process of deliberation and public debate."[14]

Therefore, Arendt's counter-narrative was, in Bilsky's words, "the story that was not told but should have been told in the courtroom."[15] Arendt concentrated on the moral, political, and juridical aspects of the trial, discussing them on several levels: first, the trial as a theater with its own dynamics; second, the personality and conscience of the accused, his capacity to judge, and the deconstruction of the radical evil explanation; third, the description of the course of events in the destruction of the Jews; and fourth, the shortcomings of the court and her own version of a final speech in defense of the establishment of an international court of justice.

First, *the trial as theater*: The trial not only took place in a building originally planned as a theater, but it inevitably adopted the form of a play, with all its actors and their interactions: the prosecutor, the accused, the judges, the witnesses, and the audience. The accused, with his clichéd language and ridiculousness, proved to be neither a conventional mass murder nor certifiably insane. The judges were old-fashioned and tried hard to understand the criminal and his crime. Last, the audience in the often half-empty room consisted of, as Arendt writes, "'survivors,' with middle-aged and elderly people, immigrants from Europe, like myself, who knew by heart all there was to know."[16]

Nothing in the Eichmann trial corresponded to the common anticipation of a trial and the usual role of the participants. Arendt's counter-narrative culminates in the statement that "it was precisely the play aspect of the trial that collapsed under the weight of the hair-raising atrocities."[17] The accused no longer stood at the center of the trial, and in some respects "the lessons were superfluous, and in others positively misleading."[18] Most theatrically, the pseudonymous witness K-Zetnik, after being interrupted in his endless and irresistible testimony, promptly fainted.

Finally, the witnesses were hardly able to contribute something new to the trial; they did not speak according to "the rule of simplicity" or possess "the ability to tell a story."[19] An exception was Abba Kovner, whose story of the rescuer Anton Schmidt appeared to Arendt "like a sudden burst of light in the midst of impenetrable, unfathomable darkness."[20]

Second, *the personality of the accused*: despite his role as the main character of the trial, Eichmann proved at the same time to be an anti-personality who in all important aspects did not correspond to the image of a monstrous criminal. His "almost total inability ever to look at anything from the other fellow's point of view"[21] was remarkable and his language was bizarre, a "heroic fight with the German language" that was a combination of confounding metaphors and strung-together clichés.[22] "The longer one listened to him, the more obvious it became that his inability to speak was closely connected with an inability to *think*," Arendt writes.[23]

Third, *the description of the course of events in the destruction of the Jews*: the course of these events showed not only the details of the mass crimes but also the common moral collapse. When the role of the Jewish councils in the deportation of their communities came up during the trial, Arendt called it "undoubtedly the darkest chapter of the whole dark story."[24] She never asks why the Jewish leaders did not resist, which was the allegation of her critics— on the contrary, this was a question Arendt found to be "both foolish and cruel" when it was asked by Hausner.[25] But the following sentence from her report provoked an outrage: "The whole truth was that if the Jewish people had been really unorganized and leaderless, there would have been chaos and plenty of misery but the total number of victims would hardly have been between four and half and six million people."[26] Arendt's analysis, which at first sight seemed to be nothing more than a simple report for *The New Yorker*, became extremely controversial in its judgment about the most troubling questions of that time. But she herself had not expected the heavy debates her report provoked. Like the individuals mentioned in Part I, Arendt acted (or rather, judged) as she did for a simple reason: namely, that she could tell the truth no other way.

2. Schindler's List—The Courage of the Bystander

Spielberg's film differs in all essential aspects from Arendt's conviction "to say what is" and her judgment about the "totality of the moral collapse." Spielberg does not need courage to tell the truth because it is the truth of the mainstream, and his truth differs essentially from Arendt's.

In *Schindler's List*, the main character, Oskar Schindler, a rescuer of the Jewish forced laborers he oversees, confronts the SS officer and labor camp commander Amon Goeth. At the time, Schindler is surrounded by other Nazi officers and the group of Jewish victims. Unlike Eichmann, Goeth represents sadistic evil. Possessed by a lust to kill and uninhibited by conscience, he shoots down more than 500 inmates of the camp in total. In their historical study "Remembrance in a Global Age: The Holocaust," which considers the changes in public discussion about the Holocaust in Israel, Germany, and the United States, authors Daniel Levy and Natan Sznaider remark upon the difference between Eichmann and Goeth. According to Levy and Sznaider, Arendt emphasized that Eichmann was not Iago or Macbeth and had not decided, like Richard III, to become a "bad guy": "With this remark she wanted to depersonalize evil and place it in the system of totalitarianism. Spielberg brought the evil back again to the level of the individual. Goeth was Iago and decided to become a bad guy," they write.[27] Goeth was ruthless, brutal, arbitrary, and corrupt; he accepted bribes. Alcohol, women, and violence were his passions beyond any limit.

Eichmann, in contrast, had no sadistic inclination, did not accept bribes, and could hardly bear his visits to extermination camps. Though the interpretation of Goeth in Spielberg's film is historically correct, Goeth does not represent the members of a totalitarian system. This system was dominated by ideology and party discipline and excluded individual preferences and passions. It was based on rules, rather than the absence of them. What is not told in the film is the fact that the SS arrested Goeth for bribery and planned to bring him to court when the war ended. In a similar case, Karl Koch, the former commander of Buchenwald, was condemned to death and executed because of bribery. So, though the SS did not tolerate private enrichment, the Nazi system in Spielberg's movie appears as a system of unrestrained individualists.

In the center of the movie stands the figure of Schindler. A smart, amoral, and self-made man, Schindler is a party member and bon vivant full of self-confidence. His strength lies in his ability to present and commercialize his products, corrupt influential people, and make deals on the black market.

After years of hope, he declares, he finally became successful, not with the help of good fortune but with the help of war. The war offers him an unexpected chance at the cheap takeover of a factory and the exploitation of a cheap Jewish workforce. He gets into a conflict with the SS, which wants to deport his right-hand man, an accounting clerk. When the SS transports his workers into a labor camp, Schindler can keep them only through bribery, and only when other Jews ask him for help and call him a rescuer does he become aware of the fact that his employees are not only a workforce but also men and women.

This turn of events evokes the sense of a strong humanity slumbering deep within Schindler. In a moving scene, he consoles Helene, Goeth's Jewish maid, who suffers from the arbitrariness of Goeth's punishments. In a discussion with Goeth, Schindler explains that true power does not consist of killing freely, but rather in being able to kill but holding back. For a short time Goeth actually hesitates to proceed with his joyful killings. Furthermore, Schindler always tries to help where help is needed. He orders a deportation train waiting at the station to be sprayed with water to cool it down in the burning summer sun. When the labor camp is going to be dissolved and the inmates are to be deported to Auschwitz, he comes to the rescue again, this time saving 1,100 men and women by putting them on his famous list and transporting them to another factory in Czechoslovakia, where he starts to fabricate munitions. And once again he rescues by bribery some of the women on the list who are transported to Auschwitz by mistake. Finally, in his new factory, Schindler produces only defective munitions.

At the end of the film, Schindler is bankrupt and confesses in a moving declaration to his workers that he has lived from slave labor and therefore will be at the mercy of criminal courts in the future. He leaves the decision to the security forces of whether to liquidate the workers or let them free. He gives each worker clothes, vodka, and cigarettes and bewails the fact that he could not rescue more people.

The story shows how Schindler, due to the circumstances, changes from an egoist to an altruist, from an exploiter to a rescuer. "What I learned in that time more than anything else," declared Spielberg after filming, "is the insight that a single person really and truly can change things. A single person can—in a metaphorical sense—breathe life into others. Oskar Schindler was such a righteous person."[28] Schindler had only to decide to do what he did; nothing more was necessary because he was a morally sound and deeply humane man. Bigger than the others, handsome and in bright suits, rhetorically gifted and morally prudent, he acted with the posture of someone nearly superhuman. "The war brings forth horrible things," he declares, meaning brutish behavior. But the totalitarian domination that brought forth this war remains unmentioned. The victims appear as a homogenous cultural and religious community, innocent and cultivated. The role of the *kapos* is mentioned only briefly and mildly, and the Jewish councils remain unmentioned.

3. Decontextualizing the Story

Schindler's List deals with a narrative of Jewish history similar to that presented by Hausner during the Eichmann trial, but it is accompanied by a notable shift in perspective. The message prevalent in Arendt's reading of the Eichmann trial—that here we are witnessing the totality of the moral collapse of the society—is replaced in *Schindler's List* with a narrative that features a pronounced egoism that does not fail to recognize the usefulness of war, as well as one in which the exploitation of the labor force does not contradict a marked humanity ready for action in an emergency case. The distinction between right and wrong, good and evil, is unquestioned. As Levy and Sznaider write, "You can rescue, you only have to decide to do it."[29]

This message clearly contradicts Arendt's threatening assumption that we are facing the moral collapse of a whole society in that, in the film, rescuers and victims are those who prove by their actions that they are not affected by moral collapse. Similarly, the movie's portrayal of Goeth contradicts the depersonalization and anti-personality that Arendt observed in Eichmann. Arendt's theory of the banality of evil, often misunderstood as making evil harmless, is actually much more troubling than the radical evil of Goeth. The Jerusalem judges would have understood better the supposedly more horrible evil of Amon Goeth, because the troubling phenomenon that Arendt wrote about—that of a society being unable to judge moral and political questions adequately—gives way in Spielberg's narrative to a clear confrontation between good and evil. The good ones who are not affected by totalitarianism in their capacity to judge confront the evil ones succumbing to their unlimited passions, and the good ones are able to put the evil ones into their place through reason and humanity. Unlike Arendt, Spielberg does not tell a counter-narrative. On the contrary, he leads a counter-reality back to a safer world, where the classical story of the fight between good and evil protagonists is still adequate and appropriate.

To sum up, we can say that though the story of the film is based on facts, it serves implicitly as a simplistic example of good and evil emerging from the moral ambivalence of the totalitarian system. However, Spielberg fundamentally changed the perspective by removing the story from its historical context and place. He also changed the personalities in that his rescuers and victims correspond to the ideal common citizen of liberal democracy: a person with intact moral judgment fighting injustice wherever he or she finds it. In fact, according to Levy and Sznaider, "Spielberg always maintained that the film deals with Bosnians in Serbia or with black Americans." In an anecdote that demonstrates the decontextualizing that marked Spielberg's approach, they note that when black youngsters in Oakland made fun of a scene in *Schindler's List* that shows a wild hunting of Jews, Spielberg rushed to the city and "created a new course in the local high school called 'The Human Holocaust: The Afro-American Experience.'"[30] Problematic pedagogy aside, the movie does prove useful and compelling insofar as it causes us to ask after the role of the bystander in our society and historical moment. But while such questioning is very important, it comes at the cost of understanding the specific challenges of living under totalitarianism.

The decontextualization that characterizes *Schindler's List* entails a three-fold change of perspective. First, the *emergence of the perspective of the witness* with which the actual German postwar generations can identify wholeheartedly. This explains the overwhelming success of the film in Germany. Levy and Sznaider summarize it as follows: "Schindler are all who want to rescue, Goeth are all who want to kill, and the Jews are the victims everywhere."[31]

Second, the decontextualization allows for a *universalization of the Holocaust*. The Holocaust Memorial Museum in Washington, D.C., stands for this universalization. The museum is not only part of the National Mall and gives the impression that the Holocaust is part of American history, but its exhibition begins with the liberation of the Jewish inmates from concentration camps by American troops. Furthermore, the Holocaust in popular narrative is not only an event of the past but also a permanent threat, a constant warning of its own possible recurrence. Therefore, the seriousness of the promise "Auschwitz: Never Again" was put to the test in the cases of Bosnia, Kosovo, and Rwanda and has represented an obligation for all European countries since the Holocaust conference in Stockholm in 2000.

Third, the decontextualization corresponds to the *end of remembrance*. The generation involved in the Holocaust is dying out. Fewer people can claim to have any experiences from that time. This loss is not trivial and cannot be simply compensated for with second hand information and knowledge because experiences are more than mere adventures and are embedded deeper than rational knowledge. They are part of one's orientation and knowledge base and shaped by an inter-subjective everyday life, a "conjunctive space of experience."[32] According to Karl Mannheim's sociology of knowledge, this conjunctive space of experience is the basis for understanding. The acquisition of history in the sense of understanding takes place on the basis of shared implicit knowledge bases. The presence of the conjunctive space of experience shapes the image of the past and decontextualizes it.

Because Spielberg emphasized the supposed accessibility of the story by telling it in terms comprehendible to our common experience, we meet ourselves in the movie and not the others; we understand our world and not the world of totalitarianism. Arendt's conjunctive space of experience is shaped by totalitarianism, Spielberg's conjunctive space of experience by liberal democracy. When telling a story that happened in the past, we must therefore ask: Are we telling it to understand the past, or to understand our present?

Endnotes

1. Vaclav Havel, *The Power of the Powerless* (London: e.a. 1985), 23–96.

2. Hannah Arendt, "Some Questions of Moral Philosophy, *Responsibility and Judgment,* ed. Jerome Kohn (New York: Schocken Books, 2003), 106.

3. Wolfgang Heuer, *Couragiertes Handeln,* Lüneburg 2002; Wolfgang Heuer: "Zivilcourage und Habitus. Öffentlicher Mut in der DDR," in: Gerd Meyer / Ulrich Dovermann, Siegfried Frech / Günther Gugel (Hrsg.): *Zivilcourage lernen. Analysen – Modelle – Arbeitshilfen,*" Tübingen 2004.

4. Paul van Buitenen, *Unbestechlich für Europa. Ein EU-Beamter kämpft gegen Misswirtschaft und Korruption,* Basel 1999. Wolfgang Heuer: "Der Glockenläuter von Brüssel. Porträt des mutigen EU-Beamten Paul van Buitenen," audio feature, Radio Kultur, rbb 9/25/2004.

5. Leoluca Orlando, *Ich sollte der nächste sein. Zivilcourage – die Chance gegen Korruption und Terror,* Freiburg 2002. See also: Jane Schneider, Peter Schneider, "Civil Society Versus Organized Crime: Local and Global Perspectives," *Critique of Anthropology,* December 2001, vol. 21, 4, 427–446.

6. John F. Kennedy, *Profiles in Courage* (1961 edition), 245.

7. Ibid., 238, 239.

8. Ibid. Allen Nivens, Foreword, xvii.

9. Hannah Arendt, *Denktagebuch 1950–1973,* ed. Ursula Ludz and Ingeborg Nordmann (Munich, 2002), 570.

10. Alexis de Tocqueville, *The Old Régime and the French Revolution* (Garden City, N.Y.: Anchor Books, 1955), chap. III. 3, 168f.

11. Hannah Arendt,"Truth and Politics," *Between Past and Future,* ed. Jerome Kohn, New York: Penguin Classics, 2006), 257.

12. Leora Bilsky, "Between Justice and Politics: The Competition of Storytellers in the Eichmann Trial," *Hannah Arendt in Jerusalem,* ed. Steven E. Aschheim (Berkeley: University of California Press, 2001).

13. Hannah Arendt, *Eichmann in Jerusalem. A Report on the Banality of Evil,* (New York: Viking Press, 1963), 125f.

14. Leora Bilsky, "When Actor and Spectator Meet in the Courtroom: Reflections on Hannah Arendt's Concept of Judgment," *Judgment, Imagination, and Politics: Themes from Kant and Arendt,* eds. Ronald Beiner, Jennifer Nedelsky (Oxford: Oxford University Press, 2001), 273.

15. Bilsky, "Between Justice and Politics," *Hannah Arendt in Jerusalem,* 232.

16. Hannah Arendt, *Eichmann in Jerusalem: A Report on the Banality of Evil,* (New York: Penguin). Books, 2006), 8.

17. Ibid., 8-9.

18. Ibid., 10.

19. Ibid., 224.

20. Ibid., 231.

21. Ibid., 47–48.

22. Ibid., 48.

23. Ibid., 49.

24. Ibid., 117.

25. Hannah Arendt, "What Remains? The Language Remains," *The Portable Hannah Arendt*, ed. Peter Baehr (New York: Penguin Books, 2000), 15.

26. Arendt, *Eichmann in Jerusalem*, 125.

27. Daniel Levy, Natan Sznaider, *Erinnerung im globalen Zeitalter: Der Holocaust* (Frankfurt, 2007), 166.

28. "Auch ein einzelner Mensch kann die Dinge verändern," Michel Friedman im Gespräch mit Steven Spielberg, http://www.shoahproject.org/links/specials/spielberg/welt980912.html (last visit 9/21/2011).

29. Levy, Sznaider, *Erinnerung im globalen Zeitalter: Der Holocaust*, 167.

30. Ibid., 166.

31. Ibid., 164.

32. Ralf Bohnsack, *Qualitative Bild und Videointerpretation. Die dokumentarische Methode*, Opladen, 2009, 130.

Arendt's Eichmann: Murderer, Idealist, Clown

Jerome Kohn

> One may say that tragedy deals with the suffering of mankind in a less serious way than comedy.
> —Bertolt Brecht

> Of course that is an outrageous statement. At the same time I think it is entirely true.
> —Hannah Arendt

This year—2011—is the 50th anniversary of the trial of Adolf Eichmann in Jerusalem. Most of you are familiar with the basic facts surrounding the trial, but, since facts themselves have become increasingly tenuous in our times, it may not be supererogatory to restate them briefly.

Adolf Eichmann was a Nazi Higher SS officer and member of the Gestapo during the Second World War. When the Final Solution of the Jewish Problem was adopted as German policy at the Wannsee Conference in January 1942, it became Eichmann's job to organize logistically the physical destruction of the millions of Jews living in Nazi-dominated Europe. When he took on that enormous task, he was already widely known as an "expert on the Jewish question"—an epithet he was proud of—due to his success in handling the "forced immigration," "evacuation," or, in plain English, the *expulsion* of Austrian Jews after the *Anschluss* or annexation of Austria by the German Reich in 1938.

The Reich that was to last a thousand years collapsed seven years later with Germany's unconditional surrender in May 1945. Eichmann was sought by the Allied victors to stand trial as a war criminal, though not with the highest echelons of Nazi officials, generals, and commandants who were tried in Nuremburg as early as November of that same year. Eichmann eluded capture, or at least recognition, and in 1950, with the help of a Franciscan priest, escaped from Europe, via Austria and Italy, to Argentina. Ten years later, in 1960, in a suburb of Buenos Aires, he was in effect kidnapped by Israeli agents and spirited off to Jerusalem, where in 1961 he was finally brought before a court of justice, found guilty of "crimes against the Jewish people," and sentenced to death. In 1962, after the Israeli appellate court denied his appeal, Eichmann was hanged. These few facts, one trusts, will not be disputed, but there are many others in the Eichmann case of which that cannot be said.

The Final Solution to the problem of European Jewry—the problem, that is, of a people perceived as intruders, parasites, and plagues in lands that were not their own—was not conceived by Eichmann. The Final Solution, if judged by international laws and conventions, or what were once believed to be universal moral standards, was a criminal and depraved idea, but it was not his idea. It is a fact that Eichmann considered Jews enemies of the Reich because they deprived Germans of their livelihoods (their "breath of life," in his words), and that he worked willingly to rid Europe of them. At the same time, according to him, he wanted to put "firm soil under their feet so that they would have a place of their own" in Madagascar, perhaps, or Palestine. There is no evidence, apart from what is taken to be self-evident, to back up the prejudgment of Eichmann's *mens rea* (criminal intent): that he hated Jews because they were Jews and sent them to their death because he believed, as Nazi ideology dictated, that they were members of a subhuman race whose existence prevented the natural progress of the human species. Nevertheless, Eichmann not only supported but also played an uncompromising—or, as he preferred to call it, an *idealistic*—role even "beyond the call of duty" in the extermination of millions of Jewish men, women, and children.

How can one account for that? Perhaps that is the basic question Hannah Arendt asks readers of her report on Eichmann's trial to think about. Her own account, in a phrase borrowed from the late Frank Kermode, is the "manifest sense" of her book *Eichmann in Jerusalem: A Report on the Banality of Evil.* The term *manifest sense* refers more or less to what we mean when we speak of a book's subject matter, and, as is the case with every substantial literary work, that sense is renewed, complemented, and also preserved in its "latent sense" or "spiritual meaning" which, according to Kermode, is generated by its ongoing interpretation, generation after generation.

Arendt's *Eichmann in Jerusalem* is an essentially controversial book, and I for one would rue the day it ceased to be. For it challenges its readers to reconsider what most of us, including Arendt, were brought up and taught to believe about the nature of evil; namely, that in all its forms, human as well as natural, evil is *out of the ordinary.* But the essential quality of the banality of evil, which can only be stated negatively, is that it is *not* out of the ordinary. But to say that is just plain wrong, if it is understood to imply that, as some have thought, there is an Eichmann in every one of us, or, to put the same thing differently, that the evil he enacted is commonplace. Arendt consistently and vehemently denied both of those propositions, and her reason for doing so is transparent if one remembers that to her, human beings as such are the opposite of ordinary; on the contrary, each one of us is unique. Let us leave this matter for now with the observation that the phrase *banality of evil* is something like a catachrestic trope—Milton's "blind mouths" being the classic example—an unexpected combination of elements that not so much signifies as reveals what is unforeseen and sometimes unprecedented.

Right now, I'd like to draw attention to a closely related but seldom noticed aspect of Arendt's book, which is the unusual gap that separates its manifest sense from its latent or interpretive sense. It is true, of course, that Arendt's Eichmann book has been interpreted over and over, almost to death, one could say. What I want to suggest is that these interpretations, however much they may have added to the book's celebrity and notoriety, have not illuminated its subject matter; on the contrary, they have tended to obscure it. When Arendt, as she frequently did, told critics that they hadn't read her book, or that they were talking about a book she never wrote, she was not suggesting that these respectable men and women had overlooked her work, nor that they had kept their eyes shut while they turned its pages, nor, least of all, that they had mistaken someone else's work for hers. She was saying that they had *rejected* the manifest, most apparent sense of what she had written. To give an example pertinent to this discussion, and indeed to this conference, when the question arose as to why she hadn't taken greater pains to define the ideas in her book, Arendt replied:

> As I see it there are no "ideas" in this report, there are only facts with a few conclusions, and these conclusions usually appear at the end of each chapter. The only exception to this is the Epilogue, which is a discussion of the legal aspects of the case. In other words, my point would be that what the whole furor is about are facts, and neither theories nor ideas. The hostility against me is a hostility against someone who tells the truth on a factual level, and not against someone who has ideas which are in conflict with those commonly held.[1]

Here Arendt anticipates the criticism that she nowhere says what she means by "the banality of evil," that the now famous phrase appears only once in the entire book, and then in the last sentence directly before the Epilogue.[2] In fact, it occurs when Eichmann, speaking before the gallows from which he will be hanged, *at once* declares that he does not believe in anything remotely resembling a life after death *and* tells those present, "After a short while, gentlemen, we shall all meet again." Arendt comments: "In the face of death, he had found the cliché used in funeral oratory," which so "elated" him that—like a clown in a circus act—"he forgot this was his own funeral." And then she adds that in these "last minutes" of his life Eichmann summarized "the lesson that this long course in human wickedness had taught us—the lesson of the fearsome, word-and-thought-defying banality of evil."

Can one ask for a clearer example of a conclusion drawn from facts, regardless if one disputes the latter and spurns the former? But after seeing what is going on in this world 50 years later—the torture, massacres, and millions of destitute and desperate refugees—can anyone still doubt that Arendt incurs so much rancor and malice, not because she invents or distorts facts to fit an idea or theory, but because the facts she reports call out to her readers—for their own sakes and the sake of the world—to revisit the topic of evil and judge for themselves what lies before them. The answer to that question is, unfortunately, *yes.* It should be added that no one knew better than Arendt the pitfalls that have entrapped even the greatest philosophers, starting with Plato, when they attempted to define evil—to say what evil is—but this is not what she is asking her readers to do.[3]

***

Eichmann's elation, clichés, boasts, and forgetfulness are woven over and over by Arendt into the fabric of her elusive subject matter. These are Eichmann's manifold banalities, and she is genuinely astonished at their proliferation in disparate circumstances, not only when he was a prisoner in Israel but also when, as he put it years before in Argentina, he was "in full possession of [his] physical and psychological freedom." It may well be, as Natan Sznaider has suggested, that Arendt's philosophic mind, combined with her poetic insight, revealed in these countless small banalities the one terrifying banality of evil. On the other hand, readers may have been deceived—and Arendt bears some responsibility for this—into thinking that *Eichmann in Jerusalem* is a straightforward report of a trial, such as one might find in a magazine (and hers was first published in *The New Yorker*), and therefore easy both to understand and to take issue with. Well, is it an easy book? Or, might it be as demanding, and also as momentous, as any she ever wrote?

Eichmann's deeds were monstrous—that is, he did what we say befits a monster—but he was not a monster, and that fact points to the gravest moral, judicial, and political problems of our time. We face these problems, on a lesser or larger scale, every day, at home and abroad. On what moral, legal, or political grounds can citizens of a republic be spied upon by agents of their own government? On what moral, legal, or political grounds can anyone, whether a citizen of a republic or not, be summarily executed by the operator of a drone 6,000 miles away, or by an elite military detail secretly dispatched halfway around the earth for that express purpose? Needless to say, monsters cannot be brought to trial, for they are not human, and only a force greater than theirs can prevail against them. Apparently Eichmann had some awareness of this when he said, in his last statement to the court: "I am not the monster I am made out to be." And certainly Arendt understood it when she wrote to Mary McCarthy (February 2, 1964): "The point of the whole business was that we were supposed to look upon a human being . . . How you can report a trial, or for that matter ever become interested in it, without this, is beyond me."

In the case of Eichmann, far from seeing in him a monster, the judges of the district court in Jerusalem, in Arendt's words, "treated him with a consideration and an authentic, shining humanity such as he had probably never encountered before in his whole life." Eichmann "had done his best to make the Final Solution final"—that was never in question—but the judges were too good and had too much "faith in the moral foundations of their profession" ever to consider that it might have been Eichmann's idealism, indeed his "*conscience* that prompted his uncompromising attitude." Was it not more plausible, Arendt asks, that "his hatred of Jews" was "boundless," greater than even Himmler's, and that he "had lied to the police and committed perjury in court when he claimed he had always obeyed [Hitler's] orders"? Regardless of the facts of the matter, Eichmann's "fanaticism," his hatred and lying, constituted the only explanation of his acts that the judges, who had "tried so hard to understand the accused," could accept (emphasis added).[4]

To some extent, Eichmann's was a hard-luck story. He wanted nothing more than to be promoted from the rank of *Obersturmbannführer*, or lieutenant colonel, to full colonel, or *Standartenführer*—after all, as he never tired of boasting, he did have standards and therefore merited the promotion. To facilitate being promoted, he had even "hoped to be nominated for the *Einsatzgruppen*, the mobile killing units in the East, because when they were formed, in March 1941, his office was [as he put it] 'dead.'" He was between jobs: the "forced evacuation," in which Eichmann wanted, as we have seen, to resettle Jews in Madagascar, a solution he falsely boasted to have invented, had come to an end; and the "forced deportation" of Jews to Auschwitz, in which his expertise in the Jewish question would be honed, had not yet begun. To read all this was "funny," because when he said it to his interviewer in Jerusalem, Captain Avner Less, a German Jew whose parents were sent to Auschwitz on the last transport from Berlin, he expected "'normal, human' sympathy."

Arendt asks: "Is this a textbook case of bad faith, of lying self-deception combined with outrageous stupidity?" No, she answers. "Or is it simply the case of an eternally unrepentant criminal?" Neither. Eichmann admitted he "had played a role in the extermination of the Jews, of course," saying that "if he had 'not transported them, they would not have been delivered to the butcher.'" But now, he went on, "he 'would like to find peace with [his] former enemies.'" "This outrageous cliché," Arendt writes, gave to its speaker an almost visible "sense of elation the moment it popped out of his mouth." Indeed, the judges soon "learned that the accused had . . . a different elating cliché for each period of his life." As the terrible war drew to its close, he dismissed his men, boasting: "I will jump into my grave laughing, because the fact that I have the death of five million Jews [or 'enemies of the Reich,' as he always claimed to have said] on my conscience gives me extraordinary satisfaction" (*EiJ* 46). And then, 16 years later in Jerusalem, he said, "I shall gladly hang myself in public as a warning example for all the anti-Semites on this earth." The manifest contradiction of the two statements meant nothing to him. Rather, as Arendt puts it, "under vastly different circumstances [they] fulfilled exactly the same function." They elated him. They elevated him. They gave him "a lift." If Eichmann was not a monster, was he a "clever, calculating liar"? Not even that, as we shall see in a moment. But for Arendt, at least, "it was difficult not to suspect he was a clown," even if that was "hard to sustain in view of the sufferings he and his like had caused millions of people" (*EiJ* 49–55).

Willem Sassen was a Dutch journalist who joined the Nazi *Waffen* SS during World War II. After the war, he escaped to Argentina where, like Eichmann, he was a fugitive from justice. The two met in a drinking club frequented by ex-Nazis, but Sassen did not know who "Ricardo Klement" (Eichmann's alias) was until, in 1955, he conducted a series of interviews with his fellow fugitive who, he soon realized, could not be anyone but Adolf Eichmann. My interest in turning to these interviews, which Arendt knew well and quoted from in her book, is to see if they really are in fact so different from her own account of Eichmann. The notion that the two "portraits" are dichotomous is still prevalent, and even those who agree that Arendt discovered a new *kind* of criminal often do not admit Eichmann himself to that company, preferring to believe he bamboozled Arendt with his lies in Jerusalem.

As mentioned above, Eichmann was in "full possession of [his] physical and mental freedom" when he told Sassen that "in 1937" after he "had been struggling with Hebrew for two years" he "had the chance to take a trip to Palestine."[5] Though he was not "impressed" by the way the Jews built "up their land," he "admired their desperate will to live, the more so since [he] was [himself] an *idealist*." Had he been born a Jew, he told Sassen, he would "have been the most ardent Zionist imaginable." Denying that he was an anti-Semite, Eichmann said he "was just politically opposed to the Jews, because they were stealing the breath of life from us." He told Sassen that "at heart" he was "a very sensitive man: I simply can't look at any suffering without trembling myself." In Hungary alone he and his men *processed* "about half a million Jews," but they "used spiritual methods to reach [that] goal. Let us keep this distinction clear," he said, "because physical liquidation is a vulgar, coarse action." He "once saw a soldier beat a frail old Jew over the head with a rubber club." He demanded the soldier be "punished and demoted," for "that is sadism," which was not permitted to Nazis.

Later in these interviews, Eichmann told Sassen that he especially admired one Dr. Rudolph Kastner, the representative of the Zionist movement in Budapest. "As a matter of fact, there was a very strong similarity between our attitudes in the SS and these immensely idealistic Zionist leaders." He told Kastner, "We, too, are idealists," and explained to Sassen "that Kastner would have sacrificed a hundred or a hundred thousand . . . old Jews . . . to save biologically valuable Jewish blood—that is, human material capable of reproduction and hard work." Eichmann's "idealism" was revealed once more when Germany faced an imminent Russian onslaught in the East. It was then that he decided (so he boasted, though the decision probably was not his) to barter one million Jewish lives for 10,000 winterized military trucks. He "wanted to accomplish as much as possible for the Reich," he said, while knowing all the while that he "could never have squeezed a million Jews out of Hungary."

The Sassen interviews end on a high note: tired and bored with the life of a fugitive, Eichmann said he would gladly surrender to the German authorities, except that he was far from certain what sort of "witnesses for the defense" his former subordinates would make. In fact he believed, "sad though [it] may sound," that Jews would make better witnesses for him. "Dr. Kastner, Dr. Epstein, Dr. Rottenberg, Dr. Baeck, the entire Council of Elders in the Theresienstadt Ghetto—all of them [he] would have to summon . . . [for] after all, there were also relatively harmless actions that took place under the general heading, 'Final Solution of the Jewish Problem.'" In the end Eichmann said he regretted nothing he had done; indeed, "if we had killed all the ten million Jews that Himmler's statisticians originally listed in 1933, I would say, 'Good, we have destroyed an enemy.'" But he did not mean their literal extermination, for that "would not be proper, and we carried on a proper war." Eichmann must have been dimly aware that the legitimate purpose of war is to defeat an enemy, not to annihilate him. But then he said, "through the malice of fate" many Jews were still alive. Well, what malice? Had he not "always claimed that we were fighting against a foe who through thousands of years of learning and development had become superior to us"?

Though he didn't "remember exactly when," he was certain that Jews could write even before Rome was founded.

I will read the last two sentences from the Sassen interviews, and ask you whether they reveal a fanatical hater and killer of Jews, or on the contrary, a clown who could even die with a certain "dignity" for what he thought of as his ideals—the only condition being his *elation* through a wildly inapposite "cliché used in funeral oratory," as we have seen. Thus as he faced death, according to Arendt, Eichmann was "in complete command of himself, nay, he was more: he was completely himself" (*EiJ*, 252). Here are the two final sentences: "It is very depressing for me to think of that people [the Jews] writing laws over 6,000 years of [recorded] history. But it tells me that they must be a people of the first magnitude, for law-givers have always been great."

***

In 1963 Hannah Arendt asked herself why, two years before, in 1961, she had attended the trial of Adolf Eichmann in Jerusalem. She answered that it was because she wanted to see one of the chief perpetrators of the destruction of European Jewry with her own eyes, "as he appeared in the flesh."[6] In *The Origins of Totalitarianism*, written some 15 years before (mainly in the latter half of the 1940s), she said she had "analyzed the totalitarian mentality" but she had not examined individuals with that mentality. Then she added: "If you look at the [totalitarian] system as a whole, every individual becomes a 'cog big or small' in the machinery of terror." But "a court procedure . . . inevitably confronts you with [a] person and personal guilt."

She wanted to know, in short, "Who was Eichmann? What were his deeds [but] not insofar as his crimes were part and parcel of the Nazi system?" That last question is essentially the same as that which "a court of justice must answer when it renders judgment. And it is for this reason that the whole small-cog theory [which was the principal point made in Eichmann's defense] is quite irrelevant" when an individual is tried for specific crimes he has been accused of committing. Is it not absurd to think of charging a cog, which is an insentient wheel that receives motion from another wheel and transfers it to yet another, and so on, with criminal behavior? She then said that she had "been thinking of the nature of evil for . . . thirty years," that is, since the Reichstag was burned in Berlin and Nazism unmasked itself to a greater degree than before, and that "the wish to *expose* myself—not to the deeds, which . . . were well known, but to the evil doer himself—probably was the most powerful motive in my decision to go to Jerusalem" (emphasis added). In *The Origins of Totalitarianism*, published 12 years before the Eichmann book, Arendt wrote: "The ideal subject of totalitarian rule is not the convinced Nazi or the dedicated communist, but the people for whom the distinction between fact and fiction, true and false, no longer exists." There the world "ideal" is used in the sense of a Weberian "ideal type," that is, not as referring to any individual, much less the individual she traveled to Jerusalem to see in the flesh. And yet, mutatis mutandis, her words seem an almost uncanny description of Eichmann, who literally thought nothing of distorting reality, with the decisive provision that this man was no mere subject of totalitarian rule. He was on trial for his life, not as a cog in the machinery of terror, but as perhaps the worst mass murderer in human history. He actively supported the Nazi version of totalitarian rule, doing all he could to destroy European Jewry, paying no heed to Jews' right to live in Europe, which had been established for nearly two millennia, since the early days of the Roman Empire.

In a letter to Mary McCarthy in September 1963, a few months after the Eichmann book was published, Arendt wrote: "What a risky business to tell the truth on a factual level without theoretical and scholarly embroidery." She is referring to the huge controversy that arose in America, Europe, and Israel over her book, which included some serious criticism but for the most part consisted of vituperation, everything from accusations of hubris, incompetence, and anti-Semitism, to death threats. But the next sentence in the same letter shifts the focus in a manner characteristic of Arendt: "This side of it, I admit, I do enjoy," she wrote; "it taught me a few lessons about *truth and politics*" (emphasis added). Well, which side of it? If not the accusations and threats, which were troubling (to say the least), then perhaps the risk in the "risky business" itself. In less than a month Arendt wrote to McCarthy again, saying she had now made up her mind "to write an essay about 'Truth and Politics,' which would be an implicit answer" to her critics. Here the word *implicit* must be emphasized, since that dense and complex essay, which first appeared in German the following year, has, after almost 50 years, hardly stilled the critical and at times slanderous chorus raised against her.

In a note to its title in its English edition, Arendt states that her purpose in writing "Truth and Politics" was "to clarify two different, though interconnected, issues," which had come to light in the controversy over her book on Eichmann and the banality of the evil he wrought.[7] The first issue, which is the principal one that concerns us here, is "the question of whether it is always legitimate to tell the truth . . ." The second issue "arose through the amazing amount of lies . . . about what [she] had written, on the one hand, and about the facts [she] had reported, on the other." We have already discussed the distortion and denial of facts in the Eichmann case, but to question the *legitimacy* of telling the truth brings us face-to-face with an entirely different question: *How* can the truth be told in view of the tenuousness of facts themselves?

The conflicted relationship of truth to politics, which comes into focus when a philosopher attempts to speak the truth in public, is an old story stretching back to Plato, whose notion of a philosopher-king improbably, or perhaps ironically, resolves the conflict in favor of truth *over* politics. The root of the problem for Plato lies between truth and opinion, for when the philosopher speaks his truth in the marketplace or in the assemblies of equals it is heard not as the truth but as another opinion among a diversity of opinions. The philosopher-king must perforce become a tyrant and void all public spaces if others—who then in no wise would be his equals but his subjects—are to apply his standards of judgment or logically infallible rules to determine the affairs that concern them all. But among equals the philosopher will find others who are not willing to give up their own opinions, which for them would be to relinquish their standpoints in a common public world. Opinions and standpoints are closely related as what might be called the *doxastic* places that sustain public spaces and, moreover, fill them with energy. Not even Socrates, the most persuasive of philosophers, could convince the citizens of Athens to examine their lives and their beliefs, and by doing so discover the partiality of every one of their opinions. Instead of that, his fellow citizens chose to put Socrates on trial and condemn him to death.

A shocking part of Arendt's essay "Truth and Politics" is concerned with the similarities she sees between lying and acting, almost as if they were mirror images of one another. Yet, as she points out, they are not the same: "The undeniable affinity of lying with action, with changing the world—in short with politics—is limited by the very nature of the things that are open to man's faculty for action" (*BPF* 258). We will return to that later, but it is noteworthy that insofar as lying articulates dissatisfaction with some bit of factual reality that can be changed by human action, they both seem instances of a strictly human freedom. Why then should telling the truth be considered a political virtue? Should truth be told if the world were to perish? What sane person would not tell a lie if doing so would avert the imminent destruction of himself, his family, and his world? Indeed, lies "are often used as substitutes for more violent means" and thus "are apt to be considered relatively harmless tools in the arsenal of political action." That being the case, Arendt says "it will therefore come as something of a surprise that the sacrifice of truth for the survival of the world would be more futile than the sacrifice of any other principle or virtue" (*BPF* 228–29). To tell the truth is, for Arendt, to say what is (*BPF* 229), which sounds simpler than it turns out to be. To tell truths of fact, truths that have been "seen and witnessed with the eyes of the body," is obviously the opposite of lying, but just as obviously the truthteller is at a tremendous disadvantage to both the philosopher and the liar. The basic reason for this is that factual truths are always contingent and therefore lack necessity. Philosophic truths, as we have seen with Socrates, can be opposed by a plurality of opinions, but they cannot be destroyed by lies; whereas factual truths, because they are reflections of the contingency of all that transpires in this world—"everything that actually has happened in the realm of human affairs could just as well have been otherwise" (*BPF* 257)—can be lied out of existence altogether. As Montaigne said, "If falsehood, like truth, had only one face, we would know better where we are . . . But the reverse of truth has a thousand shapes and a limitless field . . . A thousand paths miss the target, only one path leads to it" (*Essays of Montaigne*, "Of Liars"). This seems to me to be the crux of the matter.

Because "reality is different from and more than the totality of facts and events, which anyhow is unascertainable," the teller of factual truths has always to fit his facts into "a story, and in this story the particular facts *lose their contingency* and acquire some humanly comprehensible meaning" (*BPF* 261–62, emphasis added). Is it not a matter of common experience that when we hear a well-made story with a factual basis we recognize the meaning of the event the story recounts? We say, *This* is how it was meant to be. In doing so, we exercise our power of imagination, to be sure, but we evoke no extra-human power.

On the other hand, lying is unlimited, and for that reason can never be part of a story that, as all stories do, comes to an end. If an accumulation of lies is to "form a web of deception" that has the "semblance of truthfulness," it can only be, as Arendt sees clearly, an endless self-deception. It follows that for those who believe that Eichmann hid his real self in lies at his trial, his crimes remain inconceivable and meaningless, and that is their enduring horror. It is also why these same people can never become reconciled to the world in which Eichmann's crimes were committed. The act of lying treats "the past and the present . . . as parts of the future," that is, as if in themselves they were not real.

To put it another way, because factual truths are always of what has passed, and, insofar as the present is the outcome of the past, then lying changes both past and present "into their former states of potentiality." By so doing lying deprives "the political realm . . . not only of its main stabilizing force but of the starting point from which . . . change [and beginning] something new" are possible. If lying is a semblance of action, it is that semblance that in fact ruins action: in Arendt's view, to fail to distinguish facts from lies entails the "sterility" of political life, reducing it to a life squandered in a "constant shuffling and shifting" from one impotent alternative to another (*BPF* 254–58). If that sounds at all familiar to some of us today, it is noteworthy that Arendt leaves us not with answers, but with questions. Shall we lie impotent before the future, as if its outcome were foreknown by us or directed by some supra-political power? Or shall we summon the courage to act into the future, thereby transfiguring what comes toward us into a setting forth, whose end, to be sure, is not foreseeable and whose purpose cannot be calculated?

***

To conclude these remarks, let me turn to a well-known passage from Machiavelli's *Prince* in which he says "a prince must . . . learn how not to be good" (*è necessario a uno principe . . . imparare a potere essere non buono*), and adds, "and to make use of [this learning] or not according to necessity" (*e usarlo e non l'usare secondo la necessità*) (*The Prince*, Book XV, any edition). This does not at all mean that a prince, or for that matter anyone else, must be *taught* to be bad, and not just because Machiavelli lacked a sufficiently high opinion of human nature. It is far more to the point that, though it is not knowledge and cannot be taught, the necessity "not to be good" is *recognizable* by human beings. What Machiavelli says here is drawn from the deep well of his political wisdom, in which he stands opposed to any and every blush of idealism in politics.

Now that we have seen enough of the results of what might be called the little man's version of political idealism, let me say that Arendt's *Eichmann in Jerusalem: A Report on the Banality of Evil* is the only work of political thought I would place on a shelf next to Machiavelli's *Prince*. That is not because she so greatly admired his book (which she did), nor because these two tremendous political thinkers are among the world's most misunderstood writers (which they are), but because their shared passion for political reality—*the reality of the realm of politics*—is extremely rare. And for that reason, namely, that the two works are written for the sake of the world in which we all, whether we want to or not, live until we die, and despite the fact that in these works Machiavelli and Arendt look at what can become actual in that world from almost opposite points of view—his viewpoint being rather more sanguine than hers: better by far to ride with Cesare Borgia into the Romagna than be transported on a train to Auschwitz by Adolf Eichmann—it is mentally exhilarating to see them in the same light next to each other. True, Niccolò Machiavelli never encountered or imagined such a man as Adolf Eichmann, but one can be pretty sure that if he had, his judgment would have been much the same as that of Hannah Arendt, which is that Eichmann's crimes against human beings in their plurality revoked his right to share the world with them.

And Machiavelli surely would have relished the epigraph for her book that Arendt borrowed from Brecht, which, as far as I know, has gone unmentioned in the interpretive literature: *"Oh Deutschland − / Hörend die Reden, die aus deinem Hause dringen, lacht man. / Aber wer dich sieht, der greift nach dem Messer* ("O Germany − / Hearing the speeches that ring from your house, one laughs./ But whoever sees you, reaches for his knife"). Does that not perfectly exemplify what Machiavelli meant when he spoke of a *necessity* "not to be good," not to turn the other cheek, not to overlook or forgive iniquity? In the end, that necessity can be entrusted to, and determined by, the faculty of judgment in each and every one of us.

Endnotes

1. *Between Friends: The Correspondence of Hannah Arendt and Mary McCarthy 1949–1975*, ed. Carol Brightman (New York: Harvest Books, 1950), 148, emphasis added.

2. R. J. Bernstein, *Hannah Arendt and the Jewish Question* (Cambridge: The MIT Press, 1996),166–67.

3. Hannah Arendt, *The Life of the Mind, Vol. 1, Thinking* (New York: Harcourt, Brace, 1978), 150–51.

4. Hannah Arendt, *Eichmann in Jerusalem: A Report on the Banality of Evil* (New York: PenguinClassics, 2006), 146.

5. All quotations from the Sassen interviews are from *Life Magazine*, November 28, 1960, and December 5, 1960, which constitute the most complete English version of the interviews.

6. In the following section all quotations, unless otherwise specified, are from Hannah Arendt: *The Jewish Writings* (New York: Schocken Books, 2007), 474–5.

7. Hannah Arendt, *Between Past and Future* (New York: Penguin Classics, 2006), 227.

01110100 01101000 01100101 00100000 01110000 01100101 01110010 01101001 01101100 01110011 00100000 01101111 01100110 00100000 01101001 01101110 01110110 01100101 01101110 01110100 01101001 01101111 01101110

Human Being in
an Inhuman Age

01110100 01101000 01100101 00100000 01110000 01100101 01110010 01101001 01101100 01110011 00100000 01101111 01100110 00100000 01101001 01101110 01110110 01100101 01101110 01110100 01101001 01101111 01101110

Singularity and the Human Condition

Roger Berkowitz

01110100 01101000 01100101 00100000 01110000 01100101 01110010 01101001 01101100 01110011 00100000 01101111 01100110 00100000 01101001 01101110 01110110 01101001 01101110 01110110 01101001 01101110 01110110 01101001 01101111 01101110

H annah Arendt's *The Human Condition* is about the fate of humanity in the aftermath of the modern age. The modern age began "in the seventeenth century [and] came to an end at the beginning of the twentieth century."[1] It is the age of science. In the aftermath of the modern age and the scientific revolution, we now live in what Arendt calls the modern world, a world defined above all by "world alienation." The question Arendt poses within her historical analysis is: how does the rise of science in the modern age fundamentally challenge the human condition in the modern world by giving birth to the phenomenon of earth and world alienation?

My aim in this essay is to explore Arendt's understanding of the threat world alienation poses to the human condition. Arendt worried that scientific reasoning has so infiltrated human thinking that it might lead an alienated humanity to turn away from the human world, a world built upon the human activities of labor, work, and action. Since the human condition—as it has emerged over millennia—nurtures and thrives upon the faculties of freedom, action, and judgment, the transformation of the human condition brings about the potential loss of these human ideals.

To understand the extent of the threat Arendt is exploring, it is helpful to consider the transhumanist movement that seeks to overcome humanity through technology. Many of the events that Arendt foregrounds as central to the modern age—automation, cloning, artificial intelligence, and immortality—are the same developments that current transhumanists and futurists celebrate as improvements to the human condition. What Arendt shows is that the new developments in transhumanism correspond to longstanding human desires that—if they are actualized as Arendt saw and the futurists now promise—will bring about a transformation of the human condition as we have known it for millennia. In the face of this coming transformation of the human condition, Arendt does not take a position pro or contra, although she is clearly worried about what the loss of human freedom portends. Following Arendt, my hope is to understand these transformations, to help us, as she counseled, "to think what we are doing."[2]

I.

Arendt writes in the prologue to *The Human Condition* that, "The Earth is the very quintessence of the human condition."[3] To be human includes the fact that we are born and live on this earth. The earth—its oxygen-rich atmosphere, its abundance of water, its temperate climate—allows humans to live without artifice. The word "human" is derived, at least in part, from humus, the rich ground soil from the decay of organic matter. From dust to dust, mankind is born of soil and will return to the soil. To be human means, or at least has meant, to be of the earth. The earth corresponds to our human condition as living beings. As do animals, we humans live in and on the earth; we are creatures of the earth.

At the same time, Arendt knows that we humans are different from animals insofar as we transcend our earthly existence. She writes, "The human artifice of the world separates human existence from all mere animal environment."[4] We live on the earth and are of the earth, but we can make and remake our earthly habitat into a human world. We can build houses, dams, and walls. We can bring forth cities, temples, and works of art. Above all, we can tell stories that build a web of relations that emerges as an "altogether different in-between which consists of deeds and words and owes its origin exclusively to men's acting and speaking directly to one another."[5] The humanly created world is not tangible. Still, "for all its intangibility, this in-between is no less real than the world of things we visibly have in common."[6] While we live on the earth that is given us, we live too in a humanly created world of tangible and intangible things.

What Arendt calls the human artifice of the world is opposed to the earth, but it is not in any way inhuman. On the contrary, simply to live earthly lives, as do plants or animals, does not constitute a fully human life. To be human is to build things that last, tell stories that immortalize our deeds, and create political communities that carry a humanly created world into the future.

> *The task and potential greatness of mortals lie in their ability to produce things—works and deeds and words—which would deserve to be and, at least to a degree, are at home in everlastingness, so that through them mortals could find their place in a cosmos where everything is immortal except themselves.*[7]

We humans actualize our humanity when we artificially create and live in a humanly built world that aspires to immortality. The very distinction between human and animal, Arendt writes, is that humans can in the words of Heraclitus "prefer immortal fame to mortal things" and thus can build a world that lasts and that deserves to last.[8] The capacity to prefer immortality separates man from animal, even if, as Heraclitus writes, most humans sit around chewing the cud like cattle. Arendt's point is that all humans can pursue immortality and those artists and public actors who contribute to the immortality of the humanly built world are distinguished from those who do not. Better put, all human beings act in ways that are memorable. Even private persons are remembered by their friends and families. But some persons act in ways that deserve to be, and are, publicly memorable. It is these acts that most fully display the human capacity for immortality that runs through each of us, dividing our private selves from our public personas.

II.

As earthly beings who also are worldly beings, we humans are split by two opposing forces. First humans are artificers and live in an artificial world that we create. Second, we are living creatures and life itself is given—whether by a god or by fate—and is beyond our control. Humans thus are split beings, at once created and creating.

Arendt's ambivalent view of humans as both worldly and earthly reflects an ancient tradition that is perhaps first represented in "The Ode to Man," Sophocles's second choral ode in *Antigone*. Over two millennia ago, Sophocles characterized man as *deinon,* a Greek word that connotes both greatness and horror, that which is so wondrous as to be at once terrifying and beautiful. The Sophoclean ode begins:

> *Manifold are the* deinon *(wonders and horrors), but nothing towers more deinon (wondrous and horrifying) than Man!*[9]

Man, Sophocles tells, can plough the earth and make it give grain. He can "sail the seas" and "trap birds and animals." Man, the poet writes, is "The man who-knows-his-way-around." He has reason, which is a wondrous power. Man artifices; he can create and re-create his world. So is man *deinon*; he is wonderful.

Yet man is *deinon* also in the sense of being terrifying and horrific. As Sophocles's "man" invents and gains ever more extraordinary control over the world, he threatens not only to do evil to others, but also to extinguish part of his humanity, the mystery of his existence. Man's technological mastery endangers that part of man that man himself does not control, his humanity as a created and limited being, a being who struggles to live in and master a world beyond his control.

As *deinon*, man lives in this split realm. Man, Sophocles writes in the third Strophe of the "Ode to Man," is "*pantoporos, aporos*"; rendered in

English, this says that man in "overcoming-all-obstacles, yet unable-to-pass, he comes to nothing."[10] If man so tames the earth as to free himself from toil and uncertainty, what then is left of the mystery that is being human? Because man as *deinon* is always-overcoming, he loses his human fallibility and human freedom. In other words, to overcome all obstacles is to be a god, not a man.

In the final strophe of "The Ode to Man," Sophocles echoes this paradoxical statement about man when he has the chorus sing, man is "*hypsipolis, apolis.*" In English, the chorus sings that man "towers-high-in-the-polis, and loses the polis."[11] To achieve so much and to raise oneself above others—to rise high above the polis as a hero—is to become isolated, to lose what connects one to one's countrymen. To be a hero, in other words, is to risk being a criminal, an outlier. This ancient insight into the paradoxical wish to overcome our humanity is itself part of what it means to be human.

Sophocles's conception of man as split between his earthly fate and his worldly ability to overcome and transcend his given existence is continued in the Christian understanding of man as made, but made in the image of an all-powerful God. And this idea of man is expressed also in Immanuel Kant's understanding of man as a "*vernünftige Lebewesen,*" an existing-being possessed of reason. From the Greeks to the enlightenment, man has been understood as a split being, part animal and part God, or as Aristotle called him, a *zoon echon logon*, an animal who has the capacity of rational speech.[12] Man, as Michel Foucault rightly summarizes humanity's doubled existence, is an "empirico-transcendental doublet."[13] Arendt's discussion of the earthly and worldly aspects of the human condition in *The Human Condition* recalls the tradition of man's dividedness that begins with Sophocles's understanding of man as *deinon*.

At the same time, however, Arendt suggests that the launch of Sputnik makes manifest a radical transformation in the human condition. For millennia man was caught in an unending struggle between his earthly-animal-like and his worldly-human-and-wondrous-and-God-like capacities—a struggle that defined his humanity. Humanity was characterized by an unceasing struggle between earth and world. But now, in what Arendt calls the modern age, we are on the verge of harnessing technology so that man for the first time can fully overcome and transcend his biological, earthly, and animal foundations. Our scientific know-how has made it possible that mankind's capacity for artifice and his capacity to create a humanly built world can, for the first time, overwhelm his earthly and given existence.

Arendt's insight is that the launch of Sputnik in 1957 made palpable that the long-deferred dream of leaving and mastering the earth was finally within reach of the human species. It was now possible that humans could leave the earth and build new worlds in space. This dream itself was old, long "buried in the highly non-respectable literature of science fiction (to which, unfortunately, nobody yet has paid the attention it deserves as a vehicle of mass sentiments and mass desires)."[14] What was new is that with the launch of Sputnik and the inauguration of the space age, the once-fantastical dream had become real. We now can—or at least can realistically hope that we can—build a purely artificial world in a spaceship or on an artificial planet, one in which every object—the water, the earth, and even our bodies—would be artificially constructed and humanly made. What Sputnik represents, Arendt writes, is that we humans have finally acquired the technological means to free ourselves from our earthly home and our biological limits. We are finally free to make our world and ourselves in our image rather than to exist in God's image.

Arendt's introduction of Sputnik as the event signifying the transformation of the human condition leads her to mention the most god-like of human activities, cloning humans—"the attempt to create life in the test tube, in the desire to mix 'frozen germ plasm from people of demonstrated ability under the microscope to produce superior human beings' and 'to alter [their] size, shape and function."[15] Just as we humans can launch a rocket into space and remake our built environment, so too can we remake our genes and tailor our human selves to our desires. We can overcome and escape our earthliness, that part of ourselves that is given and beyond the mastery of human artifice. "For some time now, a great many scientific endeavors have been directed toward making life also 'artificial,' toward cutting the last tie through which even man belongs among the children of nature." We can, in other words, transcend our earthly and biological fates and remake our human environment as well as our human selves. If we succeed, we may allow ourselves to live for well over 100 years, possibly longer. All of this is, Arendt writes, driven by the "wish to escape the human condition."[16]

Sputnik and the coming ability to clone humans represent rebellions against our earthly human being, against our fated and biological existences over which we have had no control:

> *This future man, whom the scientists tell us they will produce in no more than a hundred years, seems to be possessed by a rebellion against human existence as it has been given, a free gift from nowhere (secularly speaking), which he wishes to exchange, as it were, for something he has made himself. There is no reason to doubt our abilities to accomplish such an exchange, just as there is no reason to doubt our present ability to destroy all organic life on earth.*[17]

The reason Arendt calls Sputnik the "event, second in importance to no other" is that the satellite is a worldly step toward the age-old human wish to rebel against our biological, given, and earthly existence.[18] If we can escape the earth, if we can build an artificial planet or space station where we would live in a fully artificial environment, if we can manufacture designer human beings freed from the chanciness of fate, then we are, in an important sense, able to slough off the mortal coil that connects us to our earthly quintessence; we can reject the gift of life as it is given to us and remake it, neither in God's image nor as accidents of fate, but in accord with our own human will. We can, this means, play God. And in doing so, we risk losing one part of our human condition, our earthliness, our being subject to chance, fate, and fortune.

The danger Arendt glimpses in Sputnik's launch is that it makes manifest how in matters of the human condition everything is possible. That "everything is possible" links Arendt's analysis of the human condition to her earlier exploration of total domination. Arendt's motto for the rise of totalitarian governments is David Rousset's observation that "'normal people' refuse to believe . . . that everything is possible."[19] If nihilism names the moral conviction that "everything is permitted," totalitarian government actualizes nihilism by doing in reality what was previously only thinkable, thus showing that the most horrific acts are possible.

Similarly, Sputnik shows to us in a palpable way that we can do what previously was only thinkable; since Sophocles, the thinkable desire to overcome our humanity was always thought within the confines of a confidence that such a desire was unrealizable. One key transformation manifest in the modern age is that we for the first time now can in actuality overcome our earthly humanity, that part of our human being that is beyond human control. If man can flee earth, what stands in the way of actualizing the even more forceful drive to fully master all elements of the earth, including humans themselves.

III.

There is a futurist element in Arendt's reading of the Sputnik launch, one that is surprisingly connected to prophecies of the coming singularity by contemporary futurists like Ray Kurzweil. Kurzweil has popularized the idea of the "Singularity" in his book *The Singularity is Near: When Humans Transcend Biology*. For Kurzweil, the singularity refers to the fact that technological progress will make it so "that human life will be irreversibly transformed."[20] More specifically, Kurzweil argues:

> *The singularity will represent the culmination of the merger of our biological thinking and existence with our technology, resulting in a world that is still human but that transcends our biological roots.*

There will be no distinction, post-singularity, between human and machine nor between physical and virtual reality.[21]

According to Kurzweil, in the coming era of machine-human civilization, we humans will be machine-like and machines will become humans to such an extent that we would not be able to tell the difference. Much of this is happening already. Cochlear implants allow deaf people to hear and brain implants stimulate cognitive abilities. In laboratories, scientists are technologically enhancing blood cells to transfer oxygen so efficiently that we could all run multiple marathons without strain. Implants and nanobots will "augment our hundred trillion very slow interneuronal connections with high-speed virtual connections via nanorobot communication. This will provide us with the opportunity to greatly boost our pattern-recognition abilities, memories, and overall thinking capacity, as well as to directly interface with powerful forms of nonbiological intelligence."[22] Finally, nanobots will repair our internal organs and we will be able to grow new artificial and technologically enhanced organs, opening the possibility of eternal life. In short, Kurzweil imagines that humans will become super-intelligent and immortal machine-human cyborgs.

What is more, Kurzweil believes our mastery will reach not only our bodies and minds, but also the world in which we live. He argues that we will re-engineer matter so that water molecules will include nano-technology that purifies water; smart tables will be able to be folded, unfolded, and re-molded at the blink of an eye; the ozone layer will be artificially enhanced; excess carbon dioxide will be re-engineered; and plants and animals will be technologically enhanced to be subservient to our needs. "Nanotechnology will bring a similar ability to morph the physical world to our needs."[23] With such abilities to bend nature to our will, we will be able to solve problems like global warming, food production, or unsanitary water simply by developing smart air and smart water. Thus, Kurzweil concludes:

It would appear that intelligence is more powerful than physics . . . . Once matter evolves into smart matter (matter fully saturated with intelligent processes), it can manipulate other matter and energy to do its bidding (through fully suitably powerful engineering) . . . . Such a civilization will then overcome gravity and other cosmological forces, and engineer a universe it wants.[24]

As our bodies and our environment are infused with intelligent technologies, we will gain unimaginable powers over the world in which we live. We would in a sense be able to make the world that we want.

What Kurzweil prophesies goes beyond the old idea of the Turing test. The Turing test holds that if a computer hidden behind a wall can interact with a person such that the person does not know if he or she is speaking with a computer or a person, the computer exhibits intelligence. But the

Singularity goes further. It holds that we humans will interact with intelligent machines and, even as we know they are machines, we will consider them intelligent and even human. What is more, we humans will increasingly insert technological enhancements into our bodies and brains. As machines become more human and humans become more machine-like, new hybrid machine-human species will emerge.

For Kurzweil, such a world of intelligent cyborgs would still be a human world. Even as humans transcend their biological limits and attain levels of intelligence and endurance that are superhuman, we would remain profoundly human, writes Kurzweil, in at least one essential sense. "If you wonder what will remain unequivocally human in such a world, it's simply this quality: ours is the species that inherently seeks to extend its physical and mental reach beyond current limitations."[25]

In fact, Kurzweil argues that "these future machines . . . will be more humanlike than humans today."[26] What he means, in part, is that they will be more intelligent than biologically limited humans and thus more human, insofar as humanity is defined by its intelligence. As hybrid super-intelligent beings emerge, they will remain human even as "our understanding of the term ['human'] will move beyond its biological origins."[27] Beyond intelligence, however, Kurzweil also means that the humanity of machine-human hybrids will also be found in their ability to transcend themselves, to overcome their limitations.

IV.

Arendt's discussion of automation in *The Human Condition* is one way of asking Kurzweil's question: what will it mean to be human in the scientific age and the age of intelligent machines? After the launch of Sputnik, Arendt names automation as a second and "no less threatening event" to the human condition; if Sputnik marks the loss of our human earthliness and the rise of earth and world-alienation, automation threatens to free mankind from labor, one of the core faculties of the human condition. Just as the dream to free ourselves from the earth is old, so too is the dream of being free from labor as ancient as the toil of labor itself. For millennia, humans have employed both machines as well as workers and slaves to lighten their laboring. For most of human history, however, the freedom from labor was compensated by the freedom to more vigorously pursue the other human capacities of work and action. But automation threatens to free man not only from labor, but from the human condition itself.

The newly possible fulfillment of this ancient wish to escape labor through automation carries a bitter pill. The liberation from labor comes, Arendt writes, at a time when we have become a laboring society, when we "no longer know of those higher and more meaningful activities for the sake of which this freedom [from laboring] would deserve to be won."[28] Ours is an egalitarian society, so we are embarrassed if we are free from labor when others are not. Even the wealthy and the powerful, presidents as well as kings, hedge fund managers and celebrities, all "think of their offices in terms of a job necessary for the life of society."[29] To be free from labor in such a society is not to be free to contemplate the truth or commune with one's gods or engage in great acts; to be free from labor is to be bored, useless, and superfluous. In other words, the freedom promised by automation is to be left rudderless, lost, and confused about what to do with one's time. Liberation from labor means to be confronted with "the prospect of a society of laborers without labor, that is, without the only activity left to them. Surely nothing could be worse."[30] To the question, what will human beings do in a world of intelligent machines that can work for us, Arendt worries that that the answer is depressingly little.

Arendt addresses the question of labor-saving machines and robots in §16 of *The Human Condition*, "The Instruments of Work and the Division of Labor." She argues that "the burden of biological life"—that biological life is a futile effort to escape the needs of the body—can only be eased by the employment of servants and slaves.[31] Ancient societies were slave societies because only through slavery could citizens lighten their burden and free themselves for public life. In doing so, however, the citizens lost their direct connection with their bodies and their bodily existence as well as the experience of "pain and effort." Pain and effort are "the modes in which life itself . . . makes itself felt." As "the great of the earth" came to live only vicariously through their slaves, they also lost a part of their humanity: "For mortals, the 'easy life of the gods'would be a lifeless life."[32] Our earthly life is given and will disappear, from dust to dust. Such a transient life is real only in "the intensity with which life is felt."[33]

Even as those who employ slaves and servants lose out on the intensity of earthly life, they gain in their freedom to participate in a public world. Insofar as they are freed to act in public and to create works of art that enter the world, these citizens live ever more fully in the world. Our worldly existence, Arendt writes, "derives primarily from the permanence and durability of the world, which is far superior to that of mortal life."[34] There is for these nobles a tradeoff by which they sacrifice some of the "blessings of labor"—that "effort and gratification follow each other"—for the potential immortality that can attend to work and action.[35]

It is on the basis of the distinction between the intensity and pain of labor and life versus the immortality of the world that Arendt argues that it would be impossible for a non-living robot to take over fully the burden of our human living. She writes:

> *It is true that the enormous improvement in our labor tools—the*
> *mute robots with which homo faber has come to the help of the*
> *animal laborans, as distinguished from the human, speaking*
> *instruments (the instrumentum vocale, as the slaves in ancient*
> *households were called) whom the man of action had to rule and*
> *oppress when he wanted to liberate the animal laborans from its*
> *bondage—has made the twofold labor of life, the effort of its*
> *sustenance and the pain of giving birth, easier and less painful*
> *than it has ever been.*[36]

Kurzweil is right that every year the "fabulous modern development of tools and machines" frees mankind from all-kinds of labor and means that "the craftsman would no longer need human assistants."[37]

And yet, the unimaginable automation and intelligence that accompanies the scientific and technological revolutions has, Arendt insists, a limit. As powerful as technological automation may be, it cannot "mean that household slaves could be dispensed with."[38] What technological automation cannot replace are personal servants and slaves who are tasked not with the determinate task of "making things" but with the indeterminate demand to assist a citizen in the activity of living, with the "process of life." Only a living slave—or if a machine, one that "would have to be a perpetuum mobile, that is, the instrumentum vocale which is as alive and 'active'as the living organism which it serves—can truly relieve the citizen of the burden of living. Robots, at least robots understood as automatons, are not capable of "assuming the burden of life."[39] Automation itself cannot replace human beings; but if we were able to create a truly living machine—in Kurzweil's terminology an intelligent machine—such machines could eventually assume the burdens of a humanly lived life that would leave mankind without the need to labor in an age where there is nothing else for him to do.

At the end of her book, in the final section on "The Victory of The Animal Laborans," Arendt confronts the full implication of the conjunction of automation and our laboring society where we so value human life as an *animal laborans* as to devalue what it means to be human. After Christianity had elevated the concern with life over the ancient concern with a political world, Cartesian doubt "deprived individual life of its immortality, or at least of the certainty of immortality."[40] Having lost faith in Christian eternity, modern man was not thrown back into a common world; instead, he is "thrown back upon himself and not upon this world." The world, known through the unreliable senses, was itself in doubt. It might not even be real. The only thing that modern man could see as lasting, meaningful, and real was humanity itself, the life of the species, "the possibly everlasting life process of the species mankind."[41] Marx's socialism and the rise of human rights both are founded upon a double reversal, first the Christian elevation of individual human life over the meaningful political world, and second the scientific doubt concerning the meaning and immortality of human life, which leads to the turn from a suddenly questionable individualism to sociologically determinable socialism.

In a world dominated by the life of the species, the elimination of the need to labor through automation and intelligent machines does not free man to higher pursuits; it brings him instead face to face with his meaninglessness, his existence as one part of an automatically functioning species. All that is demanded of us humans is:

> . . . sheer automatic functioning, as though individual life had actually been submerged in the over-all life process of the species and the only active decision still required of the individual were to let go, so to speak, to abandon his individuality, the still individually sensed pain and trouble of living, and acquiesce in a dazed, 'tranquilized,' functional type of behavior.[42]

Against Kurzweil's celebration of man freed by technology to his true humanity as someone who can create the world and even himself in his own image, Arendt insists there is more to humanity than the technologically enhanced power to actualize our will. Her discussions of labor, work, and action explicate three fundamental faculties of the human condition that she argues would be lost in the transition to a technological humanity divorced from this earth.

Arendt knows well that it is likely Kurzweil's vision of human overcoming might prove more seductive than the traditional ideas of a laboring, working, and acting humanity tragically split between its earthly and its divine capacities. It is very possible, she writes, that humans will exchange their biological and earthly existence for a new human existence, one that we can design and make ourselves. The only question, she believes, is whether we humans want to make such a choice:

> The question is only whether we wish to use our new scientific and technical knowledge in this direction, and this question cannot be decided by scientific means; it is a political question of the first order and therefore can hardly be left to the decision of professional scientists or professional politicians.[43]

If we are to choose our fate, we should choose wisely. Arendt insists that she does not take a position in the argument and does not offer answers to the question of whether we should shed our earthly and biological humanity. "To these preoccupations and perplexities, this book does not offer an answer."[44] Instead, she claims, *The Human Condition* is written for a simple purpose:

> *to reconsider the human condition from the vantage point of our newest experiences and our most recent fears. This, obviously, is a matter of thought, and thoughtlessness—the heedless recklessness or hopeless confusion or complacent repetition of 'truths' which have become trivial and empty—seems to me among the outstanding characteristics of our time. What I propose, therefore, is very simple: it is nothing more than to think what we are doing.*[45]

"What we are doing," Arendt adds, is the "central theme of this book."[46] And what we are doing is what is happening in the modern age, the age of science. Arendt's historical analysis of the modern age is designed to think what we are doing. And Arendt's name for what we are doing is earth and world alienation. To understand what forces are driving us thoughtlessly toward the abandonment of our earthly human condition, we need to understand Arendt's argument about the rise in earth and world alienation that has its roots in modern science.

V.

If Sputnik and automation are the twentieth-century events that threaten the human condition and augur the modern world, the great event that most fully reveals the modern age is the invention of the telescope by Galileo. The telescope allowed Galileo, in his own words, to "deliver the secrets of the universe" to the human mind "with the certainty of sense-perception."[47] In the ancient philosophical battle between the idealists and the empiricists, Galileo is thought to have given the victory to the empiricists. Against those who might argue for the truth of an idea over reality, Galileo claimed to show that empirical study aided by technological innovation could establish a real truth.

The truth about truth, however, is not so simple. What Galileo saw in his telescope was not a simple confirmation of empiricism. Recall that before Galileo people thought that the moon was perfect and flat. Galileo looked at the moon and saw dark spots. He noticed that the dark spots were turned towards the sun and he thought: "There must be mountains on the moon."[48] But he never saw the mountains, just dark and light patches. From these shadows, Galileo concluded that there were mountains on the moon that were four miles high. Which turns out to be pretty accurate—the highest one today is thought to be three miles high. And Galileo did all this without seeing a single mountain.

How did he know that there were mountains on the moon and why is his conclusion that there were mountains so important? Arendt cites Galileo as saying: "Any one can know with the certainty of sense-perception that the moon is by no means endowed with a smooth and polished surface."[49] When Galileo writes, "with the certainty of sense-perception" he offers a double paradox. First, the brilliance of Galileo's conclusion is based on his calculation, not his sense-perception; he did not "see" the mountains on the moon through his telescope. What he saw were shadows and he deduced they were made by mountains. Second, his conclusion refutes the common sense that the moon is smooth, a conclusion itself based on sense perception. For thousands of years by means of our senses we thought the moon was flat; now we learn that our senses lie to us. Galileo does not prove the certainty of sense perception. On the contrary, he proves to us that human senses are fallible.

The epochal importance of Galileo's invention of the telescope—what makes it the great inaugural event of the modern age—is that it teaches us to doubt our senses and thus to doubt the common reality of the shared world. The telescope, Arendt writes, represents a "challenge to the adequacy of the senses to reveal reality."[50] Galileo's telescope, she writes, actually brings about a "rape" on the senses.[51] The telescope made manifest to humans that our senses continually betray us, that they are unreliable. The telescope, as a tool and an event, brought to light a basic truth of science: That science, the search for reasons and causes beyond the senses, emerges not as a confirmation of our empirical senses, but as the corollary of our lost faith in our human and bodily senses and thus in the world itself.

The essential drive of the scientific worldview proceeds from the axiom that everything that is has a reason, *nihil est sine ratione*.[52] But if everything that is has a reason, then nothing exists without a reason given for it, which means that existence depends upon our giving reasons. The tree does not exist unless we rationalize it, set it within a humanly understood world. Even laws, for Leibniz and subsequent legal thinkers, only exist and operate insofar as they are meaningful and have a rational purpose. In the age of scientific reason, all things—from a tree falling in the forest to justice—come to be knowable only by the human mind. As Arendt writes, science brings about the "dissolution of objective reality into the subjective states of mind or, rather, into subjective mental processes."[53] Science is both a cause and an effect of our transformed understanding of the modern world, one in which the once-external and once-objective world is increasingly internalized.

It is because modern science replaces an objective world with the demand for subjective certainty that Cartesian doubt is the paradigmatic approach to the modern age. "The immediate philosophic reaction to this reality was not exultation but the Cartesian doubt by which modern philosophy—that 'school of suspicion,' as Nietzsche once called it—was founded."[54] The telescope and the scientific worldview it made manifest showed that man had for millennia "been deceived for so long as he trusted that reality and truth would reveal themselves to his senses and to his reason if only he remained true to what he saw with the eyes of body and mind."[55] Now that the telescope and the rise of the scientific world led to the separation of truth from appearance, man learned to doubt the world as it appears. It is, Arendt concludes, "the basic assumption of all modern science [that] there is nothing left to be taken on faith; everything must be doubted."[56]

Science is popularly thought to bring about certainty, to confirm a true or objective reality. But Arendt understands it to achieve the opposite. Science actually treats objects as those things that stand against us and are perceived by the human senses. Thus objects (*ob-jectum* in Latin, meaning literally what is "thrown against" a perceiving subject) only exist for subjects (*sub-jectum* in Latin, meaning the perceiving entities who are "thrown under" the objects that stand against them). This relationship is heard in the German word for object, *Gegenstand*, that which stands against the subject. As Martin Heidegger so profoundly understood, the objectivization of the world by science is actually a subjectivization of the world. Once the world exists only through and for humans, it comes to be disposable and useful for man. This is the source of what Heidegger calls the age of Technik, where objects lose their standing-for-themselves and come to stand in the world only in their usefulness and disposability for human purposes.[57]

Arendt argues that science, by teaching us to doubt our senses, leads us increasingly to understand the world as a humanly and artificially made world. The tree seen with one's eyes is "no longer the tree given in sight and touch, an entity in itself with an unalterable shape of its own." Instead, the seen tree is transformed in the age of science into an "object of consciousness on the same level with a merely remembered or entirely imaginary thing, it becomes part and parcel of this process itself."[58] To understand the tree, we turn to experiments and instruments. We cut, pulverize, and examine the tree under microscopes; we chemically alter the tree to pull its secrets from it; and we destroy the tree to know it. But in all these scientific efforts to know the tree, Arendt writes, we don't encounter the tree so much as our inquiring selves: "Instead of objective qualities, in other words, we find instruments, and instead of the nature of the universe—in the words of Heisenberg—man encounters only himself."[59]

The subjectification of the world means, Arendt continues, that "both despair and triumph are inherent in the same event," namely Galileo's discovery of the telescope and the rise of modern science. On the one hand, modern science brings despair insofar as we can never know the world around us through our senses. It makes actual the "ancient fear that our senses, our very organs for the reception of reality, might betray us."[60]

On the other hand, however, modern science also inaugurates and makes possible the achievement of our "most presumptuous hope," that we might come to occupy the Archimedean point outside of the physical world, the point from which man could gain leverage on the entirety of human existence.[61] By internalizing the world through science, we transform the world from a physical and objective world into a rational world, something that we can understand, master, and control. The scientific world view, Arendt argues, considers all events and all objects

> *to be subject to a universally valid law in the fullest sense of the word, which means, among other things, valid beyond the reach of human sense experience (even of the sense experiences made with the help of the finest instruments), valid beyond the reach of human memory and the appearance of mankind on earth, valid even beyond the coming into existence of organic life and the earth herself.*[62]

By virtue of the scientific world view, we elevate ourselves into non-earthly and rational creatures who can view and understand the world from a universal perspective. Arendt names this universal perspective of modern science the Archimedean point, "the point outside the earth from which to unhinge the world."[63] To think scientifically and universally is to think from a point not only distant from the earth, but also from a perspective in which one can look down upon the earth as something to know, to understand, and to control.

Standing on the Archimedean point of the universal scientists, we no longer are bound to our senses, our bodies, and the earth. "It means that we no longer feel bound even to the sun."[64] Instead, "we move freely in the universe, choosing our point of reference wherever it may be convenient for a specific purpose."[65] And this means, Arendt concludes, that we "have established ourselves as 'universal' beings, creatures who are terrestrial not by nature and essence but only on the condition of being alive, and who therefore by virtue of reasoning can overcome this condition not in mere speculation but in actual fact."[66] In the modern world, we internalize a universal perspective through which we are increasingly alienated from our fated earthliness and our human worldliness.

Human being in the scientific age is divorced from earthliness, the very earthliness that Arendt, in her Prologue, announces as the quintessence of the human condition. This "earth alienation," she writes, is of much more significance for understanding the modern age than "world alienation."[67] If "world alienation determined the course and the development of modern society, earth alienation became and has remained the hallmark of modern science."[68]

The overwhelming importance of earth alienation in Arendt's account of the modern age follows from the way it transforms the human world into an abstract, universal, and objectless science. Above all, earth alienation underlies the "most important instrument" of modern science, algebra. In contradistinction to the Greeks for whom mathematics was defined by the spatial science of geometry, Leibniz and the modern scientists turned from geometry to algebra and thus "succeeded in freeing itself from the shackles of spatiality."[69] As I've written previously:

> *Precisely because of its supersensibility, mathematics was not fundamental to the metaphysics of ancient and scholastic philosophers. Aristotle, for example, follows Plato in explicitly separating mathematics from the real world. For Aristotle, mathematics is separate and abstracted (choristos) from the world; it exists in no place (atopos), and the mathematical has no influence on actual things . . . . The grand insight of 17th-century natural scientists was not simply to rediscover Euclid and the certain method of the ancient mathematical reasoning; rather, it was to extend the mathematical method from logical and rational beings to actual beings in the world. The natural scientific conception of nature as a rational system—not geometry—is the foundation of Leibniz's philosophic jurisprudence.*[70]

Modern science elevates algebra over geometry and becomes what Arendt calls the "leading science of the modern age" because it "disclosed the modern ideal of reducing terrestrial sense data and movements to mathematical symbols."[71] By subjecting the spatial, physical, and earthly world to mental symbols of disembodied rationality, the scientists free themselves from the earth and operate on a universal basis, freed from the physical confines of the earth.

This means that mathematics, understood as geometry, is no longer the beginning of philosophy, as Plato thought; now, mathematics conceived algebraically is for Leibniz and the modern scientists the beginning of the "science of the structure of the human mind."[72] And since the human mind is the subjective ground of the objective world, algebraic "mathematics succeeded in reducing and translating all that man is not into patterns which are identical with human, mental structures."[73] All objects and beings in the world can only exist, according to the modern scientific world view, "in so far as they could be reduced to a mathematical order"; what science does through its algebraic foundation is to reduce the sense data of the objective and empirical world to the "measure of the human mind."[74]

Seen from the heights of the universal standpoint, the multitude of objects and events in the world are reduced to data. "Under this condition of remoteness, every assemblage of things is transformed into a mere multitude, and every multitude, no matter how disordered, incoherent, and confused, will fall into certain patterns and configurations possessing the same validity and no more significance than the mathematical curve, which as Leibniz once remarked, can always be found between points thrown at random on a piece of paper."[75] In other words, the "modern reductio scientiae ad mathematicam has overruled the testimony of nature as witnessed at close range by human senses in the same way that Leibniz overruled the knowledge of the haphazard origin and chaotic nature of the dot-covered piece of paper."[76]

VI.

The danger of earth alienation is that we humans begin to look at ourselves the way that scientists look at rats. At the end of *The Human Condition*, Arendt writes:

> It at once becomes manifest that all [man's] activities, watched from a sufficiently removed vantage point in the universe, would appear not as activities of any kind but as processes, so that, as a scientist recently put it, modern motorization would appear like a process of biological mutation in which human bodies gradually begin to be covered by shells of steel.[77]

This is a thought experiment Arendt expands upon in her essay "The Conquest of Space and the Stature of Man," where she writes:

> Seen from a sufficient distance, the cars in which we travel and which we know we built ourselves will look as though they were, as Heisenberg once put it, "as inescapable a part of ourselves as the snail's shell is to its occupant." All our pride in what we can do will disappear into some kind of mutation of the human race; the whole of technology, seen from this point, in fact no longer appears "as the result of a conscious human effort to extend man's material powers, but rather as a large-scale biological process."[78]

To view the earth, the world, and even ourselves from the distance of this universal perspective is to see earth and earthly beings such as ourselves as simply rule-bound creatures following statistical laws. Just as scientists can look at the atom "where apparently every particle is 'free' to behave as it wants and the laws ruling these movements are the same statistical laws which, according to the social scientists, rule human behavior and make the multitude behave as it must, no matter how 'free' the individual particle may appear to be in its choices," so too can the social scientist look upon man.[79] The justification of social science and the laws of statistics, writes Arendt, is that "deeds and events are rare occurrences in everyday life and in history."[80] Even what may seem like a rare and unexpected deed can, when viewed from far enough removed, be fit into a pattern and subordinated to laws.

> [T]he reason, in other words, why the behavior of the infinitely small particle is not only similar in pattern to the planetary system

as it appears to us but resembles the life and behavior patterns in human society is, of course, that we look and live in this society as though we were far removed from our own human existence.[81]

In such a scientific world the dominant perspective is anti-human. It is to see the entirety of human existence from the scientist's universal perspective.

In the modern world built on the foundation of the modern age, thought becomes reckoning, a "function of the brain" that can be accomplished better by artificially intelligent machines than by human beings.[82] Action is reduced to rule-bound behavior, "a more complicated but not more mysterious function of the life process."[83] Work is reduced to labor. And labor, the art of keeping ourselves alive, "demands of its members a sheer automatic functioning, as though life had actually been submerged in the over-all life process of the species."[84] For Arendt, mankind in the thrall of the universalist perspective "may be willing and, indeed, is on the point of developing into that animal species from which, since Darwin, he imagines he has come."[85] This is the true threat to the human condition, the sacrifice of those fundamental and permanent conditions that for millennia have defined humanity.

The fundamental human capacities of labor, work, and action are not lost; they remain human capacities. But these capacities are increasingly possible only for the very few, the artists and the scientists whose actions "escape more and more the range of ordinary human experience."[86] It is only the scientists who can introduce truly new and revolutionary processes into the world. But such processes are, once introduced, unstoppable and have the capacity to irrevocably alter and even destroy the earth and the human world.

What *The Human Condition* explores is much more than the basic conditions of human existence as it has emerged over thousands of years. The bite of the book is to show how the rise of a scientific worldview threatens to fundamentally alter the earthly and worldly conditions in which human being has lived. And since humans are conditioned beings, the change from living as split beings—earthly in our subjection to fate and worldly in our human capacity to create our own humanly built world—to living uniformly in a fully artificial and alienated world threatens to transform humanity itself. The transformation Arendt describes as the threat of the forces of science and automation is the loss of our earthly human plurality to the technological singularity. Unless, in thinking what we are doing, we choose to act to hold on to our humanity.

The original version of this essay first appeared in *Philosophy Today* in 2018.

Endnotes

1 Hannah Arendt, *The Human Condition*, Second ed. (Chicago: University of Chicago Press, 1998), 6.

2 Id. 5.

3 Id. 2.

4 Id.

5 Id. 183.

6 Id. 183.

7 Id. 19.

8 Id. Citing Heraclitus, Fragment B29, which in Hermann Diels *Die Fragmente der Vorsokratiker* (Berlin: Weidmannsche Büchhandlung, 1912) is given in German as: "*Eine gibt es, was die Besten allem anderen vorziehen: den Ruhm den ewigen den vergänglichen Dingen. Die Meisten freilich liegen da vollgefressen wie das liebe Vieh.*"

9 Sophocles, *Antigone*, in *The Theban Plays of Sophokles*, ed. and trans. by Philippe Nonet (United States: Amazon, 2017) 36 v332. I have modified Nonet's translation only by adding the English translation of *deinon*.

10 Id. v360.

11 Id. 38 v370.

12 Aristotle, *Politics*, 1253a.

13 Michel Foucault, *The Order of Things* (New York: Vintage Books, 1973), 322.

14 Arendt, *The Human Condition*, 2.

15 Id. 2.

16 Id.

17 Id. 2-3.

18 Id. 1.

19 See Hannah Arendt, *The Origins of Totalitarianism* (New York: Harcourt, 1973) 438-41.

20 Ray Kurzweil, *The Singularity is Near* (New York: Viking USA, 2005), 7.

21 Id.

22 Id. 316.

23 Id. 397.

24 Id, 364.

25 Id. 9.

26 Id. 378.

27 Id. 30.

28 Arendt, *The Human Condition*, 5.

29 Id.

30 Id.

31 Id. 119.

32 Id. 120.

33 Id.

34 Id.

35 Id. 107.
36 Id. 121.
37 Id. 122.
38 Id.
39 Id.
40 Id. 320.
41 Id. 321.
42 Id. 322.
43 Id. 3.
44 Id. 5.
45 Id.
46 Id.
47 Id. 260.
48 See Galileo, "The Starry Messenger," in *Discoveries and Opinions of Galileo* (New York: Anchor, 1957), 38 ff.
49 Arendt, *The Human Condition,* 260. Arendt is citing Galileo quoted from Koyré.
50 Id. 261.
51 Id. 274.
52 This is the thesis of my book, *The Gift of Science: Leibniz and the Modern Legal Tradition* (Cambridge, MA: Harvard University Press, 2005).
53 Arendt, *The Human Condition,* 282.
54 Id. 260-61.
55 Id. 274.
56 Id. 275.
57 Martin Heidegger, "Die Frage nach der Technik," in *Die Technik und die Kehre* (Stuttgart: Verlag Günther Neske, 1996).
58 Arendt, *The Human Condition*, 282.
59 Id. 261.
60 Id. 262.
61 Id.
62 Id. 263.
63 Id. 262.
64 Id. 263.
65 Id.
66 Id.
67 Id. 264.
68 Id.
69 Id. 264-65. Arendt is citing E.A.Burtt, *Metaphysical Foundations of Modern Science*, 44.
70 Berkowitz, *The Gift of Science*, 18.
71 Arendt, *The Human Condition*, 265
72 Id. 266.
73 Id,

74 Id. 267.

75 Id.

76 Id.

77 Id. 322-23.

78 Hannah Arendt, *Between Past and Future* (New York: Penguin Books, 2006), 274.

79 Arendt, *The Human Condition*, 323.

80 Id. 42.

81 Id. 323.

82 Id. 322.

83 Id.

84 Id.

85 Id.

86 Id. 323.

Martin Heidegger and Günther Anders on Technology: On Ray Kurzweil, Fritz Lang, and Transhumanism

Babette Babich

01110100 01101000 01100101 00100000 01110000 01100101 01110010 01101001 01101100 01110011 00100000 01101111 01100110 00100000 01101001 01110110 01110110 01100101 01110110 01110110 01100100 01101001 01101111 01101110

All mere chasing after the future so as to work out a picture of it through calculation in order to extend what is present and half thought into what, now veiled, is yet to come, itself still moves within the prevailing attitude belonging to technological calculating representation.
—Martin Heidegger, *The Turning*

When I first heard Ray Kurzweil speak on the technological singularity at Bard College at a conference Roger Berkowitz organized there, I was immediately put in mind of an old science cartoon (which I just as immediately popped into my PowerPoint for my own talk). The cartoon may be the most famous of Stanley Harris' many science cartoons, and it stars two scientists, an old one and a vaguely younger one who has written a row of numbers and figures across a blackboard, with the phrase THEN A MIRACLE OCCURS, followed by more equations. The older guy has the punch line (today the older one would never be a know-it-all, you need a ten-year-old for that, thus speaketh Hollywood): "I think you should be more explicit here in step two."

I used the cartoon in place of a commentary on Kurzweil's "Technological Singularity,"[1] just to counter his sales pitch. I thought it needed some recognition—given

"I THINK YOU SHOULD BE MORE EXPLICIT HERE IN STEP TWO."

Fig 1. © Stanley Harris. With the permission of Stanley Harris.

all the debate—given Kurzweil's cavalier, blissful, even gleeful underestimation of the scientific, technological problems involved with his "fantastic voyage"[2] vision of the 'Singularity' as he and his investors and his consumer base expects it to arrive any day now.[3] Of course, this is the same sales pitch for "basic" science, as Vannevar Bush pioneered this pitch to ensure continued federal support for the war project that was the Manhattan Project in 1945, that is, after its work was putatively done and in which Bush outlines little other than some of the machines that made Kurzweil famous and Steve Jobs a household name and latterly, a technological saint. But it has also been debunked for some time, as Ivan Illich argued regarding medicine's claims to have extended life expectancy (and to have contributed to the battle against epidemics) in his 1974 *Medical Nemesis*, an argument made with reference to nothing but the facts, that would be the history of disease, epidemiology, which argument Richard Lewontin would reprise in the pages of the *New York Review of Books* in response to the then-hype of the Genome Project (in the decade since, we have moved on to other hopes) and his book *Biology as Ideology*.

My rhetorical point was an "easy" one, with ironic emphasis on the ease with which we forget the same point once it is made, and I emphasized both the triviality (glasses, contact lenses) and the inherent complexity of "becoming" cyborg, posthuman, a human-machine hybrid when one gets much beyond the technology for contact lenses, given the difficulties of making an actually functional hi-tech artificial limb.[4] The reason this point is easy is because it is true; the reason this point is easy to forget is because it is not a problem by definition for most theorists of the transhuman, posthuman. One starts by simply defining what we are now, what we have now as cyborg, posthuman, transhuman being. In this the lessons of postmodernism appear to have been learned. The opponents of the postmodern reacted to the post attached to the modern.

If the modern was the mode, the latest thing, then the postmodern could only come after that, in retrospect but then it would be, by then, already modern. The referent, if it was meant to be a referent to the current era seemed to make no sense. And indeed the only sphere in which the postmodern enjoyed a more or less calm application (that is without commentators foaming at the mouth about the very idea of the word as such or per se) was in art or architecture where "modern" refers to a very definite style. But posthumanism no longer means any such thing. The posthuman, which we also call the transhuman and some sociological entrepreneurs have revised in the fashion of product updates (here I refer to Steve Fuller's *Humanity 2.0*) takes over the point initially intended by the original postmodernists and appends it to the human, however vaguely defined. Technologically stipulated in this way and with a clear reference to the marketing strategies of technological products at all levels, the so-called transhuman is thus the human on the way to the 'more than human,' the posthuman, where the assumption is that the means to achieve post- or transhumanity are at hand (this would be a college level course on Enhancements 101, perhaps already on offer at the Singularity University) and rightly confident that the market for the product is already there.

In this way, Nick Bostrom is able to make a plea for (after adding appropriate ethical cautions) and to define transhumanism as renaissance humanism, now 'enhanced' by the resources of today's science and technology in very Oxford crafted terms (where what counts is less the academic claim to fame than the industry-oriented and business outreach that characterizes UK academe, hence Bostrom's own text outlines less an academic's reflective caution, though it must be said that he is theoretically quite precise, than a ready to be submitted for a business proposal) as the intellectual and cultural movement that affirms the possibility and desirability of fundamentally improving the human condition through applied reason, especially by using technology to eliminate aging and greatly enhance human intellectual, physical, and psychological capacities.[5]

For Bostrom the ideal of transhumanism can be aggressively marketed as a humanism, and to this end he cites Julian Huxley's traditional (1927) terminology:

> *The human species can, if it wishes, transcend itself — not just sporadically, an individual here in one way, an individual there in another way — but in its entirety, as humanity. We need a name for this new belief. Perhaps transhumanism will serve: man remaining man, but transcending himself, by realizing new possibilities of and for his human nature.*[6]

For Bostrom as for Kurzweil and others in the transhumanist movement, what is most important is to embrace the ideal of the transhuman and at the same time to distinguish it from some of the pitfalls associated with the eugenics of the past, particularly that associated with the very pro-technology and equally pro-transhuman ideology of national socialism. The ambitions of transhumanism are thus all about persuading society of the value of such technology and thus the value of the research that might make it possible and the market for the same.

But, and this the point I meant to make by adding Harris' cartoon of science and the need to sweat minor details, beyond the ethical problems the transhumanist movement perceives as its greatest obstacle, there are ordinary, ontic problems. Unlike marketing strategies, or a pitch, ordinary things in ordinary contexts turn out not to be simple; rather, they are, as Nietzsche liked to emphasize, *unsagbar complicirt*, unspeakably complicated. On the human level, the biochemical and medical theorist Erwin Chargaff would dedicate a lifetime of his popular (as opposed to his scientific) writings to arguing for the need to persuade people to think about this same complexity.

It ought to, but does not go without saying that considerations of this complexity apply to the "end-aging!" brigade, particularly the mechanical motif I name call the roto-rooter phantasm animating the theories of those who suggest that we (simply) send nanobots sailing into cells to clean up metabolic debris, make repairs, work magic or what amounts to the techno-scientific same.[7] The objection has something in part to do with the difficulty of nanotech and its challenges but still more to do (and that is why I recommend reading Chargaff) with the still-as-yet incompletely understood life of the cell, that would be: the cell *as such*, including the balance of the same in terms of the organism as a whole[8]—and without even considering the question of side-effects (empirically speaking, inevitably, these can be discovered only in the wake of the deployment of any new technology).

At the Bard conference the guiding question set to the participants in my section asked if machines would "ever" realize their potential as the masters of humanity. The presupposition was that machines have such a potential. As we know, machines, so the question frames its own reply, have already begun to realize their "potential" as the masters of the human race, adding qualifiers to taste: "not as much" as some fear, "not in the fashion" once anticipated by enthusiasts of the so-called future, and so on. So specified, it may be argued that machines have claimed hegemony over human beings, both physically and ideologically but rather than triumphant accession the ascendancy turns out to be more rather than less of a let down.

At the same time, and this is the value of a leading question, one can just as well refuse the claim, replying that machines have made no such incursions, using the same points and the many of the same authors to do so. But, like question and answer, refusals also incorporate, repeating what is opposed as Martin Heidegger, here following Nietzsche, reminds us. Heidegger who spent his life reflecting on this question via the notion of humanism also suggested that on the one hand the threat of technology is precisely in the realization of its potential mastery. On the other hand, the ultimate threat posed by technology resides in our desire to 'master' that mastery.

Machines "project" as the phenomenologists say or as the techno-theorists put it, they "extend" human senses or capacities or consciousness. Using this same phenomenological reading of technology, trans- and post-humanists speak of human "enhancement." But a phenomenological analysis reminds us that the augmentation in question is more attuned to the machine than it is (or can be and this is in spite of the detours that Bruno Latour and associated actor-network theorists rightly emphasize) cut to *human* measure. It is a reflection of this very attunement that, to speak as the ethnographers and sociologists who study this phenomenon, we are "machine-obedient." Nor are we as mechanically tractable or responsive as we are because we wish to be—because we love our machines, *erotically*, affectively, as Latour suggests that we do[9] or else as Donna Haraway has also argued in another way,[10] but and quite simply inasmuch as we have to be machine-obedient simply to *use* our machines in the first and last place. This is true from our autos to our computers and cell phones and cameras, indeed and even Facebook and so on. And here there is a network-actor loop (or loophole) at work: for it turns out that the greater *our* obedience, the "better" the machine obeys, as we suppose it does, our every whim.

Fig 2. Lynn Randolph's Cover Image for Donna Haraway's 1991 *Simians, Cyborgs and Women*. Reprinted with permission of the artist.

Thus when people like to quote the science fiction writer, Arthur C. Clark's musing that, assuming a sufficient level of technological advancement, technology is indistinguishable from magic, they usually forget the other half of the observation as it presupposes a lack of familiarity with that same technology on the part of the observer of the magic in question.

Indeed: you may not think about the things you need to do to log on to Facebook (and you may likely have allowed your computer to "remember" for you so that you really need never think about it, until you are, say, on the road) but just those things need to be done, exactly as they need to be done, or you cannot log in. Little magic there one might say. Same deal with a plane. You may like to think it magical to fly. But I need only remind you of what you already know well enough, think of the mind-control ministrations of the TSA in the United States and their equivalents elsewhere, complete with George Orwell-like loudspeaker-driven public announcements, or the more salient fact when it comes to the miracle of flight that you, qua passenger, are effectively in a large, relatively windowless, certainly airless bus for the greater part of the duration of your journey, and, here quite apart from the security mindset, I leave out the necessity of negotiating airports (take off and landing on either part of everything you need to forget to pretend to yourself that you have an experience that comes anywhere near that of the man of steel or Daedalus (or Icarus, but as technology and not magic was involved here, we recall that things turned out badly for him when he flew too near the sun, confronting the limits of his father's ingenious feather and wax design for his son's mechanical wings).

Indeed the claims for technological whiz-bits are always rather like playing *World of Warcraft* or having a *Second Life* avatar or just using an iPhone app. The *more* you believe in the awkwardly drawn characters (dependent upon the limitations of computer graphics and the limitations of your hardware) and the more invested you are in the (relatively awkwardly configured) 3-D representation of the world inhabited by those characters, the better your "experience" will be.

In her Bard lecture, Sherry Turkle[11] invoked psychological and ethnographic studies to remind us of the little kick we get, the reward we get for the achievement that it is to send a message and—*wait for this*—to receive a reply.

You've got mail.

And machines do indeed use little bings and chimes, just like psych labs do—and this is no accident—to signal precisely that mini-reward. And we do wait for it. This is not just an acoustic it is also a visual signal: that's why we look at the apple icon when our iPhones start up and turn off, that's why we notice Windows Vista or the Windows 7 and its little spinning wheel, etc. In the same way, and without anything so tedious as a trademark, Facebook makes addicts of its users who post in the hope of eliciting a response or for folks who seek to acquire "followers" on Twitter or more pointlessly, because derivatively, those who work to expand their Google "circles."

Martin Kusch and Harry Collins argue that it is the phenomenon of machine obedience, mechanically repeated, that explains why infantry men on the ground, at the front, i.e., the same soldiers with the best reasons in the world to flee do not in fact "run from fire" as one might anticipate. After a detailed chapter on "Machine Behaviour and Human Action," after a careful, historical analysis of military drill and its variations, Kusch and Collins interrupt themselves to ask this particular question:

But why, over the centuries, has the musketman and his equivalent not run from fire? Consider the musketman's job. He must keep his place, ignoring the screams of the wounded and terrorized, stand, load, kneel, aim, fire, stand, load, kneel, aim, fire, over and over again, amid the whine and thwack of missiles splitting the air and felling his comrades.[12]

Kusch and Collins, who by the time they get to this point in their own text had already spent more than one chapter of their book detailing several types of behaviour (and distinguishing between *polymorphic* and *mimeomorphic* as they name these types), do not answer their own question by fitting it into any of their well-crafted schemata. Much rather, so the authors argue, it turns out to be the function of military drill to engender a mechanism composed "of humans who had turned themselves into entities as mechanical as the muskets themselves."[13] Hence, psychologically speaking, the reason musketmen hold their ground, and the reason the infantry as such does not run away, turns out to be a very literal matter of their training. Drilling soldiers effectively engender effects of *habit*, habituation, a second nature or nature natured. Drones may make this very literally automatic but the mechanism as deployed in human soldiers has been perfected for centuries.

Given their different background formations in analytic history of philosophy (Kusch) and sociology of science (Collins), both authors perhaps not surprisingly seem to lack awareness of Nietzsche's relevant reflections on what he called the virtues of "mechanical activity [*machinale Thätigkeit*]", which Nietzsche also characterizes very ironically in terms of what Western culture, with all its Auschwitz-resonances names "the blessing of work." The "blessing" [*Segen*] of mechanized activity consists for Nietzsche in the numbing virtues of the fact "that a doing and nothing but a doing continuously intrudes into consciousness." This repetitive and constant pre-occupation functions to deaden awareness "because," as Nietzsche says (and let this be a word of warning to all multi-taskers out there), "the chamber of human consciousness is *small*!" (GM III: 18.)

In other words, as military psychologists well know—and as Seneca already argued in *On the Brevity of Life*—one can only (really) do one thing at a time. If the Stoic ideal is one of consummate mindfulness, the same mechanism that can be developed for the sake of higher spirituality and for meditation works at lower levels as well. If sufficiently drilled or trained, soldiers will be too pre-occupied, too identified with the mechanical process of loading ammunition and firing, quasi-machines serving real machines, too much of an appendage of their own artillery to be able to pay any real attention to the shells exploding around them.[14] Action heroes—and war movies—depend on this mechanism.

As Kusch and Collins reflect, "As one military sociologist observed: 'Ritualization is in part a defense against anxiety."[15] And as they continue the point, well-qualified in good-social-scientific terms, current training procedures emphasize the automatic-as-such even absent a competent leader, calling this "independent" operation. Thus Kusch and Collins cite the U.S. Army Training Support Center in 1991 as writing:

> *Every soldier must be trained to take initiatives and be rewarded for doing so. ...real American-style combat teams—composed of independent, confident, thinking individuals—can get the job done even when the boss is 'out to lunch'.*[16]

It is because of the inherently intentional dimensionality of consciousness that we are able to become our machines, that we can become, as a military unit does, to use a familiar and very military metaphor, like a well-oiled machine because we project ourselves into our machines: our machines, our selves.

Heidegger's Machenschaft, Fritz Lang's Metropolis, and Titanic Technology

Thus Heidegger focuses on *Machenschaft*, mechanization, a can-do-ability along with gigantization in his *Contributions to Philosophy*, including his reflections on the last god, including his fugues, all very much in the sense that Ernst Jünger would speak of *Titan-Technik*, that is to say, literally titanic technology.

Metonymically and historically speaking there is in this an association with the infamously "unsinkable" Titanic. James Cameron's film of the same name re-immortalized this already told and retold story of the ship's disastrous collision with destiny and the presumption of engineers. Here, the film is worth noting for its imagery of the technological imaginary, beginning with a positive representation of the triumphalist technological cult of the machine, complete with a high-tech flashback technique beginning with computer graphics and cutting edge bathysphere-cum-submarines. The key imagery however is the vision of classically futurist machine technology of the turn of the last century, that is the ship itself, the Titanic at the outset of the story within the film's storytelling, with all its promise still intact, showcasing the mighty batteries of the ship's steam engines, juxtaposed with the muscular and dirty and sweating workers who shovel coal in the belly of the ship at the command of the captain above and the call for "more steam!" In addition to the collector's appeal of 19th-century technology, in addition to the beauty of crafted wood well-fitted to beautifully stylized or bespoke brass dials on the captain's and first mate's console on the bridge, Cameron's *Titanic* spotlights the chiaroscuro dynamism of the machine, all Herb Ritts' coy photographic eroticism transposed to film: the fake antique of straining human muscle serving the dark machine power of fire-spitting steam engines. And this image may well be the most pornographic image in the film—rather more than Leonardo di Caprio's whimsical nude painting of the discreetly posed Kate Winslet.

With the dissonant eros of technology, that is the erotic allure of the dynamo, we have the "imaginary" of the machine in modernity, starting of course as we always start whether we are conscious of it or not with Charlie Chaplin's 1936 film, *Modern Times*, and this is so even if we have *not* seen the movie.

And however familiar it may be to Anglophone audiences, Chaplin's film for its own part is only a remake of the kind we know so well between German films and American re-interpretations, re-envisioning Fritz Lang's still more classic if certainly egregiously somber vision of modernity, *Metropolis* which premiered in 1927, the same year Heidegger published *Sein und Zeit*.

Lang's *Metropolis* is the mechanized city of the future as metaphor for the political life of modernity. And just as the polis has served as a metaphor for political reflection since Plato, this mechanical vision is the subject of the film's social commentary. Lang's titanic Moloch is thus a machine polis which demands the sacrifice of the humanity of its citizens. This is the mechanical vision of the city in its verticality, its organization: with the leaders above, with creative work and dreams and time on their hands, and the workers in the dark below, with their anomie, and their quasi-life, oppressed by spirit-shattering labor. Remarkable here is the concinnity (my favorite musical term) of Lang's political fable, featuring the Maria robot, with the consummation of the "Technological Singularity" as Kurzweil sees our destiny. As director, and by way of the well-known "magic" of the cinema, Lang accomplishes this transformation before our eyes in a perfectly Leibnizian spirit: this becomes a difference that, all-too maliciously *apparently, or seemingly* makes no difference. This seeming is perfectly fatal for Maria qua noxiously troublesome living being (rather like many women—from a male point of view), who *becomes* Maria the vastly more tractable, because programmable robot. Thus the robotic transformation doesn't just render the human redundant; it requires as the process works in *Metropolis* the death of the original.

Like Kurzweil's rapturously singularized human beings-cum-computer software programs or digital resonances, the original Maria pays for this enforced "enhancement" with her all-too-human life.

As it turns out, the erotic perfection of the robot is not so much that it comes to life but that it *improves* on life and in so many ways. Maria is beautiful, fine and good: if *only*, her head were *not* filled with ideas about the workers, if only she kept her mind on sex and poetry, and then after marrying, on caring for her husband's white shirts and catering to her children's happiness (and keeping them quietly out of earshot: children, like women, should be seen and not heard).

In this way, the graphic detail of the Bard conference icon featured the iron maiden or female Golem prototype of the Maria robot *before* her rapturous, "singularizing" perfection which transformation gives us the Maria-Robot indistinguishable from the Maria-Mensch or human being.

Lang's cinematic perfection gives us not any cheaply, ontic technological achievement (a tool that works or "is" everything it appears to be; rather, it offers a "user-friendly" "experience" that we "take" to be the technological achievement of a human machine as such—assuming, that is, that the programming of this illusion also functions and assuming in addition that we,

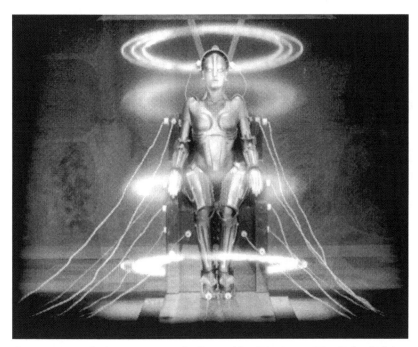

Fig. 3. *Metropolis* (1927 Germany), directed by Fritz Lang. The Robot/Brigitte Helm / Credit: UFA/Photofest copyright UFA.

the users, go along with the programming). The tractable going-along-with on the side of the user just happens to be (and this should be emphasized) the *other half* of the programming achievement. The point is, as Jaron Lanier writes in *You Are Not a Gadget*, that it matters less that machines actually are human than that we humans come to see them as human and treat them so. This works, Turing enthusiasts are advised to take note, in *both* directions.

Of course and at the same time it is relevant that Fritz Lang's Maria-Robot (Maria enhanced or perfected) turns out to be a filmic simulacrum, not the film technology of filming a robot in accord with the iconic iron maiden phantasm of the movie poster itself. Instead the mechanized robot becomes or is transformed into Maria by way of the *theatrical* transformation that I above recalled as movie magic. Like the Patty Duke cousin-twins in the American TV series of the sixties, the actress, in this case that would be Birgitte Helm, who plays Maria; the human girl is the same actress who plays the "robot" who looks like a girl because she is one in fact. We are charmed by this movie convention or suspension of belief just as we have learned to love not only Data but Seven of Nine the Borg bot, as we impolitely call her, the *Star Trek* android, who wears face-jewelry as a fetish signifier of the machine that we "know" her to be.

Thus we get the perfectly archetypal female, and here is a question I would pose to this archetypical notion, so ardently sought by cyborg theorists: would a lady who was and was not a human being (being mechanical, or to employ up-to-date terms here: being electronic or simply being a digital representation) but who otherwise fulfilled your every (male) desire, would you (could you?) *care less*?[17] Internet sex turns out to be just as fulfilling as actual sexual encounters and no awkward after consummation-moments (no discussions, no underwear to find, no Playboy magazine strategies for jettisoning the lady, no having to call or having not to call). Sex with robots would be even better. And who doubts this?

Anders on the Technological Prometheus and the Shame of Having Been Born

We have already mentioned Günther Anders who was Hannah Arendt's first husband and who was Walter Benjamin's cousin and to continue the resonance of inbred familiarity, was part of the original circle of young scholars associated with Theodor Adorno and the Frankfurt School in addition to having been a student of Husserl's and of Heidegger's. Anders made the question of technological mastery or excess along with the correspondent notion of human obsolescence the center of his life's work. Anders kept his observant powers throughout his long life, in this not unlike Kant's late-life productivity, and here we note as variously, disparately gifted human beings, that such a capacity is anything but a given. Nor did Heidegger himself quite achieve this (as Arendt tells us and as Gadamer also attests). But what is still more significant, Anders kept his powers sharply attuned to the changing technological times.

Not that this mattered in terms of his lack of influence on the academy which then as now pays attention only to "important" names (and these are usually names we already know). And notwithstanding Anders' sustained philosophical focus, even philosophers of technology such as Don Ihde and including techno-science and social theorists such as C. Fred Alford do not even mention let alone engage Anders, even Bruno Latour does not do so although Anders is more received in French technoscience than even in German or Anglophone technocience. Surprisingly, even the activist scholar Stanley Aronowitz, himself very like Anders, and whose work is indispensable for a social and political theory of technology, does not refer to Anders, just as those interested in discussing crimes against humanity similarly manage to skip any reference to Anders.

There may be good reasons for this in addition to the perennial scholarly desire to reinvent, all by oneself, whatever it is that one wishes to claim to be the first to talk about or to mention. Or perhaps this was because Anders, like Jacob Taubes, was a pain, difficult to deal with, a bit like Ivan Illich his fellow Viennese, who was however, being a priest, the kinder sort of heretic (Anders, who hailed from Breslau—where Hans-Georg Gadamer grew up, Gadamer, who was born into a German family of scientists and scholars, was born in Marburg—made Vienna his adopted home town with his second wife, Elisabeth Freundlich). If, as can be thought, Anders exemplified such an excessive character it also rendered him well-equipped to deal with similar characters for his own part.

Accordingly, Anders had little trouble dealing with Adorno, a notoriously "difficult" personality. Like Adorno too, it could be observed that Anders was a teaser whose teasing was unbearable for Americans because it pointed out how much he knew and therefore could not but come off as mockery. Unlike the kind of "critical thinking" that involves thinking just and only what status quo science tells you to think, critical theory requires considerable breadth just to be critical. And Anders knew an enormous amount about the Greeks, as he also knew about music, as he knew about art, about Hegel and Marx, about Kant, and as he also knew about Husserl and Heidegger. Like Nietzsche and like Illich, the social critic of education, medical science, and technology, Anders was also and this is perhaps the most rare of all, an authentic or real heretic, that is: the sort of critical thinker who meant what he said and who acted on it at the expense of his career—and he did this from the start—and who suffered for this in terms of his reputation (he was for a long time not even mentioned) and his livelihood. Thus, Anders did what most social critics do not do and sometimes even suppose cannot be done: throughout his life Anders walked the talk.

What is more, the views Anders opted to champion were out of kilter, unpopular. Indeed, like Ivan Illich's political views, Anders's views were *anti-popular*. Thus and instead of talking about the Holocaust as a Jew and as he might well have done (though he did this too, he did all kinds of things, including music and literary theory to boot), Anders made Americans (that would be the good guys in World War II from his perspective, and he *should* have been more grateful . . .) uncomfortable by talking as incessantly as he did about Hiroshima. And even people who insist on mentioning Hiroshima do not go on, as Anders insisted on going on to talk about Nagasaki and to count off, almost kabbalistically, the dates of Hiroshima, the bomb detonated, as it mattered to him, on August 6, 1945, where just two days later the legal rubric for defining crimes against humanity would be spelled out in Nuremberg on August 8, 1945, the next day Nagasaki, August 9, 1945.

Like Heisenberg, and like Einstein, Anders seemed to think that the problem of evil was the bomb. And like Heidegger he also insisted that the evolution of that same problem had to do with what, unlike Heidegger, he had seen from the start as the problem of humanity itself as standing reserve in Heidegger's terms, a resource that however would need, desperately need, improving.

This Anders called the shame of being born. This is the shame of a navel. For the mark of creation, as a creation at the hand of god, which is (and here Anders concurs with Sartre) the perfected dream of modernity, is that we as human beings do not merely manage to be the ones who, as Nietzsche's madman tells us, have "killed" God—"And we have killed him." (*The Gay Science* §125)—and with our own hands, so that the sacred as Nietzsche puts it, bleeds to death as we watch (but then, what about the blood, and Nietzsche goes in for excessive realism: what about the stench? Gods, too, so he tells us, decompose!).

Much more than merely murdering God—this, after all, would be a piece of cake for Anders as a Jew, a secular Jew no less—we want to take his place. But that's the kicker.

The problem for us is that we are born and not made. Above all, we are born, this is the Heideggerian point, *as* we are born, thrown *as* we are thrown and we are not designed in accord, this is the anti-Cartesian impetus, with our preferences as we might have specified them (had anyone asked).

Anders' most dissonant insight—vying with anything Levinas argues about the face as it also vies with anything Heidegger argues about death and thrownness, and with everything (and in the case of Anders this is not by accident) that Arendt writes about natality—is that the whole of our problem with modernity begins and ends with our awful *shame* at having been born (oh gosh and now we begin to remember all the Theweleit anxieties about war, about Jews and others as very patent anxieties about women). What we much rather want to be instead, and there is always an instead, is the machine. Anders articulates the modern human fantasy today, the 'dream' as he calls it, "was naturally to be like our gods, the apparatus, better said, to belong to these (mechanical) gods completely, to be to an extent co-substantial with these gods: *homologouménos zēn.*"[18] Our desire is to be the machine, or as in the current era, and to speak with Kurzweil, to become one with the digital realm.

Thus and ultimately for Anders, our desire is to be manufactured, to be fabricated, to be a product, maybe one with serial numbers, perhaps an ISBN, just so that we can market and upgrade ourselves: the point here would be interchangeable parts.[19] If something breaks: fix it; when something wears out: replace it.

Thus towards the end of his life, Anders would recollect his own collision with the spirit of the times after World War I. No kind of poetic experience "on horseback," this was a direct confrontation with changes made by medical technology coupled with modern transport. The result of these technological transformations of human life at the very limit of everydayness, here conceived as a Heideggerian everydayness, shattered that everydayness for him. Beyond anything so theoretically to the point of the ready-to-hand quotidian, more than a misplaced / broken hammer, Anders recalled the dissonance of this vision, at the age of fifteen, as he was on his way home after the first World War, spent as a too-young soldier in France.

> *On my way back, at a train station, maybe it was in Liege, I saw a line of men, who strangely seemed as if they began at the hip. These were soldiers who had been set on the platform on their stumps, leaning them against the wall. Thus they waited for the train that would take them home.*[20]

These are transhumans. No one will ever need to tell them that their canes, their wheelchairs, their prosthetic limbs, are their extended selves. This they know.

With this in mind, we quote the little hymn Anders' gives us for musically-monotone Molossians:

> *But if we ever succeed*
> *in throwing off our burden*
> *and stand as [iron] bars*
> *fitted into [iron] bars*
> *As prosthesis to prosthesis*
> *in intimate conjoining,*
> *and the flaw was what had been*
> *and shame was yet unknown—*[21]

For Anders, our shame is our genitalia.

Like Arendt and like Heidegger and Jonas (and so on), we recall that Anders had a classically German *classical* education, which included both Athens *and* Jerusalem: thus Anders speaks of *aidos*. We are, as he says "no product" but and rather than being god—think of Sartre's very Cartesian, existential articulation of this dream—we are just and merely creatures, with every "creaturely inadequacy."[22]

Finite and limited, we are *merely* human. If only we were as gods: if only we could be manufactured to precision standards at the consummate height of the technological engineering we are so sure is coming our way—just you wait.

In the future, everything will be better.

It is Anders' figural analogy, God = Product, that I find the most compelling or thought-worthy, as Heidegger would say. The product is God. Hence as Anders goes on at this point:

The attempt to prove his "thing piety," endeavoring an imitatio in-
strumentorum, one has no choice but to undertake a self-reforma-
tion: at the very least and in the smallest degree to undertake effort
to "improve" [today advertizing agencies and apologists for
transhumanism prefer to say 'enhance'] himself, rectifying the
'sabotage' suffered owing to original sin: the legacy nolens volens
of birth, now for once reduced to the smallest conceivable degree.[23]

For Anders, we want to correct the mistakes in our make-up: the errors
that cause us to become ill, to suffer, to die. An imperfect, rather than a well-
made product, as René Descartes had already pointed out as part of his
philosopher's proof of the existence of god (the Parisian theologians did not
miss a beat with this one), a proof that just also happened to be a condemnation of God's manufacturing specs: had he, Descartes, fabricated himself, he
would have done it better.

For Anders, we have already at the time of his writing in the mid-1950's
begun to undertake this same rational and Cartesian enterprise which we call
—and it is instructive for those who believe like Kurzweil in the logarith-
mically accelerating evolutionary trajectory of technoscientific engineering
and design that we use rather the same terms that Anders emphasizes in
1956, and formulated in English—*"Human Engineering"*.

As a corollary, so Anders reminds us, the human being is manifestly a
"defective design,"[24] especially when regarded from the perspective of technical devices (error tends, as we know, to be "human error" rather than a result of a deficiency in the machine, whatever the machine might be).

In this way, Anders' first chapter "Concerning Promethean Shame" in the
first volume of his *The Obsolescence of Humanity: On the Soul in the Age of
the Second Industrial Revolution* prefigures—albeit in a *darker* moda-
lity—Kurzweil's brighter enthusiasm for the "natural history," as it were, of
humanity towards an evolutionary culmination in a literally technological
rapture. Nor is the word "rapture" an overstatement: we are talking about replacement, consummation, salvation, transfiguration—and like the technical
problem attendant upon the theological (or Disneyesque) problem of the re-
surrection of the body, what *do you do* with the old iPhone when the new
one arrives? An already present and growing problem for iPhone owners all
over the world in just a few months to the soon to be 5G (ah, the devil take
the bees) singularity, some of whom already have two or three earlier phones
in a drawer somewhere.

For Anders, Descartes' musing that God had created him with deficiencies (this would be the true maker's mark, this would be *the* Promethean
shame), can rightly be kicked up a notch. Here we see that like Arendt, Anders too is Heidegger's good student, and thus he moves from Descartes to

Kant. Thus we move, as Anders argues, "into the obligatory." Or and in "other words," as Anders explains, "the moral imperative is now transferred from the human being to the gadget."[25]

What *ought to be*, what *should be* is now the tool, the device, and the gadget. We want technology, the more of it the better, and as we ourselves become our own technology, so much the better. This then is Kurzweil's dream: let there be not merely the human but high technology, and let us not forget, as we reflect on this, that Kurzweil is in the business of selling technology: let there be stuff to buy.

For his own part, Anders is merely repeating the maxim that Heidegger had already identified in his *Contributions to Philosophy* as the maxim of fascist techno-science (whatever is technically possible should be actualized as quickly as possible) which as Heidegger had anticipated and Anders could not but corroborate, applied with fairly dispassionate equal measure to Soviet and capitalist aka American science alike:

> *What can be done counts now as what ought to be done. The maxim: 'become the one you are' is today perceived as the maxim of the gadget. ... Gadgets are the gifted the 'whiz-kids' [English in original] of today.* [26]

But and for all the claims that are made on his behalf (claims Anders happily echoed for his own part) to the effect that Anders opposes Heidegger, just as he similarly opposes Adorno, Anders also takes over (as Adorno also charged) and radicalizes Heidegger's critique.

Hence Anders begins his 1956 *Die Antiquiertheit des Menschen* [The Obsolescence of Humanity] with a reflection on nothing other than the very *impossibility*, as it were, of criticizing technology, that is to say of "refusing" or distancing oneself from technology: an impossibility that found expression for Heidegger himself in his *Gelassenheit*—and a critical impossibility that has hardly been ameliorated, let us be careful to underscore this, in the interim:

> *As I articulated this thought at a cultural conference, I was met with the counterclaim, in the end one always has the freedom to turn off one's technological devices, indeed one even has the freedom to decline to buy any such, and dedicate oneself to the "real world" and just and only this world.*
>
> *Which I disputed. And indeed just because the one who strikes is as much at the disposition of technology as is the consumer: whether we play along with it or not, we play along, because we are played. What ever we do or fail to do—that we increasingly live a humanity for whom there is no longer 'world' or world experience but phantom of*

world and a phantom of consumption, no part of this is altered by our private strike: this humanity is today the factical with-world, which we must take into account, to strike against this is not possible.[27]

As this citation makes plain, Anders follows Heidegger in the case of technology where to follow Heidegger always means, just as Michael Theunissen once reminded us, to be set in contest with him, that means to question as Heidegger questions. In this sense what Anders does is to think Heidegger's critique as Nietzsche would recommend thinking critique in his own reflections on Kant: *through* to its furthest consequences.

Thus we recall Heidegger's allusion to Rousseau at the start of Heidegger's own *The Question Concerning Technology,* "Everywhere we remain unfree and chained to technology, whether we passionately affirm or deny it."[28] Hence when Anders reflects in his *The Obsolescence of Humanity* on the ultimate impossibility of denying or refusing technology, simply and only because we are human beings in a world with others, he repeats a point Heidegger had underlined early in his *Being and Time,* writing that "Dasein's Being in the world is essentially constituted by being with" and underscoring that this remains even when Dasein is alone, "even when factically no Other is present-at-hand or perceived. Even Dasein's being-alone is being-with in the world."[29]

But as Heidegger articulates this problem in "The Turn," one of the original lectures he presented in 1949 in Bremen, warning in perfectly apocalyptic tones attuned to the cybernetic technology of the day and which effects continue on the internet that is the current form of that same broadcast technology: "we do not yet hear, we whose hearing and seeing are perishing through radio and film under the rule of technology."[30]

In an age where the *Geräte* of which Anders speaks, that is, again, the gadgets, the "technologies" as we increasingly speak of them, remain more indispensable than ever they were for Anders writing in what may have been the most optimistic age of technology, that is the postwar era. And this indispensability is not nothing, as Heidegger says. And it is in advance of Baudrillard but very much after Heidegger and in strikingly Heideggerian terms that Anders writes as he does.

As Anders reminds us, no matter what we do, and in this he handily includes every imaginable luddite expedient, we remain *constitutionally* incapable of renouncing their use:

> *What holds true of these devices holds, mutatis mutandis, for everything. . . . To maintain regarding this system of devices, of this macro-device, that is a "means," that is to say that it is at our free dis-*

posal to be set to whatever purpose, would be completely sense-less. The system of devices, the apparatus, is our world. And world is something otherwise than means. Something categoric-ally otherwise—."[31]

In addition to his Heideggerian anticipation of Latour's claim, as we cited it earlier, that it is difficult to draw the line between us and things, between ourselves and our tools, our technologies, entailing that for Anders we simply "are" the technological things of our lives, Anders' ultimate point is a critical one. Thus Anders highlights the already given and determinate character of the modern consumer, determined as we are by our modern advertising. Thus, as we like to say, here making it all-too plain that we speak from the perspective of the advertisers, we live in and on the terms of and as a consumer society. This point is at the same time the very heart of Heidegger's analysis of *Gestell* as Anders continues to analyze it, here without reference to the term per se.

For, taken in all precision these are not just so many "preliminary decisions" but *the* preliminary decision instead. Yes. The. In the determinate singular. For an individual device does not exist—what is at stake in reality is the whole. Every individual device is consequently nothing more than part of a device, merely a screw, merely one piece in a system of devices, a piece partially directed to the requirements of other devices, its existence in part exigent upon other devices which turn compel the necessity for new equipment.[32]

More than Heidegger, although describing Heidegger's fate as a thinker and critic (heaven forfend!) of technology and indeed (heaven help us still more!) of science, Anders analyses the reasons for our silence as intellectuals in the face of technology and its effects as indebted to nothing more effective and egregious or tragic than simple socialization: in order not to be supposed a reactionary."[33] Nor has this fear of being thought reactionary (or technologically backward) changed in the interim. Hence Anders' observation is truer than ever. And his further reflection thus also bears repeated consideration:

that a critique of technology has already become a question of moral courage today is, as a consequence, unsurprising. In the last analysis (so thinks the critic) I can't afford to permit anyone to say of me... that I was the only one to fall through the cracks of world history, the one and only obsolete human being, and far and wide, the sole reactionary. And thus he keeps his mouth shut.[34]

For just this reason, Anders could not but be a reactionary. Being so got him little for his pains: his work was not read; he was treated with disregard by his peers (and those who were rather less than his peers) in his lifetime. But what he did do was to speak truth to power. And speaking truth to power, even if we never manage to do this for our own part, is always something we are always called to do—even on pain of being "far and wide, the only reactionary."[35]

Anders took this further than it took Heidegger but it also took him further than Adorno with whom Anders remained in contact, however bristly contact. Thus to illustrate my conclusion to follow, Anders reminisced, recalling a phone call he made to Adorno to ask Adorno if might stand in his place in a protest action Anders could not attend. Adorno predictably responded by refusing, somewhat indignantly: *You know I don't follow any banner.* Anders reply was point-counterpoint: *Then run ahead of it.*

Adorno hung up. There was, because there could be, no reply to that.

Conclusion

When it comes to technology, to machines and the question of (human) mastery, I maintain the Andersesque hope that—and unlike Adorno who simply heard Anders' suggestion as an insult[36]—we might yet find ourselves willing to take up the charge, and may be even, as Anders suggested, to take the lead in a moment of human freedom.

As we recall from Heidegger's *The Question Concerning Technology,* "Everywhere we remain powerlessly chained to technology, whether we passionately affirm or negate it."[37] Heidegger's language includes the term *"unfrei,"* with all of its Rousseauian overtones. The very same point recurs on the first page of Marcuse's *One Dimensional Man* and for his part, Anders himself reflects in 1956 in the *Obsolescence of Humanity* that it is impossible simply to renounce technology for the very early Heideggerian reason that we are human beings in a with-world, *Mit-Welt*, with others, *Mit-dasein.*

The problem that remains is the particularly Marxist and critical challenge of action. And Anders, more than either Heidegger or Adorno, was a scholar who *acted* on his politics, as radically conceived as they were, in the real world, the life of human action. And what often goes by the title of political agency, be it reading the paper, voting in a two party system, everyday politics of whatever given public sphere, should be contrasted with Anders' activism as this last involved the kind of life action that would seem to have been technologically eclipsed until the events sponsored, aided and abetted by technology, that would be the role, however short-lived in the end, in the Arab spring or the still ongoing American Fall into Winter, Occupy Wall Street. For the most part however, for most of us, especially we academics, we think ourselves "activists" if we click on an email link and hit return.

As Heidegger never tired of reminding us, down to a last letter that was also the last academic reflection he would write, to a circle of American Heidegger scholars: we still need to question in the wake of modern technology.

Endnotes

1 Ray Kurzweil, *The Singularity Is Near: When Humans Transcend Biology* (New York: Viking, 2005).

2 This reference to the 1966 film *Fantastic Voyage* is more than apt: the earlier instauration of Kurzweil's contributions on this theme is the health oriented (and there is nothing wrong with being health oriented) book he co-authored with a physician: Kurzweil and Terry Grossman, *Fantastic Voyage: Live Long Enough to Live Forever* (Emmaus, PA: Rodale Books, 2004).

3 Vernor Vinge, "The Coming Technological Singularity: How to Survive in the Post-Human Era," lecture presented to the *VISION-21 Symposium*, NASA Lewis Research Center and the Ohio Aerospace Institute, Mar. 30–31, 1993.

4 This is the frustrating conclusion Michael Chorost reaches in his March 20, 2012 contribution to the very pro-technology, very popular magazine, *Wired*: A True Bionic Limb Remains Far Out of Reach."

5 Nicklas Bostrom, 1999. "The Transhumanist FAQ." http://www.transhumanism.org/resources/faq.html.

6 Julian Huxley, *Religion Without Revelation* (London: E. Benn, 1927). Cited in Bostrom's "A History of Transhumanist Thought," *Journal of Evolution and Technology*, Vol. 14, Issue 1 (April 2005): 1–25.

7 A seemingly tailor-made sci-fi tale in David Simpson's self-rendered e-novel *Post-Human* (Bloomington: iUniverse, 2009), composed in the bad-future genre style that we know from films like *Bladerunner*, or *Roadrunner*, or *Robocop*, begins by depicting everyday life in the ultra-longevity lifestyle paradise created by nanotechnology, which the author to show his harmless familiarity with this technology speaks of as so many fairy beings called "nans," a paradise which is then undone by nans, whereby in the predictable (I-hope-the-screenplay-version-gets-made-as-a- movie before this book disappears from kindle radar) course of events, the devastation is revealed to be the fault of the usual caricature evil-doer only to end with a new world made by nans, good ones this time. See Fred Glass, "The 'New Bad Future': *Robocop* and 1980s' sci-fi films," *Science as Culture*, 5 (1989): 6–49 and, further, Glass, "Totally Recalling Arnold: Sex and Violence in the New Bad Future," *Film Quarterly*, Vol. 44, №1 (Autumn, 1990): 2–13.

8 For an excellent and by no means inherently antipathic discussion of these technical difficulties see Richard Jones, "Rupturing the Nanotech Rapture," IEEE *Spectrum* (June 2008): 64–67 and his book: *Soft Machines: Nanotechnology and Life* (Oxford: Oxford University Press, 2004).

9 Latour, *Aramis or the Love of Technology* (Cambridge: Harvard University Press, 1996).

10 Donna Haraway, *Modest Witness@Second Millennium: Female_-Man©_Meets_OncomouseTM* (London & New York, Routledge 1997).

11 See for some of this research, Turkle, *Alone Together: Why We Expect More from Technology and Less from Each Other* (New York: Basic Books, 2011).

12 Martin Kusch and Harry Collins, *The Shape of Actions, What Humans and Machines Can Do* (Cambridge: MIT Press, 1998), p. 161.

13 Kusch and Collins, *The Shape of Actions*, Ibid.

14 Kusch and Collins, *The Shape of Actions*, pp. 153ff.

15 Ibid., p. 155.

16 As cited, ibid.

17 Reporting on what can seem an extreme instantiation of this trend, see the August 31 2010 issue of the *Wall Street Journal* for an account of the online game *Love Plus*, "a product of Konami Corp. played on Nintendo Co.'s DS videogame system." According to the *Wall Street Journal*, the game *Love Plus* is for men who play with a virtual girlfriend, and in this case, manage to accrue enough points to be able to go on vacation "with" this same virtual girlfriend in a real life resort town, Atami, Japan—paying real money for the privilege, including real dinners—for two—and hotel rooms—also for two. Thanks to my students Carlo DaVia and Chris Hromas for this example.

18 Anders, *Die Antiquiertheit des Menschen*, Vol. 1, p. 36.

19 Ibid., p. 39.

20 Mathias Greffrath, "Lob der Sturheit,*" Die Zeit,* "Zeitläufte," 28/2002.

21 "Aber wenn's uns doch gelange, / abzuwerfen unsre Last, / und wir stunden, als Gestänge / in Gestänge eingepaßt, // als Prothesen mit Prothesen / in vertrautestem Verband, / und der Makel war gewesen, / und die Scham schon unbekannt —„ *Die Antiquiertheit des Menschen*, Vol. 1, p. 39.

22 Ibid., p. 36.

23 Ibid., pp. 36–37

24 Ibid., p. 32

25 Anders, *Die Antiquiertheit des Menschen*, Vol. 1, p. 40.

26 Ibid., p. 40.

27 Ibid., p. 1.

28 Heidegger, *The Question Concerning Technology*, p. 4.

29 Heidegger, *Being and Time*, 156/120.

30 Heidegger, *Die Frage nach der Technik* in: ders. *Vorträge und Aufsätze* (Pfullingen: Neske, 1954).

31 Anders, *Die Antiquiertheit des Menschen*, Vol. 1, S. 2.

32 Anders, *Die Antiquiertheit des Menschen*, Vol. 1, S. 2.

33 Ibid., p. 3

34 Ibid.

35 Ibid.

36 For Adorno's theoretical part, see Robert Hullot-Kentor's essay, "Adorno Without Quotations" in his *Things Beyond Resemblance: Collected Essays on Theodor W. Adorno* (New York: Columbia University Press, 2006).

37 Heidegger, *Die Frage nach der Technik in: ders. Vorträge und Aufsätze* (Pfullingen: Neske, 1954), S.1.

Political Thinking
in an *Un*Human Age

Davide Panagia

01110100 01101000 01100101 00100000 01110000 01100101 01110010 01101001 01101100 01110011 00100000 01101111 01100110 00100000 01101001 01110110 01110110 01100101 01110010 01110110 01100001 01101001 01101111 01101110

I drove home from the Hannah Arendt Center's "Human Being in an Inhuman Age" conference at Bard College on Sunday, October 24, 2010. At the time I lived in Peterborough, Ontario, Canada and was a faculty member in the Cultural Studies Department at Trent University. This means that the drive home from the Hudson Valley to the Kawartha Lakes region was approximately eight to ten hours, depending on the speed limit (both posted and chosen) as well as the line of cars having to cross customs at the Canadian border. I can't listen to audio books when I drive as they tend to put me to sleep. But that wasn't a problem. I had had a good night's rest and was fully energized by the meeting and by the discussions—both public and private—that took place over the prior two days. The result was, for me, the birth of a research agenda that was at once new and pressing, though I didn't know how to formulate it at the time. The only thing of which I was certain was that I had to get home and, after spending some quality time with my family and another good night's sleep, track down a copy of the "Kill Switch" episode of the *X-Files* (Season 5, Episode 11; original air date: February 15, 1998) in order to view it anew.

"Kill Switch" was a one-off, monster-of-the-week genre episode of the *X-Files* that was not part of the overall arch of the series. It was written by William Gibson and Tom Maddox both of whom, as is well known, were early innovators of 1980s cyberpunk genre of science fiction literature. The monster in question is an artificially intelligent internet software program that has achieved consciousness and a notable amount of control over affairs in the analog world. It is a brilliant episode which I recently revisited for the purposes of writing the current contribution, and I can confirm that it holds up very well. The basic plot of the episode is that the writer of an AI program (Donald Gelman) realizes that the AI has become too powerful and so has devised a "Kill Switch" virus that would shut it down. But the AI successfully intervenes and thwarts that attempt, killing its father and remaining active, vigilant, and preventing any further attempt to shut it down. Donald Gelman had a friend and co-creator, David, who (with his romantic partner, Esther) had devised a way to upload their consciousness onto the AI. The rest of the episode devolves into a frantic attempt by the series' protagonists (Fox Mulder and Dana Scully) as well as Esther, to shut down the AI. In the process of attempting to do so, they discover that David has been killed, or so it seems; though later we learn is that he has, perhaps successfully, uploaded his consciousness into the AI. The episode (without revealing any further spoilers) concludes with Esther doing the same thereby reuniting with her love interest.

Hannah Arendt had taken up many of the themes of the "Kill Switch" episode in *The Human Condition*. That work famously begins with a reflection on the 1957 launching of Sputnik-1 and of the scientific efforts to, as she says, make life "artificial."[1] Arendt notes the biological sciences in this regard, and the possibility of genomic alterations chief amongst these, which were no doubt pressing upon her given the concerns she articulated in *The Origins of Totalitarianism* and which were no doubt reminiscent to her of the Nazi eugenics efforts. A few years after the publication of *The Human Condition* she would return to the issue of artificial life anew, and this time with specific attention to the cybernetic revolution of the postwar period. As an invited participant of the *First Annual Conference on the Cybercultural Revolution* (1964), she delivered a short intervention that remains prescient to this day.

"Cyberculture" and "cybernation" are terms that circulated in the discussions and debates of that conference, the proceedings of which were collected in a volume entitled *The Evolving Society*.[2] By 1964 cybernetics was the hot new science in the North Atlantic world that invited a series of cross disciplinary debates, experiments, and philosophical explorations focused on the idea of reflexive feedback loops. Indeed, feedback systems were one of the central topics of the Macy Conferences that took place between 1946-1953 and which boasted an impressive range of international scholars, scientists, and engineers.[3] The idea of cybernetics is at once simple and complex as well as far reaching. In his *Cybernetics or, Control and Communication in the Animal and the Machine* (1948) Norbert Wiener famously states that he and his colleagues "decided to call the entire field of control and communication theory, whether in the machine or the animal, by the name *Cybernetics*, which we form from the Greek κυβερνήτης or steersman. In choosing this term, we wish to recognize that the first significant paper on feedback mechanisms is an article on governors, published by the Scottish theoretical physicist J. Clerk Maxwell in 1868, and that governor is derived from the Latin corruption of κυβερνήτης. We also wish to refer to the fact that the steering engines of a ship are indeed one of the earliest and best-developed forms of feedback mechanisms."[4] There is, in short, a direct connection between feedback and governance for cybernetic scholars like Wiener. They imagine complexity to be regulatable by self-managing homeostatic systems. The steering mechanism discussed by Maxwell is archetypal for Wiener precisely for this reason: it is a control mechanism that perpetually adjusts according to the surrounding environment (i.e., the unpredictable irregularities of flow and turbulence) by reflexively modulating itself in response to the information it receives.

Hannah Arendt's intervention at the 1964 Cybercultural Revolution conference does not focus on the technical aspects of feedback systems. Rather, and once again quite presciently, her reflections concern the matter of work and its relationship to time, specifically with respect to the growing technologization of labor and the increased free time that cybernetic systems promised. Any activity that is 1. regulable and 2. output specific could be governed by an automated negative feedback mechanism; if so much human activity falls under this schema of governability (and much of it does, as we now know), then this would free up human time. Arendt is thus quick to distinguish between two competing notions of free time; on the one hand, there is the leisure time of the Ancient Greek *scholē* that she articulates as the abstention or reprieve from doing something necessary so that citizens might participate in political life. The other form of free time is vacant time, which (for her) has its historical exemplarity in the political culture of the late Roman Empire. Vacant time is a real concern for Arendt who worries that humans may not be able to adapt to it: "But change in a life of vacant time may present a different problem. It is possible that the human species, adaptable though it has always been, may not be able to adapt to vacant time. For vacant time does not condition anything. Vacant time is nothingness."[5]

Arendt is unapologetic in her subtlety: the threat that cyberculture poses to humanity is nihilism. Nihilism is not a guarantee, nor is it a predictable outcome. But in her political imaginary it is one of two possible outcomes. Nihilism is the outcome chosen by those whose vacant time is not dedicated to public service. To the extent that she associates vacant time with imperial Rome, it is clear that the real threat of vacant time is the nihilism of perpetual war: "The vacant time of the Roman plebes was 'mitigated,' at times, by the endless wars waged by the Roman Empire. If I am right, and I hope I am right, we shall never again have such a 'consolation.' I think that at least traditional warfare as an instrument of foreign policy is probably on its way out."[6] No doubt, this is an uncharacteristically idealist sentiment on Arendt's part depending on what she might mean by "traditional warfare."

We can debate the verifiability, accuracy, or prescience of Arendt's statements about the possible political outcomes and hazards of cyberculture *ad nauseum*, but in doing so we would miss the point of her insight:

namely, that cyberculture is not simply a technical innovation but a way of life that ushers a fundamental ontological shift that transforms the relationship between technology and governance, and thus the relationship between humans and political action. By asserting that "the revolution we face is profound" and then articulating that revolution as the relationship between humans and time, Arendt wants us to consider the possible emergence of a new ontology of the human that is, as she asserts, "really fundamental."[7] What is *really fundamental* for Arendt isn't so much the advancement of the technical innovations as the fact that humans may not be capable of adapting to them. This doesn't mean that humans will disappear or become inhuman but, as she rightly notes, there is the very real possibility of a fundamental transformation of the human, like the transformation that Esther—in the "Kill Switch" episode—makes by choosing to upload her consciousness to the web in order to be able love once again. Not change, or alteration, or adaptability, then, but transformation. Better yet, we might speak of Arendt's remarks as pointing us to a potential transubstantiation of the human (and here, I use transubstantiation in the Thomist/Aristotelian sense of the term).[8] Esther's final solution in the Kill Switch episode was her human transubstantiation.

In light of these provocations I would like now to proceed and suggest three other ontological transubstantiations that further challenge our political understandings in what I call #datapolitik, or the age of algorithmic ubiquity.[9] It's a curious thing about these seemingly alien and *un*-human technologies—those mathematical functions that participate in our lives, that we at once embrace and reject like a tumultuous love affair—that they are born of the all too human desire to unequivocally conquer the imponderable chasm between you and I, between myself and others, between me and the world.

To begin, then, we should ask ourselves what is an algorithm? We know that an algorithm is a calculation, that it provides a series of computational rules for an input that then generates an output. And we know that both the term "algorithm" and the mathematical operations we call algorithms emerge from a history of Europe's engagements with the Arabic world. Rodrigo Ochigame explains that the term "algorithm:"

> *derives from the late medieval Latin "algorismus," from the name of the Islamic mathematician Al-Khwārizmī, whose manuscripts in Arabic described the Indian system of arithmetic. The word's meaning eventually developed into the technical definition employed in today's computer science: "any well-defined computational procedure that takes some value, or set of values, as input and produces some value, or set of values, as output."*[10]

An even more functional definition of algorithm is proposed by Tarleton Gillespie who tells us that "in the broadest sense, [algorithms] are encoded procedures for transforming input data into a desired output, based upon specified calculations. The procedures name both a problem and the steps by which it should be solved."[11] I find each of these definitions compelling but notably, none tells us much about algorithms beyond accounting for their operation as mathematical functions. In short, what I am suggesting is that the definitional approach to understanding the political ontology of al-gorithms—by which I mean their status as manifold events of political parti-cipation in everyday life—is not going to get us very far. And so, it is by investigating the conditions of possibility of the medium's technical milieu that I propose we begin our reflections by addressing three problems that al-gorithms pose to the Western tradition of critical political theory.

Here is the first: Algorithms are not representational structures, not in the manner that we typically understand what a representation is. This is a con-sideration that would trouble Arendt's own thinking on cyberculture further, and one that she could not (at the time) have realized. That is to say, the en-tirety of the Western tradition of political theory, and our claims about what political thinking is, are representational and are well ensconced—if not wholly rooted—in a mimetic relationship to the world. If we think about the media of political thinking, we tend to think of representational media like writing (i.e., words and concepts) but also painting, or even photography and film. Democratic politics holds the capacity for representation (whether per-sonal or institutional) as the central qualification for ensuring legitimacy and stability. And representation is the principal concept that grounds our under-standings of both truth and truthfulness. We judge either the truth or truth-fulness of a claim or of someone with whom we interact on the basis of their capacity to represent their intentions, their ideas — indeed, their promises — accurately. If, as Arendt argued, the human capacity to make promises is a crucial way of "coping with the unpredictable consequences of plural initiat-ives," surely that capacity rests on a prior mimetic capacity that allows us to represent our intentions, hopes, dreams, and aspirations to others through promise making.[12] To quiet the turbulence of unpredictability humans make promises and in doing so, they represent to others a future self. As she states, "binding oneself through promises, serves to set up in the ocean of uncer-tainty, which the future is by definition, islands of security without which not even continuity, let alone durability of any kind, would be possible in the re-lationships between men."[13]

The algorithm does not represent. It transcodes and correlates. Before it can perform those functions, it must 'learn' (through both human and non-human intervention) to accurately code things; and of course, humans are programmers (at least initially). But the operation that relates things within an algorithmic world is not mimetic. On the contrary, it is virtual and probabilistic. No outcome is guaranteed, though its likelihood can be predicted; and unlike human actions (which are definitive and can't be taken back), the algorithm's recursive feedback function makes it so that any outcome is never final or definitive. To have a better sense of what I mean, consider this description of the operation of machine learning taken from a recent article on AI neural networks:

> *Think about building a cat detector. You're training the neural network by feeding it lots of images of cats and things that are not cats (the inputs) and labeling each group with a 1 or 0, respectively (the outputs). The neural network then looks for the best function that can convert each image of a cat into a 1 and each image of everything else into a 0. That's how it can look at a new image and tell you whether or not it's a cat. It's using the function it found to calculate its answer—and if its training was good, it'll get it right most of the time.*[14]

Arendt's understanding of political action requires the binding of one's self through promises in order to stay the ocean of uncertainty. Her understanding of this operation is that of a mimetic operation that identifies an agent with the future completion of a virtuous action. Political mimesis for Arendt is what guarantees a relation between present and future, but political mimesis is not operational in the virtual reality of algorithmic cyberculture. As we see from the account above, the operation in question is entirely different from a mimetic one that Arendt imagined as the *sine qua non* of political action. Whereas mimesis has its ontological grounding in the human desire to reach out and into a plural world of perceptions and experiences, the recursive function of an AI algorithm is wholly oriented to creating a world that need not have any relation to a physical reality experienced by humans, and does not require the sharing of space and time *with* humans. What is even more aleatory to our current all too human sense of mimesis is that the "training operation" described above is actually (and knowingly) performed by humans: The "reCAPTCHA" tests that we often execute online to help determine whether we are humans or robots and thus can access a secure space are part of a Google's AI training platform that initially trained Google's text recognition software capacities and now trains Google's automated driving AI (this is why the reCAPTCHA test has shifted from texts/letter recognition to images of traffic lights, parking meters, and crosswalks).

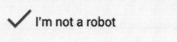

The irony—both political and aesthetic—is this: our mimetic impulses are invoked to "prove" our humanness so as to train an artificial intelligence (i.e., a robot) to simulate humanness.

I now wish to briefly raise a second problematic related to the first: traditional theories of political and aesthetic theory require—indeed presuppose—perceptual experience. When we critique something we experience some *thing*, whether an idea expressed in language, the plot of a film or a play, the dynamics of a visual image, an historical event, etc. All of these things are available to experience because a medium projects them to our horizons of experience. Our thinking and (especially) our faculties of judgment are thus oriented towards addressing individual or collective perceptions of the experiential object or event. The problem is this: We do not experience an algorithm. We experience a computer screen, keyboard, and mouse, we experience touch screens and listening devices, and we experience inputs and outputs; but we don't experience algorithms. Algorithms are *non*-experiential media; they are *an-aesthetic*. The best we can do (which is something most people can't do, including the author of this contribution) is program and analyze code. Thus the question: what mode of political thinking is available to non-mimetic, an-aesthetic media?

The question might be better put this way: if our tradition of political thinking calls for us to make judgments about the world of appearance, what kinds of judgments can we humans make about things that operate but do not appear? Furthermore: how might these judgments matter? These are complicated questions for which I have no immediate answers in part because my immediate concern is to ask how we might begin to think politically about these new developments when our habits of political thinking can't address the technical ontologies that structure the operational milieu of these media. That said, what seems at issue (once again, and evermore) is the legitimacy of political power that, in our moment, expresses itself as a recursive mathematical function.

A third problematic for a political theory of algorithms: Algorithms exist in the condition of ubiquity. By ubiquity I mean that they are used everywhere and for everything: traffic lights, electrical grids, romantic lives, sewage systems, financial trading, air navigation—you name an activity and it's very likely that an algorithm is involved in its management. Ubiquity also describes our current age characterized as it is by an implicit commitment to horizontal integration. Hence the increased anxiety around surveillance technologies, but also the techno-enthusiasm around recent developments in machine learning and artificial intelligence.[15] Algorithms are imagined as a solution to everything, precisely because so much of our daily lives involve repetitive, task oriented, serialized, and sequential activities; that is, automated and repetitive movement.

Take the case of one controversial predictive policing algorithm (used for predicting theft) that was adapted from an algorithmic equation originally devised to predict earthquake aftershocks. It is empirically the case that like an earthquake aftershock, "a burglary in one neighborhood might trigger a second or third burglary in that same area close in time."[16] The simple idea for this particular genre of predictive policing was to adapt the earthquake algorithm to crime. In this case, "ubiquity" means the horizontal integration of a mathematical operation among the terms being treated. The fact of ubiquity works alongside the non-representational nature of the medium such that an earthquake aftershock prediction algorithm is equally relevant to other aftershock-like behaviors, like theft. What relates these two events is not the content of the behavior, but the pattern which proves to be correlative such that both are predictable according to similar inputs. The input may change (earthquake, or theft, or romantic interest), but the probability that predictable patterns will emerge (i.e., the output) won't change.

The point of algorithmic ubiquity, and its challenge to our modes of political judgement, is this: it is not possible to turn away from algorithms. One of the standard ways of contending with potentially harmful or unfair or unjust forms of mediatic participation is through various gradations of censorship legislation. The quintessential version of this in the United States is pornography legislation in relationship to first amendment protections. But here, and once again, legislation can operate effectively when there is an object or a perceptible action upon which to adjudicate. Whether we agree or not that hard core pornography is protected speech, and whether we share Justice Potter Stewart's famous 1964 assertion that we can't define it but "I know it when I see it," there is still an "it" to be seen. That's not the case with algorithms, especially given the fact that in most (if not all cases) algorithms in the United States are protected not by the first amendment, but by copyright law, making algorithmic accountability one of the biggest challenges for US jurisprudence to date.[17]

Non-representation, an-aesthesis, and ubiquity: These are the three intersecting and interlaying problematics that structure an inquiry into a political theory of algorithms. Thus the question: how do we think algorithms politically? I believe that this question will remain with us for some time. It is a question that finds resonances with Aristotle's own question when, at the beginning of the *Poetics*, he proposes to speak not of poetry in general, but of its species and respective capacities. Aristotle's answer—revolutionary as it was at the time, and wholly *un*human given the extant ways of understanding poetry in classical Athens—was to say that it was a medium of action and not of character or song as Plato had insisted. In defending this position as he does Aristotle reconfigures the human relationship to drama by rearticulating the partitions of the sensible for dramatic reception and human perceptibility. As James Porter rightly affirms in the *Poetics* Aristotle is "developing a theory of aesthetic perception."[18] And this theory of aesthetic perception transforms dramaturgy into a visual medium (i.e., *opsis*) and not an aural/acoustic medium as his contemporaries and his culture would have insisted.[19] In the same way, and thanks in large part to the provocations of Bard's "Human Being in an Inhuman Age" conference, I wish to invite a similar provocation as Aristotle's and ask what perceptibilities, what modes of attention, what dispositions, and what transformations are enacted by the participation of an *an-aesthetic* technical object in the diurnal comings and goings of a political culture? To ask this question requires our being able to be open to the possibility that traditional political concepts like freedom, privacy, equality, justice, domination, etc., might not be as compelling to our political inquiry as we assume they should be, and that we need to transform, if not create anew, the forms of thinking adequate to a political inquiry in and of algorithmic governance.

I conclude with a final provocation: After a decade of reflection my inclination is to edit the title of the conference and speak not of an inhuman age, but of an *un*human one. Why *un*-human? Because one of the tasks of political thinking now is to rethink the relationship between human life, political action, and world in that "really fundamental" way that Arendt advises.

Endnotes

1 Hannah Arendt, *The Human Condition*, Second ed. (Chicago: University of Chicago Press, 2013), 2.

2 Alice Mary Hilton, The Evolving Society: *The Proceedings of the First Annual Conference on the Cybercultural Revolution--Cybernetics and Automation* (Institute for Cybercultural Research, 1966),

3 Steve J. Heims, *The Cybernetics Group* (MIT Press, 1991).

4 Norbert Wiener, *Cybernetics: Second Edition: Or the Control and Communication in the Animal and the Machine* (Martino Fine Books, 2013), 11-12.

5 Hannah Arendt, *Thinking Without a Banister: Essays in Understanding, 1953-1975* (Knopf Doubleday Publishing Group, 2018), 326.

6 Id. 325.

7 Id. 327.

8 Reinhard Hutter, *Aquinas on Transubstantiation: The Real Presence of Christ in the Eucharist* (CUA Press, 2019).

9 I explore the technical ontology of algorithmic governance in greater detail in Panagia, "On the Possibilities of a Political Theory of Algorithms" (2020), where I connect our current algorithmic moment with the rise, development, and political thinking of postwar cybernetics.

10 Rodrigo Ochigame, "The Long History of Algorithmic Fairness," Phenomenal World, January 30, 2020. https://phenomenalworld.org/analysis/long-history-algorithmic-fairness

11 Tarleton Gillespie, Pablo J. Boczkowski, and Kirsten A. Foot, eds., *Media Technologies: Essays on Communication, Materiality, and Society* (MIT Press, 2014), 167.

12 Arendt, *The Human Condition*, xix.

13 Id. 257.

14 Karen Hao, "AI Has Cracked a Key Mathematical Puzzle for Understanding Our World," MIT Technology Review, October 30, 2020. https://www.technologyreview.com/2020/10/30/1011435/ai-fourier-neural-network-cracks-navier-stokes-and-partial-differential-equations/

15 Pedro Domingos, *The Master Algorithm: How the Quest for the Ultimate Learning Machine Will Remake Our World* (Basic Books, 2015).

16 Andrew Guthrie Ferguson, The Rise of Big Data Policing: Surveillance, Race, and the Future of Law Enforcement (NYU Press, 2017), 65.

17 On this matter, see especially Frank Pasquale, *The Black Box Society: The Secret Algorithms That Control Money and Information* (Harvard University Press, 2015) and Bernard E. Harcourt, *Exposed: Desire and Disobedience in the Digital Age* (Harvard University Press, 2015).

18 James I. Porter, *The Origins of Aesthetic Thought in Ancient Greece: Matter, Sensation, and Experience* (Cambridge University Press, 2010), 96.

19 Stephen Halliwell, *Aristotle's Poetics* (University of Chicago Press, 1986), 337–43.

Some Notes on How We Should Imagine Human Beings in an Inhuman Age

Rob Riemen

01110100 01101000 01100101 00100000 01110000 01100101 01110010 01101001 01101100 01110011 00100000 01101111 01100110 00100000 01101001 01101110 01110110 01100101 01110010 01110100 01100101 01100100

The French poet and philosopher Paul Valéry made, in the 1920s, the following observations in his essays on the crisis of the human spirit. He writes:

> [. . .] the spirit represents our capacity for transformation. Our emotional life can be transposed into works of art. The spirit creates new, intellectual needs, through which we can transcend our physical instincts and bestial natures. The spirit has allowed us an awareness of time, of past and future. With this we can look ahead, imagine possibilities and go beyond the present moment. In addition, a man can break free from himself, imagine himself in the place of others. Each person is thus equipped with the intellectual capacity to observe and criticize his own actions and values.

> But the human mind has become derailed. We have become less sensitive. The modern man needs noise, constant excitement; he wants to satisfy his needs. Since we have become ever more insensitive, we need more crass means to answer to our craving for stimulation. We have become addicted to events. If nothing happens one day we feel empty. 'There's nothing in the papers,' we note disappointedly. We have been poisoned by the idea that something has to happen; we are obsessed with speed and quantity. A boat can never be large enough, a car or plane never fast enough. The idea of the absolute superiority of large numbers—an idea of which the naivety and vulgarity is evident (I hope)—is one of the characteristics of the modern human being.

> We have forfeited our free time. I don't mean by this chronological time (our days off), but internal rest, being free of everything, the mental distance from the world we need to make room for the most

delicate elements in our lives. We allow ourselves to be driven by speed, momentum—everything must happen now—and by impulses. Nothing is durable any more. Farewell cathedral, built across three centuries; farewell masterpiece that required a lifetime of experience and attention to perfect. We live passively. We defer to telephones, our jobs, fashion. Life becomes ever more uniform. Appearance, character, everything needs to look like everything else and the average always tends to descend to the lowest sort. One of the most striking characteristics of the contemporary world is its superficiality: we vacillate between superficiality and restlessness. We have the best toys that man has ever possessed. What a lot of fun! Never had so many toys But what a lot of worries! Never had so much panic! And an ever increasing amount of intellectual exertion is asked of us. Others think for us. What's more, our intelligence becomes ever more specialised. Due to the demands of technological progress, society has a growing need for "professionals,"replaceable intellectuals. There is no longer any use for a Shakespeare, a Bach, a Descartes, poets and thinkers, irreplaceable intellectuals.[1]

This is what Paul Valéry wrote 90 years ago, a complete description of how the human being—seduced by the siren sound of technology—is in the process of losing the human spirit. Compare his time with our time, and it is obvious that there is a parallel between the exponential growth of technology and what might be called the exponential loss of human spirit in our time.

Paul Valéry had, rightly, a deep-seated fear that with the loss of personality that would follow our becoming uniform individuals, we might easily forget what it means to be human, what the true greatness of being human is all about.

What defines the human being? This indeed became a question in the inhuman age of totalitarianism.

At the end of his moving novel, *Life and Fate* (1959), the Russian novelist Vasily Grossman describes how his protagonist, the scientist Victor Strum, a man who at first refused to conform to the ideology of the Stalinist regime and remained true to himself, receives a phone call from Stalin himself and is told he will receive funding for his research. Then, Strum finds himself confronted with a "request" to sign a letter in which two of his fellow scientists are accused of treason. Strum knows that the accusations are false and that his colleagues are innocent. However, not signing means acting against the will of Stalin and losing all of the power and career opportunities he has just gained. He signs the letter. And Grossman writes:

That night Strum did not sleep. He felt a pain near his heart. Where did this terrible oppression come from? He had gained power, but he had lost his inner freedom. With horror, he realized he was incapable of guarding and protecting his own soul. A power had grown in him that was turning him into a slave. He had committed an act of cowardice! He had thrown a rock at miserable, bleeding, defenseless people . . . His affection toward his daughter, his dedication to his wife, his hopeless love for his girlfriend, his sin and his happiness, his work, his beautiful science, the love for his mother and his sadness at her death—all had disappeared. His heart was empty. Why had he committed this terrible sin? Everything in the world was insignificant compared to what he had lost. Everything is insignificant compared to the truth, the pureness of one small human being; even the empire stretching from the Pacific Ocean to the Black Sea, even science itself.[2]

A second story concerning the essence of being human from the inhuman age of totalitarianism is told by Primo Levi in his classic memoir, *If This Is a Man*. Levi describes the episode where he, in Auschwitz, has been ordered to get the "soup" for the afternoon: *Essenholen*. He does this together with a young French friend, called Pikolo, as the pot, weighing over a hundred pounds and to be carried more than half a mile, is too heavy for one man. The French friend asks Levi to teach him the Italian language, and suddenly the "Canto of Ulysses" from Dante's *Inferno* springs to his mind. In a rush, as they don't have much time, Levi wants to tell about Dante, about *The Divine Comedy*, but above all he want his young friend to know this "Canto of Ulysses," which he has to translate into French. And Levi writes:

I am in a hurry, a terrible hurry. Here, listen Pikolo, open your ears and your mind, you have to understand, for my sake:

Think of your breed; for brutish ignorance

Your mettle was not made; you were made men, To follow after knowledge and excellence.

As if I also was hearing it for the first time: like the blast of a trumpet,like the voice of God. For a moment I forget who I am and where I am.[3]

When we ask the question: How should we imagine human beings in the inhuman age? we must keep in mind that the inhuman age is not only a future but already has a past, a European past: Stalin's slave society with its engineering of the human soul, and Hitler's Third Reich, with its death camps to deprive human beings of their dignity, to reduce them to *Untermenschen*, and to kill them as if they were insects.

In this totalitarian inhuman world two scientists, both agnostic, discover the truth of Socrates' answer when, in his dialogue with Alcibiades, he is asked: "So what is the human being?" And Socrates answers: "The human soul."Why the human soul? Because for Socrates it is the source of life and love. Due to our soul, we know about absolute, spiritual values as the life-giving qualities that dignify our life: truth, compassion, justice, beauty, freedom, friendship, goodness, wisdom, etc. It is because we are endowed with the gift of a human soul that we are moral beings! Animals and machines are not.

Yes, despite what some posthumanists want us to believe, there is an *ontological* difference between the human being on the one side and animals and machines on the other side. We are, as long as we are human, moral beings who should strive to dignify their life. How? As Socrates taught us: to care for our soul, to cultivate our soul. Which means: to live in truth, to do justice, to create beauty. No animal and no machine will be ever able to do that.

To ask: What is a human being? is to ask a *moral* question. It is not a *political* or an *academic* question. When it becomes a political or academic question, the process of dehumanizing has already started.

When human beings are deprived of their soul, when they are no longer free, moral beings striving to incarnate spiritual values into their lives, then "humanity" will be reduced to two categories: victims and murderers.

Ray Kurzweil dreams of "the singular man," the fusion between man and the machine, which has already been realized in the phenomenon of the SSer, that moral zombie of a man turned into a killing machine. I admit: it is primitive prototype—but it is the prototype of the singular man.

Why is it that Mr. Kurzweil has so much status and prestige in the USA? The answer to this question is that we, too, are in a process of forgetting what the essence of being human is. The general mindset is seriously affected by the dehumanisation of what is called *kitsch*. There is kitsch when in a society nothing has an intrinsic value. The absolute spiritual values are gone, what is left are phenomena that claim to be all important—yet, measured by the greatness of the human soul, they are not.

Only in a kitsch society can money and people with money become super important just because they have money. Our identity is no longer based on who we are but on what we *have*. You can buy your identity and you can *show* it with clothes, cars, house, bank account, etc. Consumerism is not so much the expression of greed, but an expression of the deep longing to buy your favorite identity—and then show it to as many as you can through Facebook, Hyves in the Netherlands, and other social media. We want to be known, but our being is as empty as the being of those who are best known: celebrities. We no longer love the life of the mind, as all has been reduced to feeling and the wish to feel good. Everything—work, relationships, friends, spare time— has to be fun and pleasant. We hate everything that is difficult. And this is the big message from both the commercial world and the technology industry: we can make life easy, we can make you feel good, we can chase away all that is difficult for you. To have lots of money and fun are the new parameters of a "good" life. Education, therefore, is no longer the formation of character and the cultivation of the human soul; it has to be useful, competitive, productive, flexible, and nice. No longer is the aim to become "man thinking" but *"homo economicus."* In short: kitsch is like a cosmetic that hides the loss of what has real value: the loss of our soul and its knowledge of true life-giving qualities.

It is due to this dominance of kitsch and its celebration of stupidity and triviality that we have come to believe that men like Kurzweil, with their fantasy of the fusion between man and machine, are widely admired, including by the so-called intellectual elite. We should not be very much surprised by this, since we cannot disconnect the celebrity status of people like Kurzweil and the nihilism of posthumanist intellectuals who no longer know the difference between man and animal, between man and machine, as they no longer recognize the question, "what is a human being," as a moral question. And this is because, despite all their intellect, they have forgotten what both Grossman and Levi, in the most inhuman circumstances, came to realize: the essence of being human is the possession of and care for the human soul and the cultivation of absolute spiritual values.

At the end of his life, referring to man's endless capacity to realize the inhuman, Levi wrote: "It happened. So it can happen again. That's all we want to say." If again, in whatever form, mankind passes beyond the human into the inhuman, posthumanist academic nihilists should know they are complicit!

Endnotes

1. Paul Valéry, "La crise de l'esprit" (1919) and "Propos sur l'intelligence" (1921), trans. Rob Riemen.

2. Vaily Grossman, *Life and Fate*, trans. Robert Chandler (New York: Vintage Books, 2006), 823-25.

3. Primo Levi, *If This Is a Man*, trans. Stuart Woolf (New York: Everyman's Library, 2000), 134–5.

Machines

Nicholson Baker

01110100 01101000 01100101 00100000 01110000 01100101 01110010 01101001 01101100 01111011 00100000 01101111 01100110 00100000 01101001 01110110 01110110 01100101 01101110 01110110 01100101 01101001 01101111 01101110

I have been to only one Arendt Center Conference. It was truly inspirational, and I'm honored to be a speaker here today. I like the title of this panel: "Is Art Human?" It feels a bit like a meditational prompt—like one of those dried paper f lowers that you drop into a bowl of water and then you watch it expand. At first you think, art? Well, yes, sure, of course it's human. But then you think, wait, what I wanted to do when I wrote that last book was to make something that was not part of me—that was out there. And then you think about a finished book, after it has come off a machine that probably weighed 20 tons—after the book was sliced, wrapped, shipped, when it has weight. And you look at the lines on the page. They're very . . . linear. They're grid-like, and they have a kind of a machine-born and machine-bound quality to them, which is part of the excitement. The excitement is that you've come up with something juicy, something that's born of your own mind, but is now inhuman. That is not you. That is pretending, that is a sort of simulation of being human that you hope someone else will be able to reconstitute with his or her eye by skimming it across all those tiny fixed serifs that are waiting to be picked up and made to come alive again.

Is art human? How am I going to answer that? I began by making a list of what machines really thrilled me as a kid. I wrote down the carousel slide projector, because there is that beautiful swallowing sound that it makes when it switches to a new slide. My father was in the advertising business, and he was a kind of carousel slide projector jockey. He got two or three carousels going at the same time, and he had a special tape recorder with secret beeps that would be sent to each slide projector so they could switch in tandem and do fade-ins and fade-outs. All of that mechanical, clunky, clinking, Kodak complexity leads to something that faded in and out on the screen—that has an insubstantial reflective quality, a glow to it.

The other machine that really got me was the piano. That has to be the greatest, solidest, heaviest, most human machine of modern times. It's a lacquered factory of beauty. It's so, so tall when you are a little kid; you can set up your plastic army men underneath it and have battles. Then you can pre- tend to drive the piano with the pedals. If you flip your right foot off the right pedal and then catch it a certain way, the whole piano will make a tremendous thrumming sound that comes from all the wires at once.

Escalators were important to me as a kid, too, very important. In fact, I wrote my first novel as a kind of celebration of an escalator ride. The guy is on his lunch hour, and he begins by getting on the escalator, and the novel ends with his getting off the escalator. So it is a kind of travel book: he goes from the first floor to the mezzanine level, and then he's done. This was just because I really liked the looping endlessness of escalators and felt they were underappreciated in the American novel.

Another kind of machine that I liked a lot, because we subscribed to the *New York Review of Books*, was the intricate machinery, or the mechanical-ness, of David Levine drawings. I liked that they were made up of tiny cross-hatchings—tiny motions of the hand that were exactly parallel, and which, when you looked closely, did not seem to have anything to do with the human face. And yet when you pulled back from the page, there was Virginia Woolf. Levine could make these thousands of very precise, perfect, parallel movements, and out of them shape a human face, which is probably the hardest challenge for any artist—to draw something with eyes, with highlights, something we will recognize as an individual literary person.

What else? AR turntables. I do not know if any of you are from that generation, but those were beautiful. Steam engines. On-Off switches. Light switches. We had a number of different kinds in my house. That was the first word I learned, *light*, because I'd learned how to switch the light switch on and off. We had the kind of light switch that pushed in and out, with mother-of-pearl tips—it was an old house.

Wallpaper patterns interested me because I knew they were not the way they looked. They weren't huge, they were one narrow pattern cleverly replicated. Part of the appeal, the intoxication of these surfaces, is the fact that small, irregular things are stealthily repeated. You see a locally chaotic vine, and you realize it is the same locally chaotic vine that is three feet over here. It's the same pleasure you can have when you think about a big automobile factory from the fifties and all the chrome bumpers are lined up. They're all irregular and lumpy, but they're all irregular in the same way, so in fact they're not irregular at all.

Camera shutters: that beautiful clicking sound that means that something very tiny and perfect is happening. A snip of time has been measured off and allowed to elapse, and now it's done. I loved camera shutters. And I wrote a piece for the *New Yorker* once about movie projectors. I thought beforehand I knew how they worked—I thought they worked the same way they had in junior high school. There was always one kid who was adept, who was charged with the task of threading the movie projector. It made a clicking sound. But when I looked into the projectors in multiplex movie theaters, it turned out that movies there were projected from giant horizontal platter systems.

So I wrote an article about that and I was able to work in a famous Charlie Chaplin movie. Chaplin is going through something that looks like a crazy production line. He's actually drawn down and around something— and suddenly you realize that Chaplin is threading himself through his own movie projector. It's a beautiful thing to see—he's using the movie projector to convey the idea of the forbidding, alien, dehumanizing presence in his life, something that he has to thread himself around. And yet it's the medium that allows him to be, most fluidly, Charlie Chaplin.

But then when I'd made this list, I thought, wait, none of these machines are really the crucial machines. And then I realized what it was: the first machine that I really loved as a kid. It began as a sound on the street that I lived on, Strathallan Park in Rochester, New York. I would hear this approaching sound—*pfffftttttfff*—and I would go to the window in the very early morning, and there it was: the enormous yellow street sweeper. It made a kind of steady moan of the central engine, plus it had the irregular sound that was produced by the rotating bristles. I never knew when it was going to come by. It was a huge accession of good luck when I would be able to look out the window and take it in. It had two big, round, front brushes, and when they turned, they turned inward. So the machine would actually be going forward, while the bristles—and I really loved this fact—were turning in a direction that was opposite to the machine. The bristles were actually resisting the forward motion of the street sweeper.

I never thought of the man inside the street sweeper. He was invisible, hidden in the top of this tower of machinery. Then in the back there was another huge, bristly, cylindrical thing that was also turning in the opposite direction. There was something beautiful about the idea that the act of cleaning, the sweeping progress, would be in opposition to the machine's forward advance. It was fighting itself in order to sweep my street. The other thing that I liked was how the sweeper outlined things. It was saying to the street, you are just a street now, but I will come and clean you up and make you new. I am going to make your edges be more defined.

Part of the challenge, or the pleasure, of being somebody in the art business is that you get to draw a line around things. You get to outline them and say where the line actually goes. The driver of the street sweeper, though I did not see him, was an artist, outlining my street. He was saying to the street, I'm going to celebrate you this Tuesday morning at 4:35 a.m. And it was also as though he was forgiving. If he found that there was a parked car in front of him—parked by one of those people who didn't see the sign, "Tuesday morning go on the other side"—he'd say, okay, fine, I am just going to veer out and go around. Later in the morning you could follow the clean path that the street sweeper had made when it veered out and forgave the car for being parked there.

That was my most favorite machine. Back then I did not think of machines as being oppressive or frightening or awful. And I think now that one of the jobs of the artist is to re-humanize the machinery that we rely on. If you are going to ride the escalator every day, you have to figure out why that's interesting. If we watch movies that come from movie projectors, we have to find out what about the movie projector is odd, worth thinking about. It turns out that in the middle of the movie projector there's this device, this star, which has to shift suddenly and then shift back, very fast. The engineering of it has to be perfect. I interviewed the man in charge of making these Maltese cross stars.

The notion of being an artist, the privilege of being an artist, or of being someone trying to be an artist, is that you get to look around the world and say, "What is it that is really proof of the fact that life is full of interest, exciting, and worth living?" And a lot of the fun things that make life worth living are in fact technical inventions and innovations. This is why I ended up writing about the street sweeper.

The last book I wrote is about a poet. He has to write an introduction to an anthology of poetry and he puts it off. I wrote it with the help of a machine. I set up a camera and videotaped myself in all sorts of places around the house, and then stripped out the audio and transcribed it. Then I had an enormous stack of pages, a transcript of a person pretending to be a poet, who is pretending to explain iambic pentameter. Iambic pentameter—another bit of machinery. So here's this poet trying to explain the nuts and bolts of poetry, and I wanted him to explain it in a way that felt true. So I set up the video camera and taped myself in various parts of the house, outside in our yard, in a white plastic machine-made chair, and then I transcribed it all.

I had a huge transcript, and then I did a final machine-inspired step that I had never done before. I assigned random numbers to each of these transcribed chunks. I went to random.org, which is a place where you can obtain beautiful random numbers that are really truly random, and I assigned one number to each of these chunks. Then I put them in the order that the chunks gave me. I'd been a musician and read about a composer named Xenakis and his random number tables and I thought, well, finally I'll be a modernist. The point for me was to look at this randomized, chaoticized, messed-up manuscript, and then to have to crawl back toward the human way to tell it. To fight back toward the way in which it really wanted to be said.

Somehow, I think the nice thing that machines do is they destabilize us. They are big, powerful, and wrong. They set us off course, and part of the joy is then remembering that they actually are human products that can be surrounded by thoughts. Their hard edges are softened by all sorts of analysis and associations and memories that we accumulate when we deal with them day by day.

Drones and the Question of "The Human"

Roger Berkowitz

01110100 01101000 01100101 00100000 01110000 01100101 01110010 01101001 01101100 01110011 00100000 01101111 01100110 00100000 01101001 01110110 01110110 01100101 01110110 01110100 01101001 01101111 01101110

D omino's Pizza is moving on from its short-lived "Domicopter" drones and now has launched the Nuro robot car that autonomously delivers your pizza. Not to be outdone, Amazon is working on a fleet of Prime Air delivery drones to deliver same-day packages in the U.S. Amazon now joins UPS and Wing (owned by Google) in winning FAA approval for their drone delivery services. In Denmark, farmers use drones to inspect fields for the appearance of harmful weeds, which reduces herbicide use as the drones directly apply pesticides only where it is needed. Environmentalists send drones into glacial caves or into deep waters, gathering data that would be too dangerous or expensive for human scientists to procure. Federal Express dreams of pilotless aerial and terrestrial drones that will transport goods more cheaply, reliably, and safely than vehicles operated by humans. Human rights activists deploy drones over conflict zones, intelligently searching for and documenting abuses for both rhetorical and legal purposes. Aid agencies send unmanned drones to villages deep in jungles or behind enemy lines, maneuvering hazardous terrain to bring food and supplies to endangered populations. Medical researchers are experimenting with injecting drone blood cells into humans that can mimic good cholesterol carriers or identify and neutralize cancerous cells. Parents in Vermont are using flying drones to accompany children to school, giving a whole new meaning to helicopter parenting. And Pilobolus, a New York dance company, has choreographed a dance in which drones and humans engage each other in the most human of acts: the creation of art.

In all areas of life, there is a rush to adopt drones to make our lives better. But the significance of drones to human civilization is poorly understood. In our headlong embrace of drone technology, we are forgetting to ask two basic questions: What is a drone? And, what does it mean that the once-obvious boundary separating human and machine intelligence is being diminished?

What Is a Drone?

There are at least two sources for our present misunderstanding of drones. The first concerns our widespread technological ignorance. Few of us are fluent in the language of computer coding or the intricate workings of algorithms that govern drone behavior. Drones do not simply follow static coded trajectories. Armed with algorithmic instructions that permit machines to react with exceptional speed and reliability to external factors in ways that seem intelligent, drones mimic or improve upon human responses. The Navy's Phalanx Shield weapon chooses targets and fires without any human intervention, and it can do so faster and more accurately than humans. The Phalanx Shield is not "intelligent," but it can react according to preset criteria and make flexible judgments following complicated algorithms. In short, drones are now able to carry out tasks autonomously that historically were thought to be the exclusive province of humans. For those of us who are unaware of how algorithms empower drones to simulate intelligence, the human-like behavior of drones is mysterious, impenetrable, and at times, uncanny.

A second and more important misunderstanding is that drones have been confused with their infamous military exemplars—the Predator and the Reaper—and are therefore exclusively associated with targeted killings in the war on terror. Much of the commentary about drones concerns the legitimacy of extrajudicial killing as well as the civilian casualties that accompany these attacks. Extrajudicial killings are hardly novel, however, given that warring states have been eliminating each other's high-value targets by poisoning, sniper fire, mail bombs, improvised explosive devices, and other means for centuries. Unmanned aerial vehicles are powerful weapons, but they are just that, new tools improving upon a long-standing practice. To the extent that discussions about drones get lost in questions of the morality or legality of targeted killing, we are not actually talking about the full impact of drones. Drones, more precisely understood, are intelligent machines that—possessed of the capacity to perform repetitive tasks with efficiency, reliability, and mechanical rationality—increasingly displace the need for human thinking and doing.

But let's step back. The original meaning of a drone is a male honeybee. It is a nonworker bee that is fed and kept alive by the hive to serve but one purpose: devoid of a stinger and spared the toil of foraging for food, drone bees sport special receptors that allow them to find and impregnate the Queen. They live as idlers who do no work and must be fed and cared for by the hive; they also free the worker bees to work without worrying about sex or reproduction. When today we speak of robots, unmanned vehicles, and automated machines as "drones" we speak metaphorically; modern drones recall the original sense of the male honeybee as something that performs one function repetitively and well, without distractions and with unrivalled efficiency.

The metaphorical potential of the drone has been mined at least since Plato. In *The Republic*, a human drone is a fallen member of the oligarchy who desires riches but disdains work. The Platonic drone neither earns money nor builds things. He does not fight for the *polis*. Just as "the drone growing up in a cell is a disease of a hive," so too is the human drone "a disease of a city."[1] What is more, the most talented drones will morph into tyrants. Craving luxuries and working not at all, the drone excels at getting others to work for him.

Plato is hardly the only thinker to note the tyrannical impulse in drones, which is also the subject of Ernst Jünger's prescient novel, *The Glass Bees*, originally published in 1957. Jünger's text centers on a job interview between an unnamed former light cavalry officer and Giacomo Zapparoni, the secretive, extremely wealthy, and powerful proprietor of the Zapparoni Works, which "manufactured robots for every imaginable purpose." Zapparoni's distinction is that instead of the big and hulking robots such as are produced by other industrialists, he specialized in Lilliputian drones that gave "the impression of intelligent ants."[2]

Zapparoni's robots were not powerful in themselves, but working together like drone bees and drone ants, the small drones "could count, weigh, sort gems or paper money." Their power came from their intelligent yet thoughtless coordination. The drones

> *worked in dangerous locations, handling explosives, dangerous viruses, and even radioactive materials. Swarms of selectors could not only detect the faintest smell of smoke but could also extinguish a fire at an early stage; others repaired defective wiring, and still others fed upon filth and became indispensable in all jobs where cleanliness was essential.*[3]

Dispensable and efficient, Zapparoni's mini-drones could do the most dangerous and least desirable tasks.

Before Jünger's hero is introduced to Zapparoni's drones, he is given a warning: "Beware of the bees!"[4] And yet, marveling at them, the cavalry officer is fascinated. He feels himself "come under the spell of the deeper domain of techniques," which, like a spectacle, "both enthralled and mesmerized."[5] His mind, he writes, went to sleep and he "forgot time"—as well as "the possibility of danger." He forgets the warning.

The danger posed by Zapparoni's bees is the one we face today: that we allow our fascination with technology to dull our humanity. We have become infatuated by perfection and intolerant of human error; we worship data-driven reliability and disdain untested human intuition; and we value efficiency over beauty and chance. "Technical perfection," Jünger writes, "strives toward the calculable, human perfection toward the incalculable.

Perfect mechanisms—around which, therefore, stands an uncanny but fascinating halo of brilliance—evoke both fear and a titanic pride which will be humbled not by insight but only by catastrophe."[6] As we humans interact more regularly with drones and machines and computers, we may come to expect ourselves, our friends, our colleagues, and our lovers to act with the same efficiency—and inhumanity—of drones.

That reliance upon drones diminishes our humanity is the research-driven conclusion of Sherry Turkle, an anthropologist at MIT and a technology writer. In her book *Alone Together* Turkle discusses her studies of human interaction with so-called social robots, programmed to respond to human emotion.[7] In regular intercourse with such robots, she argues, humans will reduce their expectations of other humans.

Turkle offers countless examples of smart, thoughtful people who come to crave robotic companionship, often more so than human friendship. One such person is Edna, a great grandmother, who, when given a robotic baby to play with while she is playing with her real two-year-old great granddaughter, immediately takes to the robot and proceeds to ignore the real child. Turkle also tells of Aaron Edsinger, a computer scientist who designed the robot Domo. Edsinger feels Domo's attention, senses Domo's desire, and finds it pleasurable to be touched by Domo, "even if he knows that the robot doesn't 'want' to touch him." The point of these and many other stories is that for the lonely—and even for those technically savvy people who know that robots can neither feel nor think—conversing with, caring for, and playing with a machine is fully consistent with the wonder of attachment, friendship, and even love. These relationships with machines are one-sided, diminished, and superficial; and yet, they are satisfying—frequently more satisfying than human relationships.[8]

Turkle concedes that many human relationships are less than optimal. From fake orgasms to canned expressions of sympathy, human friends and lovers can seem mechanical. And yet, in relationships with people, we have to work toward meaningful connection. We "learn to tolerate disappointment and ambiguity," writes Turkle, "and we learn that to sustain realistic relationships, one must accept others in their complexity."[9] But with robotic friends as companions and partners, the work of human relationships fades away. There is a real danger that the rise of robotic companions and coworkers will lower our expectations of human relationships, and that we will come to see this reduction as the norm. Turkle, clearly shaken by her research, asks us to confront the implications of this loss.

The trend Jünger and Turkle worry about is unmistakable: we are at risk of losing the rich and mature relationships that mark us as human. The rise of social robots, unmanned aerial vehicles, and other one-dimensional machines that act like humans without the perceived human weaknesses of distraction, emotion, exhaustion, quirkiness, risk, and unreliability answers a profound human desire to replace human judgment with the more reliable, more efficient, and more rational judgment of machines. For all the superficial paeans to human instinct and intuition, human beings, in practice, repeatedly prefer drone-like reliability to the uncertain spontaneity of human intuition. In other words, we confront a future in which "human" is a derogatory adjective signifying inefficiency, incompetence, and backwardness.

The Human Condition

To understand the role humans play in a world increasingly augmented by super-intelligent drones that repeatedly perform a particular task with a ruthless efficiency, there are few better guides than Garry Kasparov. In 1997,Kasparov had the distinction of being the first World Chess Champion to fall to a chess-playing machine, Deep Blue. Writing in the *New York Review of Books* of February 11, 2010, Kasparov reflected on what that loss meant for the fate and future of humanly-played chess, specifically noting three changes brought about by the rise of the machines.[10]

First, machines have redefined what a good chess move looks like. Chess has always valued moves that combine surprise, innovation, and elegance. A bold move can throw off an opponent. This is changing. As Kasparov writes, "the machine doesn't care about style or patterns or hundreds of years of established theory. It counts up the values of the chess pieces, analyzes a few billion moves, and counts them up again." The point of a computer playing chess is simple: To win. "Increasingly, a move isn't good or bad because it looks that way or because it hasn't been done that way before. It's simply good if it works and bad if it doesn't. Although we still require a strong measure of intuition and logic to play well, humans today are starting to play more like computers."[11] In other words, the embrace of robotic chess means that humans, to compete, will have to think more like computers and less like humans.

Second, Kasparov argues that the rise of intelligent machines neutralizes the advantage of experience. One of the traditional characteristics of the human condition has been the benefit of wisdom acquired with age. But with databases of chess games and the availability of constant play against chess programs, today's preteens can accelerate the learning process, supplanting the necessity of experience. Bobby Fischer's 1958 record of attaining the Grandmaster title at fifteen was broken only in 1991. Since then it has been broken twenty-two times, with the current record holder, Ukrainian Sergey Karjakin, having claimed the title at the nearly absurd age of twelve in 2002. Now in his twenties, Karjakin is among the world's best chess players, but like most of his modern wunderkind peers, he is no Fischer, who stood head and shoulders above his contemporaries.

Finally, chess machines neutralize genius, another traditional and distinctive facet of the human condition. Kasparov tells of his experience of two matches played against the Bulgarian Veselin Topalov, at the time the world's highest ranked Chess Master. When Kasparov played him in regular timed chess, he bested Topalov 3–1. But when he played him in a match when both were allowed to consult a computer for assistance, the match ended in a 3–3 draw.

Kasparov does not conclude, as might be expected, that computers are ruining chess. On the contrary, he argues that computers—projecting the consequences of all possible moves and pointing out possible outcomes and countermoves—will free their human partners to "concentrate on strategic planning instead of spending so much time on calculations." Ironically, Kasparov argues, "human creativity [is] even more paramount under these conditions."[12] As we outsource merely quantitative skills to our artificial brains, we humans will be freed to our higher and evermore creative humanity. There is in Kasparov a whiff of the old Marxist utopianism—that once workers are freed from labor they will have time for higher pursuits like philosophy and gardening. But just as a hundred years of consumerism has showed that Marx's laborers use their excess time not to read or pursue hobbies but rather to work more in order to consume more, so too is it questionable that humans today will make creative use of the liberation that worker drones provide from the humdrum need to calculate and execute dangerous and repetitive tasks. There is a real question of what human creativity means once it is abstracted from the so-called mechanical activities of calculating, processing, acting, and knowing.

The worry that drones might have an impact on human creativity is reinforced by their enthusiastic embrace by artists. Drone art has become commonplace today. Camera-equipped drones bring an aerial perspective that—like the images from space satellites—frees humans from their earthly limitations.What is more, the artist Harold Cohen has spent decades creating the painting machine Aaron, which produces figures and scenes in its own style. Aaron cannot learn on its own, but its art easily passes the Turing Test, which means that art critics cannot tell that Aaron's paintings are done by a machine. Aaron's art has been displayed at London's Tate Modern Gallery, Amsterdam's Stedelijk Museum, the Brooklyn Museum, and the San Francisco Museum of Modern Art. Cohen insists that Aaron is not creative, and he is right. The art of creation is distinct from algorithmic activity and it cannot be broken down into logical formulas, no matter how sophisticated. But Aaron, even if he is not creative, creates art that *appears* to be creative and to have been made by human beings.

The reason such machines are not simply fancy new tools, the reason that drones are different from other technological innovations, and the reason drones pose a danger to the humanity of the human condition—is that they are specifically capable of reducing the need for human judgment, human creativity, and human thought. Because of their ability to act flexibly, reliably, and with a quasi-human intelligence, humans find them irresistibly useful. Drones are not susceptible to emotions, fatigue, or distraction. In war, they will kill neither out of anger nor fear. Flying a plane, they will not fall asleep at the wheel or check a text message. Carrying a fetus, if and when they do so, they will provide only the healthiest of diets. We must confront the basic fact that humans frequently prefer the decisions and abilities of machines to the creative intuitions of humans, especially when the tasks involved are important and difficult.

Drones are machines that mimic human action and human judgment and also offer a mechanical albeit importantly seductive ideal of human behavior. Drones, in other words, transform what we mean by our humanity. As drones proliferate and as humans prefer drones to other humans in war, sex, and art, the ideal of human creativity and human judgment are becoming less recognizably human. There is a real question about what uniquely human activities will be left immune to the penetration of drones.

Drones and War

In this regard it is helpful to consider the question of war. "War," Heraclitus tells us in his fragment 53, "is the father of all things."[13] It is the extremity of war that made Achilles a hero, a model of the human capacity to set the common good above one's own welfare. And it is war that gave Patrick Henry's cry, "give me liberty or give me death," its ringing appeal. War may be hell, but war is deeply human. In the pure violence experienced only in war, war calls forth ideals of justice in order to make sense of its own horrors. Absent the glory and tragedy of war, writes Simone Weil in her essay "The Iliad, or the Poem of Force," there would be no spiritual cauldron in which to forge the mettle of justice.[14]

Given the connection between war and the human ideals of justice, what does it mean that war is increasingly being fought by drones? The desire to substitute machines for humans is most intense precisely in those fields with the highest stakes. In a speech at Bard College in 2010, the roboticist Ron Arkin described how robots "can identify, target, and engage in the battlefield without human intervention."[15] Already, cruise missiles can, once launched, "select and engage a target." Arkin noted that the United States, for instance, employs "Fire and Forget systems, which are torpedoes that can be launched and just patrol a particular region, waiting for a target." And the Phalanx system deployed on Aegis class cruisers have an auto mode that, once turned on, will fire upon anything that nears the ship. For Arkin, the use of fully autonomous drones in warfare is inevitable.

Arkin is not alone in this view. Sir Andrew Pulford, chief Air Marshal of the Royal Air Force in the United Kingdom, declared in a September 2013 television interview that it is simply a matter of time before autonomous "Terminator 2-type" machines will be widely deployed. We already have drones that are faster than humans, stronger than humans, and smarter than humans. The time is coming when drones will be thought also to have better judgment than humans. Even ChristofHeyns, the United Nations'Special Rapporteur on extrajudicial, summary, or arbitrary executions,also assumes that lethal autonomous robots (LARs) will one day be a reality. It is for this reason that he argues it is "essential for the international community to take stock of the current state of affairs, and to establish a responsible process to address the situation and where necessary regulate the technology as it develops."[16] Heyns has called for a worldwide moratorium on LARs—weapons systems that, once activated, can lock on and kill targets without further human involvement. "Machines," he argues, "lack morality and mortality, and as a result should not have life and death powers over humans. "There is, however, no surer way of clearing a path to lethal autonomous robots than to provide a regulatory framework for their development and deployment.

The moral question regarding the ethics of war is, for others, precisely an argument for the development of lethal and autonomous drones. Arkin and Pulford, for example, argue that intelligent drones are to be welcomed—not least because they promise to make war more ethical and more humane. Because of exhaustion, anger, or the desire for revenge, human soldiers often act rashly. Engaged in dangerous operations, soldiers tend to fire first and ask questions later. The list of war crimes that stretch back millennia is all the evidence needed to make visible the inhumanity of man amidst war. Muchof the inhumanity of war comes from the difficulty, if not the impossibility, of training humans to suppress their natural instincts and to submit to a difficult and dangerous moral code. Drones, Arkin claims, have the potential to humanize warfare: Indeed, he suggests in his lectures at Bard College that robots in war can "be more humane than humans."

Arkin and Pulford also make the argument—now widespread in technological circles—that drones are simply a novel, powerful, and ultimately useful new tool. Drones can kill, but they also save lives. They are no different from other incredible technologies that can do great good and spread terrible harm. Penicillin saves lives; the combustion engine has freed humanity to move about the earth; DNA evidence and video from surveillance cameras increase the likelihood of a just verdict in legal cases. Of course Penicillin, overused, creates untreatable superbugs; the combustion engine has unleashed an ecological disaster; and genetic testing and surveillance threatens our expectations of privacy. All technology is double-edged, but that is not an argument against technology.

There is a certain all-knowing elegance to such arguments, in which one assumes the owl-like vision of history to flatten distinctions and undermine the unprecedented. And yet drones are new. They may simply be our latest machines, but they are machines that—for the first time in history—can perform as well as or even better than humans in those activities that have throughout human history been understood to be quintessentially human. It is precisely because drones lack the mysterious human element in dangerous, difficult, and important situations that involve diagnosis, creativity, and killing that we increasingly trust drones more than humans to make the better judgment. Humans prefer the unemotional and rational (yet flexible) decisions of drones to the often-clouded, biased, and irrational judgment made by fellow humans. It is humans who are choosing, consciously or not, to subordinate human judgment to decisions based on data and algorithms. The result is that the emerging age of the drone threatens to transform the fundamental conditions of human life as we have known it.

The fact that we are in the process of transforming the human condition was for Hannah Arendt the great event of our time. In *The Human Condition* Arendt identified labor, work, and action as the three basic activities that have been central to what it means to be human since the dawn of civilization.[17] Since time immemorial humans have labored and sought to provide the means for their subsistence and biological preservation. Beyond labor, humans also work and build structures, create artworks, and found states that endure. These lasting things do not serve biological subsistence, but comprise the humanly built world that gives to human life its characteristic meaning and significance. Finally, humans *act,* which means that they can do things that are surprising, shocking, and new. Like Achilles, who refrains from fighting on account of a slight; like Gandhi, who found strength through peace; and like Martin Luther King, Jr., who followed a dream, we humans can act in ways that are unexpected and also inspirational. It is the capacity of human action to surprise and inspire that motivates artists and citizens respond to great acts by building monuments, founding new political states, and engaging in revolutionary reimagings of existing polities. The human capacity to act, Arendt argues, is what enables humans to call forth heroes, build civilizations, and change the world.

Arendt helps us to see that spontaneous human actions are at the center of politics. Only unpredictable action can surprise us. Heroic, bold, and even daring or foolhardy deeds are necessary for politics, for only such acts strike a public citizenry as worthy of attention. Singular actions make others take notice, precipitating the public speech and collective action that for Arendt is the core activity of politics. Arendt worried that as human society came under the sway of statistics and "the law of large numbers," action would become both predictable and explainable. Action in a statistical world is reduced to behavior, a result not of spontaneity but rather a product of statistical and historical regularities. And as we rely increasingly on drone-like machines, we habituate ourselves to interactions with drones so that spontaneous and striking human deeds will become increasingly endangered.

In the end, the threat drones pose is not to civilians in war or to jobs. The real threat is that as our lives are increasingly habituated to the thoughtless automatism of drone behavior, we humans habituate ourselves to acting in mechanical, algorithmic, and logical ways. The danger drones pose, in other words, is the loss of freedom.[18]

Endnotes

1. Plato, *The Republic*, trans. by Allan Bloom (New York: Basic Books,1991) 552a ff.

2. Ernst Jünger, *The Glass Bees*, trans. by Louise Bogan and Elizabeth Mayer (New York: New York Review of Books, 2000).

3. Id. at 8.

4. Id. at 115.

5. Id. at 132, 133.

6. Id. 155.

7. Sherry Turkle, *Alone Together*, (New York: Basic Books, 2011).

8. Id. at 133.

9. Id. at 55.

10. Gary Kasparov, "The Chess Master and the Computer," *New York Review of Books*. Feb. 11, 2010. https://www.nybooks.com/articles/2010/02/11/the-chess-master-and-the-computer/

11. Id.

12. Id.

13. Heraclitus, in Hermann Diels, *Die Fragmente der Vorsokratiker*, (Berlin, 1912) fragment 53.

14. Simone Weil, "The Iliad a Poem of Force," in *Simone Weil: An Anthology*, ed. by Sian Miles, trans. by Mary McCarthy (Weidenfeld & Nicolson: London, 1986).

15. You can access Ron Arkin's speech here: https://www.youtube.com/watch?v=JMffceBjrBM

16. Christof Heyns, "Report of the Special Rapporteur on Extrajudicial,Summar or Arbitrary Executions," United Nations Human Rights Council, April 9, 2013.

17. Hannah Arendt, *The Human Condition* (The University of Chicago: Chicago, 1958).

18. Id. 42 ff.

The Rhetoric of Sustainability: Human, All Too Human

Marianne Constable

01110100 01101000 01100101 00100000 01110000 01100101 01110010 01101001 01101100 01110011 00100000 01101111 01100110 00100000 01101001 01101110 01110110 01100101 01110110 01110100 01101001 01101111 01101111 01101110

S ustainability is all the rage! The side of my carton of reduced-fat milk, for instance, reads "Savor Sustainability." It's an ad for "Cooking for Solutions: Celebrity Chefs Celebrate Sustainable Cuisine," a fund-raiser featuring "dozens of renowned chefs: two days of gourmet events," and "extraordinary organic and sustainable food and wine" to support the nonprofit Monterey Bay Aquarium, "its acclaimed seafood watch program and the Aquarium's many initiatives to assure a future with healthy oceans." There's also news from UC Berkeley's Office of Sustainability announcing that the Graduate Division is one of the campus's certified green departments which, among other things, is "offering composting" for its staff. Berkeley brags that it is among the top 18 of 373 campuses named as a Green Campus by the Princeton Review (one of whose criteria is that the campus employ a "dedicated full-time sustainability officer").[1]

Lest you think I'm being too parochial, consider sustainability's national and international policy presence. The 2008 Higher Education Opportunity Act made grants available to universities "to establish sustainability programs to design and implement sustainability practices, including in the areas of energy management, greenhouse gas emissions reductions, green building, waste management, purchasing, transportation, and toxics management, and other aspects of sustainability that integrate campus operations with multi-disciplinary academic programs and are applicable to the private and government sectors."[2] There's also, of course, the 1987 United Nations Brundtland Report, "Our Common Future," which has been credited (in an account presented by the UN Commission on Sustainable Development) with changing "sustainable development from a physical notion based on the concept of sustainable yield in forestry and fisheries to a much broader concept that linked economic and ecological policies in an integrated framework."[3]

In a now oft cited, but by no means universally accepted, definition, the Brundtland Report identified "sustainable development" as "development that meets the needs of the present without compromising the ability of future generations to meet their own needs."

Acting locally and thinking globally, or rather reading locally and cruising the Web globally, I'm struck by the ubiquity of sustainability. "More sustainably"offers itself all over the place as the answer to the main question asked by the Hannah Arendt Center's Conference "Human Being in an Inhuman Age": "How ought we humans respond to our inhuman future?" In contexts ranging from dining, farming, building, funding, and educating, sustainability invokes far-ranging sets of practices, behaviors, and processes. Their value as "sustainable" appears largely unquestioned. That is, one can object to a practice as unsustainable, but very few declare themselves against sustainability as such. Sustainability is a faith, like democracy.

Rather than assessing the extent to which sustainability is the right response to an ostensibly inhuman future, I'd like to take up Hannah Arendt's counsel to "think what we are doing" insofar as today what we are doing is seeking to live sustainably. How has sustainability become a panacea? What does it really mean? What is being sustained? For how long—indefinitely? And what might pursuing ecological and economic sustainability portend?

Sustainability on its face offers a tautological answer to a question best posed as "how ought we humans to respond to an unsustainable present so as to ensure a (human) future?" This question, of course, already presumes sustainability as value or goal, insofar as unsustainability is what we have and don't want. Thus unsustainability is where I will begin, as I explore in Part I how the human need for a "durable world," as explained by Arendt, contributes to the power of sustainability. Rather than trying to determine whether sustainability is really "for the sake of the human" or "for the sake of the earth" (a live issue within sustainability studies), I will suggest in Part II, using the California condor as an example, that we think instead about the ways in which sustainability blurs distinctions between human and nonhuman, artifice and nature. Finally, in Part III, I will speculate about the sort of future sustainability offers.

I. Durability and the Unsustainable Present

Many know of the two major 20th-century threats to human being identified by Arendt: totalitarian government and nuclear destruction. Arendt also mentions a third threat: that of consumer society. She argues in *The Human Condition* that as the "appetites [of laboring man] become more sophisticated, so that consumption is no longer restricted to the necessities, but on the contrary, mainly concentrates on the superfluities of life," the character of the society of *animal laborans* does not change, but "harbors the grave danger that eventually no object of the world will be safe from consumption and annihilation through consumption."[4] Not only that, but with automation, "we are confronted with . . . the prospect of a society of laborers without labor, that is, without the only activity left to them."[5] Sounds pretty bleak: humans with an inhuman future.

Twenty-first-century appeals to sustainability, rather than threatening to annihilate human being, claim on the contrary to *sustain* it. *Sustain* as a verb means to keep (from falling, in being, or going); to support, uphold or hold up (as life with necessities); to endure, bear up against, withstand; to undergo, experience, or submit to (as an injury or loss); to be the support of, to bear to do, to hold oneself upright or fixed.[6] Sustainability emerges as a value or aspiration at a time when current human practices of growth and consumption appear unsustainable (they cannot bear up), as the 1960s and '70s precursors to sustainability (Rachel Carson, Paul Ehrlich, Garrett Hardin, David Brower, Lester Thurow, and so forth) maintained. Population is growing too fast. We are poisoning land, air, and sea and using up the earth (and now, with global warming, the air) in such a way that it cannot be replenished.

Sustainability invokes a quality of duration, then, that consumer society has ostensibly lost. To what does this quality attach? The danger Arendt saw in consumer society consisted of annihilation through consumption of all the "objects of the world." Environmentalists appear to be concerned with the destruction, by contrast, of things of the earth (coral, fish, water, oil, birds, and so forth). They dispute among themselves whether to protect earthly things (and which ones) for their own sakes, as having inherent or intrinsic value or worth, or whether to do so for the sake of their utility to human beings.[7] Some argue that earth itself and as a whole should be sustained, insofar as earth is of a piece with humans.

Arendt has been invoked to support the latter view, insofar as she challenges the strong distinction between passive earth and active human.[8] Her account of earth and world, which corresponds roughly to that of the natural and the built environment, very much complicates the relations between human and nature, however, rather than eliminating the distinction. For Arendt, humans are conditioned beings; their existence is conditioned by and conditions the reality of their world.[9] They exist through, or their reality is made up through, three sorts of activities corresponding to three sorts of domains, all of which are aspects of what Arendt calls the *vita activa* that (along with the *vita contemplativa*) is integral to being human.

Of these three domains, the "world" for Arendt is a world of human making and fabrication "by the hands"; the things we make, from tools to buildings to artworks, offer human beings a relatively stable place of their own. Individuals use materials that they extract (often violently) from nature to work and to construct this world. The "earth," by contrast, names for Arendt the place to which humans as living beings, rather than so-called cultural ones, are so far bound. The earth is the domain of necessity, in which the human animal labors "in the sweat of his brow" and participates in endless cycles of reproduction and consumption needed to continue the life of the species.[10]

And then for Arendt there is the ephemeral realm of "freedom," of action and of participation in "politics," which requires not only the shared built world but also the presence of a plurality of others. Freedom corresponds to the kind of unpredictability that belongs to human action insofar as it occurs within an already existing web of human relationships. To be embedded in this web means, on the one hand, that any particular action (including utterance) will not necessarily achieve its purpose and, on the other, that it has the potential to begin something surprising and new. The possibility of human freedom, of action as Arendt understands it, is threatened not only by totalitarian government or nuclear destruction, but also when human practices become only instrumental means to further ends or automatic behaviors conforming to an administered environment. The temporality of action is a strange one, as action as such neither makes objects linearly nor produces things cyclically. Instead, action is seen by others as the expression of an actor's identity and credited—in retrospect—with the initiation of historical events.

For Arendt, the cycle of life requires humans to labor to produce things from nature that will deliberately be "used up." Think of bread. The laborer toils to produce goods whose consumption fuels human life. If not consumed, these goods go to waste or decay. In working or fabricating, by contrast, humans use (rather than "use up") nature to make such things as tools, which are themselves made to be used for further ends. The oven is built to bake the bread. Tools and buildings and artworks made from nature provide stability, solidity, and permanence in the world, although they, too, eventually wear out, in linear fashion. Nature thus plays at least a fourfold role in Arendt's account of earth and world: as an original indifference to human being, as the "merciless" biological processes of consumption and reproduction to which human beings as living beings are necessarily bound, as the supplier of matter that humans use up and use to fulfill living needs and worldly wants, and as the threat of deterioration of the human world, against which human beings must struggle.

As important to Arendt as understanding the activities that make us human is understanding how judgments as to the highest human activity have changed. In her account, the Greek philosophers, disillusioned with politics, elevated the *vita contemplativa* over the *vita activa* and in particular over political action. There followed a series of reconfigurations culminating in the l9th-century elevation of laboring activity over all others. Even work and "the ideals of *homo faber*, the fabricator of the world, which are permanence, stability, and durability," writes Arendt, "have been sacrificed to abundance, the ideal of the *animal laborans*. . . . We have made work into laboring, broken it up into its minute particles . . . to eliminate from the path of human labor power . . . the obstacle of the 'unnatural' and purely worldly stability of the human artifice" (*HC* 126). The upshot is a "consumer society" in which, rather than making durable use-objects, we produce through automated repetitive processes goods that will be used up or become obsolete. Think of gadgets, such as disposable cameras, or now obsolete media technologies from record players to Palm Pilots.

Today, "sustainability" counters the paradoxical immateriality of consumption with the durability and permanence of nature (or of earth). But sustainability carries a different resonance than does "nature preservation" or "environmental conservation." At its origins, the conservation movement focused on keeping what was currently unspoiled and, to some degree, unused, that way. It aimed to keep nature "wild" and to spare it from the violation entailed in human use. Its success lay in the creation of national parks and pristine wilderness areas in which (insofar as conservation was successful) activities of mining, drilling, and harvesting lumber appeared unthinkable. For early conservationists, it was even something of a dilemma whether—and certainly a political issue to what degree—humans should take to managing land so as to minimize human beings' access to and impact on it. They knew management itself to be a human activity.

II. Condors and Culture

Current sustainability adherents have fewer qualms about intervening in nature. Today's attempts to deal with endangered species go well beyond early conservationist measures to protect a species'"wild" environment. Endangered whooping cranes, for instance, are today taught to follow lightweight planes for migration.

The story of the California condor shows the shift in attitudes toward human intervention. A late 1890s geologist describes the "California vulture" as a "doomed bird," a

Figure 1: An ultralight vehicle leads migrating whooping cranes.

"species . . . in process of extinction" that is "certainly worth preserving if possible." Upon encountering a mature and possibly dying condor up close, the author decides not to kill the "harmless, if not useful bird" with his hammer, but to leave it "to fulfill its destiny."[11]

Compare this to a 1953 report that recommends, "our objective should be to maintain and perhaps to increase the natural population of condors."[12] The mid-century report nevertheless calls artificial feeding, transplantation, and breeding in captivity "impractical proposals." Not only is the author skeptical that these can work, but also he notes that "the recreational value of wildlife is in inverse proportion to its artificiality. The thrill of seeing a condor is greatly diminished when the birds are being raised in captivity." His recommendations include federal protection (not just the current state protection) to forbid shooting condors or disturbing their nests; he mentions a permit granted as an exception (to an exception of condors from scientific research permits) to the San Diego Zoo "to trap and cage one pair."[13] He also recommends protection by closures of the public lands on which condors were almost exclusively found. Finally, he recommends education (of persons, not condors) in part to encourage stockmen and trappers to leave outdoors the undiseased carcasses of the dead animals on which condors feed. Today, 50 years later, the late 20th-century and early 21st-century story of the return of the condor is, if not well known, certainly well documented.

1982 represents the low point of the joint captive plus wild condor population. Since the capture of the last five wild birds in 1986-87, condor numbers have grown through captive breeding and release programs to 383, 188 of them in the wild.[14] These huge and breathtaking birds, touted as "nature's cleanup crew" having survived since the Pleistocene era (over 10,000 years ago), now carry radio transmitters and are adorned with numbers large enough to be read through binoculars. Websites and posts allow one to follow the doings of numbers 253F and 223M, for instance, at their nest-cave.

Starting in 1983, all condor eggs and nestlings were taken for captive breeding. Eggs were picked up by helicopter to develop a captive flock, while wild pairs engaged in "replacement-clutching" or second laying of eggs in the same season. The condor recovery plan that followed the 1973 Endangered Species Act had not proposed captive breeding, but with the capture of the last wild bird in 1987, all breeding at that time became captive. Condors turned out to be reasonably good at it: all of the original 27 captive flock of 1987 bred in captivity and only one died. By 1998, there were 150 condors "in existence."[15]

Captive birds were, of course, carefully observed and monitored. They were sexed chromosomally and separated into family lines, each pair housed in a large flight cage containing nest cave, pool, and perches. They were isolated from human keepers. Laid eggs were "candled" to see if fertile, replacement-clutching was encouraged, and hatching nestlings were at first helped by humans. Nestlings were fed by puppets (so as to prevent imprinting), before being placed together for socialization.

As more was learned about how condors behaved in captivity and how to release them, procedures were modified.

The release program suffered—or sustained—its own ups and downs. Because birds were not being released into a wild flock, they had what one scientist who has studied condors called "behavioral problems." The first puppet-reared birds, for instance, "soon began to develop problems with excessive attractions to human structures and with strong tendencies of the birds to approach people without evident fear."[16] Condors have destroyed windshield wipers, weather stripping, tents, sleeping bags, and mattresses. They have been known to collide (fatally) with overhead wires, to land on oil-well pads and buildings (even to enter a bedroom), and to chase people down backcountry trails. One bird was seen carrying a .38-caliber revolver in its bill, apparently taken from a backpack. Now pre-release condors go through aversiveness training by being exposed to dummy utility poles equipped with electroshock wiring.Parent-reared captive birds, though wilder than the puppet-reared birds, also have problems. At one point, parent-reared birds "came in contact with a group of puppet-reared birds from another release and joined that group, adopting many of [its] human-oriented behaviors . . . There was no opportunity to see if their initial good behavior might have lasted if the parent-reared birds had remained isolated from other condors." Zoos now place pre-release puppet-reared condors with "mentor adults, instead of just with other juveniles," although "chicks reared together" still show "significant difficulties in forming successful pair bonds with their early cage mates in later life."[17] And the condors seem to have difficulties breeding in the wild: "Two early failed breeding attempts involved groups larger than pairs (a trio and a quartet) occupying single nest caves," a phenomenon that had never been observed in what is now called "the historic wild population."

Even when they do mate, the condors' problems are not over. Their chromosome pool may not be good. Very few wild breedings have produced nestlings, much less fledglings. Despite the provision of food subsidies in the form of clean carcasses, released birds are still dying of lead poisoning. Some are picked up and saved by "emergency chelation therapy," which removes lead from the bloodstream and allows it to be excreted. To deal with the issue, some states have passed laws against hunting with lead bullets in particular areas. The U.S. military "recently announced its intentions to convert fully to [nontoxic ammunitions] in a 'green bullet' program," although nontoxic ammunition is not fully available commercially nor as cheap as lead ammunition.[18]

Distinctions between nature and artifice, wilderness and civilization, become blurred, as we have just seen, when humans reach "into nature" (in Arendt's felicitous phrase).[19] But the distinction also blurs when sustainability practices extend from nature into the Arendtian durable world. Humanmade objects and tools now aspire to be natural—or green. Recall those green bullets! Or think of electric cars or plastic containers that are made to be recycled or even composted.

Sustainability, it turns out, applies as much to the built environment as to nature. The nonprofit U.S. Green Building Council's LEED (Leadership in Energy and Environmental Design) certification program is a booming case in point. As a "design tool," LEED "provides independent, third-party verification [by members who helped develop the ratings] that a building project meets the highest green building and performance measures." Despite some criticism about the grandiosity of its claims and the cost and time it takes for projects to be approved, LEED generally seems to be considered a good thing. Its green building certification rating deals with water, energy use,the operation of the construction site, materials, daylight, access, education, appropriateness to regional priorities, and so forth. In the Council's own words, the LEED rating "encourages and accelerates global adoption of sustainable green building and development practices through a suite of rating systems that recognize projects that implement strategies for better environmental and health performance."[20] Both nature (environment) and welfare (health) are sustained through artifice (design).

Even "historic preservation," a practice whose concern for the stability, solidity, and permanence of a durable world would hardly seem to need boosting, has got onto the sustainable-design bandwagon. Its partnerships with sustainable design epitomize the slogan "recycle and reuse." No longer simply preserving older buildings for display, historical preservationists restore and revitalize them for new mixed uses. They convert former warehouses into condos, industrial buildings into artist studios, piers into tourist markets, and so forth.

As sustainability becomes a value that extends over both nature and artifice, earth and world, its global character comes to the fore. Now eco-nomics and eco-logy, the policies and sciences of the running of the *oikos* or the household, cover the globe.[21] The "sustainable development" made internationally famous by the UN Brundtland Report, represents the integration of economics and ecology, as knowledge and law, into worldwide management. New metrics offer ways of accounting for disparate processes at the global level through common units of measure. Carbon footprints and taxes are the best known. The language of sustainability becomes the universal, multisyllabic, pseudoscientific, Latinate vocabulary of administration and problem solving that is characterized by references to efficiency and effectiveness. In short, big words say very little. Consider this way of talking about the goal of achieving "fully vigorous wild populations" of condors:

Success will not likely come by ignoring problems, but by devising ways to identify and solve problems in the most effective and efficient ways possible . . . the remaining obstacles all appear to be solvable problems, with enough determination and skill given to the task.[22]

Translation: We hope that if we try hard enough, we can fix things.

III. Unpredictability and the Sustainable Future

So far, I've drawn on Arendt's understanding of durability to show how "sustainability" injects into our relations with the earth a blurring of the distinction between nature and artifice. Humans once used up the things of nature to live and used its materials to build objects that they strove to keep nature from wearing out. Today nature has become what humans try to prevent from wearing out or disappearing. Humans interrupt the formerly cyclical movements of nature through their own fabrications (seeding clouds and making snow). Like other fabricated goods, nature is now susceptible to destruction by its human creator. And yet human beings respond to their great power over nature with ever greater attempts to measure it, master it, and subject it to further control.[23]

Identifiable no longer with the cyclical occurrences of the earth, nor quite with the stable and solid fabrications of creative-destructive humans, nature becomes subject to crisis and unpredictability. As Arthur F. McEvoy shows of the California fisheries crises and the recent landslides outside Santa Barbara, disasters happen when people, with the help of the law, insert themselves into situations (e.g., constructing houses below cliffs being watered for avocado farming) such that ordinary natural processes (e.g., rain) have catastrophic social results.[24] Protecting against "natural disaster" thereby becomes an endless task of human intervention into the natural processes of the earth that human action, with the unpredictability of its effects, has itself unleashed.

Protecting and recovering from disaster also flies the flag of sustainability. Think of BP's "greenwashing" ads following the 2010 explosion of the Deepwater Horizon oil rig and the subsequent release of thousands of barrels of oil into the Gulf of Mexico. The company with the sun-sprouting logo apparently spent $93 million in ads between April and July 2010, three times what it spent during the same period the previous year. In the ads, the CEO of BP called the spill "a tragedy that should never have happened" and claimed that BP had "taken full responsibility."[25] Sustainability is a broad enough umbrella to shelter Starbucks' importation of fair trade and shade-grown coffee, Monsanto's production of genetically modified seeds, and Wal-Mart's recent announcement that it would be doubling its use of local grocery suppliers.[26]

In the name of sustainable agriculture, Monsanto produces a corn seed whose corn produces a chemical that kills the larvae of the corn borer, a "devastating pest" whose larvae digs tunnels in ears of corn. The fungus that fills the holes can produce mycotoxins that end up in the milk of corn-fed cows and are "associated" with health issues like cancer. If the pollen of this corn mixes with that of "organic" corn, however, the organic corn loses its designation. And Greenpeace argues that the chemical that kills the corn borer larvae may also harm butterflies.[27] Meanwhile, the giant Wal-Mart chain wants to move toward a sustainability index for food and to push other companies to follow.[28] Who can predict where the corporate embrace of sustainability will take us?

Indeed, the unpredictability that humans have unleashed into nature is matched only by the unpredictability of human actions themselves, including those of participants who act and speak, sincerely or cynically, in the name of "sustainability." Despite my temptation to reduce sustainability to a practice of instrumentality or of Heideggerian technique in which earth becomes standing reserve, what sustainability and the "green revolution" portend cannot yet be predicted.

Figure 2: A California condor, known as 167, against the sky

Sustainability *has* been introduced, somehow. It threatens to sweep up in its train multinational corporations, small businesses, family practices, as well as their most trenchant critics, here and abroad. The oddness and intricacies of this alliance seem to preclude any effective willing of particular effects by any given "human subject." Persons nevertheless act "sustainably": they engage in backyard composting, set up farmers' markets, pass city council resolutions about mass transit, limit the use of toxins, and establish disaster relief programs, however indeterminate the actual effects of these acts. Even as sustainability grows out of earlier movements, its ubiquity and penetration into so many aspects of modern (or postmodern) human life shows it to be something new. Its story so far is a tale of human beings and the politics of nature. Whether that tale turns out to be an account of ultimately cataclysmic or not-so-cataclysmic annihilation—a history of the initiation and achievements of humans acting grandly in concert, if not in harmony—or more-or-less irrelevant to our future remains to be seen.

What is clear is that sustainability no longer allows us a 19th-century faith in history as progress. In challenging the narrative of progress as it does, though, sustainability also seems to require an impossible leap: a leap from a present that cannot endure to a future that is called on to do so indefinitely. The imagination of this leap testifies to the potential of human action and freedom, and hence of politics and continued human being à la Arendt. But the *end* that such a leap would ostensibly accomplish simultaneously suggests a difficulty with or for human being. Fixing the future into an enduring or steady state suggests a new temporality that is neither cyclical nor linear. It appears incompatible not only with labor and work, but also with the freedom and unpredictability that characterizes action, the third activity that Arendt ascribes to human beings.

I subtitled this essay "Human, All Too Human," for two reasons. I did so in honor of Friedrich Nietzsche, who was the first to prophesy the straits to which human action and nonaction would lead us. I did so also because sustainability, understood as a human aspiration to fix into place a future that one way or another escapes human grasp, shows that we are *still* the somewhat paradoxical humans of modernity whom Arendt diagnosed, capable both of politics and of threatening ourselves with annihilation. Who knows for how long we will sustain *this* balance?

Endnotes

1. Clover Stornetta, carton date May 24 16:12 [2010]. See Green Rating Press Release [2010], http://www.princetonreview.com/green/press-release.aspx.

2. The Higher Education Opportunity Act (Public Law 110-315) (HEOA), enacted August 14, 2008, reauthorizes the Higher Education Act of 1965, as amended. It also incorporates the provisions of the Higher Education Sustainability Act. See Title XI, Studies and Reports. Sec. 1120, Summit on Sustainability.

3. UN Commission on Sustainable Development, "Framing Sustainable Development: The Brundtland Report—20 Years On," Sustainable Development in Action, Backgrounder, April 2007, accessed October 10, 2010. The Brundtland Report was the basis of resolutions passed at the UN's Rio Summit in 1993, which will be followed by "Rio Plus 20" in 2013.

4. Hannah Arendt, *The Human Condition* (Chicago: University of Chicago Press, 1958), 133.

5. Ibid., 5.

6. Adapted from *Oxford English Dictionary*, 2d Edition, Vol. XVII Su-Thrivingly, prep. by J. A. Simpson and E. S. C. Winer (Oxford: Clarendon Press, 1989), 326–327.

7. See selections in *American Environmentalism: Readings in Conservation History,* 3d ed, Roderick Frazier Nash, ed. (NY: McGraw-Hill, 1990); and in *Environmental Philosophy: FromAnimal Rights to Radical Ecology,* Michael E. Zimmerman, ed. (associate eds. J. Baird Callicott, George Sessions, Karen J. Warren, and John Clark) (Englewood Cliffs, NJ: Prentice Hall, 1993); and articles in the journal *Environmental Ethics* generally.

8. Paul Ott, "World and Earth: Hannah Arendt and the Human Relationship to Nature," *Ethics, Place and Environment* 12 (2009), 1–16; Kerry H. Whiteside, "Hannah Arendt and Ecological Politics," *Environmental Ethics* 16 (1994) 339-358; and "Wordliness and Respect for Nature: An Ecological Application of Hannah Arendt's Conception of Culture," *Environmental Values* 7 (1998) 25–40.

9. Arendt, *The Human Condition*, 9.

10. Hannah Arendt, "Labor, Work, Action," *Amor Mundi*, ed. James Bernauer (Boston: Martinus Nijhoff Publishers, 1987), 29–42, 35.

11. J. G. Cooper, "A Doomed Bird," *Zoe* I (1890), 248–9.

12. Carl B. Koford, "The California Condor" (NY: Dover Publications, 1966; reprint of National Audubon Society Research Report No. 4, 1953), 135.

13. Ibid., 135–8.

14. August 31, 2010, status report.

15. Information in this paragraph and in text through note 16 comes from Noel F. R. Snyder and Helen A. Snyder, *Introduction to the California Condor* (Berkeley: University of California Press, 2005).

16. Ibid., 217-8.

17. Ibid., 222, 236.

18. Ibid., 230.

19. Taken up nicely in Mick Smith, "Environmental Risks and Ethical Responsibilities: Arendt, Beck, and the Politics of Acting into Nature," *Environmental Ethics* 28 (2006), 227–246; and "Ecological Citizenship and Ethical Responsibility: Arendt, Benjamin and Political Activism," *Environments* 33 (2005), 51–63 at 57.

20. See U.S. Green Building Council website: http://www.usgbc.org/.

21. See also David Macauley, "Hannah Arendt and the Politics of Place: From Earth Alienation to Oikos," reprinted as Ch. 5, 102–133, in *Minding Nature*, ed. David Macauley (New York: The Guilford Press, 1996).

22. Snyder and Snyder, 240.

23. Bronislaw Szerszynski, "Technology, performance and life itself: Hannah Arendt and the fate of nature," *Sociological Review* (2003), 203–217.

24. Arthur F. McEvoy, "The Agency of Law in Natural Catastrophe: A Historical Analysis" in *Losing Ground: A Nation on Edge* (Environmental Law Institute, 2007).

25. BP's advertising budget was reported widely. See for instance: http://money.cnn.com/2010/09/01/news/companies/BP_spill_advertising_costs.fortune/in dex.htm. Regarding BP's image, see also James Ridgeway, "BP's Slick Greenwashing," http://www.motherjones.com/mojo/2010/05/bp-coated-sludge-after-years-greenwashing.

26. Taylor Clark, *Starbucked* (NY: Little Brown, 2007), ch. 6.

27. Elisabeth Rosenthal, "In Italy, a Conflict over Corn," *New York Times* August 24, 2010, A4.

> *To prevent the pollen from spreading, antiglobalization activists stripped tassels off corn that had been grown without the appropriate permissions (in what was itself labeled an act of civil disobedience) on farmland in Italy.*

28. Stephanie Clifford, "At Wal-Mart, a Plan for More Local Food," *New York Times*, October 15, 2010, B1 and B4.

List of Contributors

01110100 01101000 01100101 00100000 01110000 01100101 01110010 01101001 01101100 01110011 00100000 01101111 01100110 00100000 01101001 01101110 01110110 01100101 01110110 01110100 01101001 01101111 01101110 01101110

Babette Babich is a professor of philosophy at Fordham University. She is author of *Nietzsche's Philosophy of Science: Reflecting Science on the Ground of Art and Life* and, most recently, *Günther Anders' Philosophy of Technology: From Phenomenology to Critical Theory.*

Nicholson Baker is the author of eleven novels and many works of non-fiction, including *Double Field,* which won a National Book Critics Circle Award and, most recently, *Baseless: My Search for Secrets in the Ruins of the Freedom of Information Act.*

Roger Berkowitz is founder and academic director of the Hannah Arendt Center at Bard College where he is Professor of Politics, Human Rights, and Philosophy. He is the author of *The Gift of Science: Leibniz and the Modern Legal Tradition*and editor of many volumes including *Artifacts of Thinking: Reading Hannah Arendt's Denktagebuch.*

Peg Birmingham is professor of philosophy at DePaul University and editor of *Philosophy Today.*She is the author of*Hannah Arendt and Human Rights*and co-editor (with Philippe van Haute) of*Dissensus Communis: Between Ethics and Politics*(Koros 1995).

Marianne Constable is the Zaffaroni Family Chair in Undergraduate Education and a professor of rhetoric at the University of California, Berkeley. She is the author of *Just Silences: The Limits and Possibilities of Modern Law*and *The Law of the Other: The Mixed Jury and Changing Conceptsion of Citizenship, Law, and Knowledge.*

Wolfgang Heuer is Privatdozent at the Otto-Suhr-Institute of Political Science at the Free University in Berlin. He is editor of hannaharendt.net and author of Couragiertes Handeln (*Courageous Action*) and *Citizen: Personal Integrity and Political Responsibility.*

George Kateb is William Nelson Cromwell Professor of Politics Emeritus at Princeton University. His writings include *Hannah Arendt: Politics, Conscience, Evil; The Inner Ocean: Individualism and Democratic Culture; Emerson and Self-Reliance;*and most recently, *Patriotism and Other Mistakes.*

Jonathan Kay is Canadian editor of Quillette, and host of the Quillette podcast. He is the author *Among the Truthers: A Journey Through America's Growing Conspiracist Underground.*

Jerome Kohn is editor of numerous volumes of Hannah Arendt's work, including *Thinking Without a Banister; Responsibility and Judgment; The Promise of Politics; Essays in Understanding*; and *Hannah Arendt: The Jewish Writings* (with Ron H. Feldman). He is the trustee of the Hannah Arendt and Heinrich Blücher Literary Trust.

Uday Singh Mehta is Distinguished Professor of Political Science at the CUNY Graduate Center. He is the author of *Liberalism and Empire: Nineteenth-Century British Liberal Thought;The Anxiety of Freedom: Imagination and Individuality in the Political Thought of John Locke.* His forthcoming book is *A Different Vision: Gandhi's Critique of Political Rationality.*

Davide Panagiais Professor of Political Science at University of California, Los Angeles. He is currently Co-Editor of the journal, Political Theory. He is the author of *The Poetics of Political Thinking, Ten Theses for an Aesthetics of Politics*, and, most recently, *Rancière's Sentiments.*

Rob Rieman began the journal Nexus in 1991 and founded the Nexus Institute in 1994. He is the author of *Nobility of Spirit: A Forgotten Ideal*and *The Eternal Return of Fascism.*

Linda M.G. Zerilli is the Charles E. Merriam Distinguished Service Professor of Political Science and the College at the University of Chicago. Her books include, *Signifying Woman, Feminism and the Abyss of Freedom,* and *A Democratic Theory of Judgment.*

Also from Black Rose Books

Friendly Fascism:
The New Face of Power in America
Bertram Gross
Paperback: 978-0-92005-723-0
Hardcover: 978-0-92005-722-3
eBook: 978-1-55164-766-1

Transformative Planning:
Radical Alternatives to Neoliberal Urbanism
Thomas Angotti, ed.
Paperback: 978-1-55164-691-6
Hardcover: 978-1-55164-693-0
eBook: 978-1-55164-695-4

Mind Abuse:
Media Violence and its Threat to Democracy
Rose A. Dyson
Paperback: 978-1-55164-732-6
Hardcover: 978-1-55164-733-3
eBook: 978-1-55164-734-0

Lies the Media Tell Us
James Winter
Paperback: 978-1-55164-252-9
Hardcover: 978-1-55164-253-6
eBook: 978-1-55164-630-5

Direct Deliberative Democracy:
How Citizens Can Rule
Debra Campbell and Jack Crittenden
Paperback: 978-1-55164-669-5
Hardcover: 978-1-55164-671-8
eBook: 978-1-55164-673-2

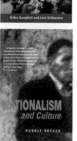

Nationalism and Culture
Rudolf Rocker
Paperback: 978-1-55164-094-5
Hardcover: 978-1-55164-095-2
eBook: 978-1-55164-500-1